Paris and the Commune
1871–78

MANCHESTER
1824

Manchester University Press

Cultural History of Modern War

Series editors   Peter Gatrell, Max Jones, Penny Summerfield and
Bertrand Taithe

Already published

Jeffrey S. Reznick   *Healing the nation: soldiers and the culture of caregiving
in Britain during the great war*

Penny Summerfield and Corinna Peniston-Bird   *Contesting home defence:
men, women and the Home Guard in the Second World War*

Centre for the
Cultural History
of War

Paris and the Commune
1871–78

The politics of forgetting

~

COLETTE E. WILSON

Manchester University Press
Manchester and New York
distributed exclusively in the USA by Palgrave

The right of Colette E. Wilson to be identified as the author of this work has been asserted by her in accordance with the Copyright, Designs and Patents Act 1988.

Published by Manchester University Press
Oxford Road, Manchester M13 9NR, UK
and Room 400, 175 Fifth Avenue, New York, NY 10010, USA
www.manchesteruniversitypress.co.uk

Distributed exclusively in the USA by
Palgrave, 175 Fifth Avenue, New York,
NY 10010, USA

Distributed exclusively in Canada by
UBC Press, University of British Columbia, 2029 West Mall,
Vancouver, BC, Canada V6T 1Z2

British Library Cataloguing-in-Publication Data
A catalogue record for this book is available from the British Library

Library of Congress Cataloging-in-Publication Data applied for

ISBN   978 0 7190 7476 9 hardback

First published 2007

16 15 14 13 12 11 10 09 08 07   10 9 8 7 6 5 4 3 2 1

Typeset in 10/12pt Minion
by Graphicraft Limited, Hong Kong
Printed in Great Britain
by Anthony Rowe Ltd, Chippenham, Wiltshire

Contents

List of illustrations

List of tables

Acknowledgements

This book is based on the research I carried out while a doctoral student at Royal Holloway College and I would like to take the opportunity to express my gratitude both to the College and to the AHRC for their financial support, to Robert Lethbridge for supervising the original thesis, and especially to Ana Carden-Coyne, Alison Welsby, Emma Brennan and the anonymous readers at Manchester University Press for all their hard work on my behalf to bring this book to publication. Very special thanks are due in addition to my colleagues at the Institute of Germanic and Romance Studies, particularly Naomi Segal and Martin Liebscher for their advice on aspects of the book, and Gill Rye for giving me the opportunity to test out my ideas by teaching a unit on the Commune on the MA in Cultural Memory, and I shall always be grateful to my students for their enthusiastic participation in my seminars. I would also like to thank the editors and reviewers of *Les Cahiers naturalistes*, *French Studies*, *Romance Studies*, the *Journal of European Studies* and *The 2001 Group*, who published early versions of some of the chapter sections. *Romance Studies* and the Institute of Germanic and Romance Studies also kindly contributed to the cost of acquiring copies of some of the illustrations.

I have presented aspects of my research at various conferences and seminars and I am very grateful to the scholars I met at these events for their questions and comments as well as to the many colleagues and friends who in their various ways helped me or facilitated my research, including: Aimée Boutin, Andrew Bowie, Alison Finch, Michael Freeman, Anne Green, Tom Gretton, Catherine Guy-Murrell, Alec Hargreaves, Susan Harrow, Alec Honey, Susan Hopkins, John House, Edward Hughes, Debra Kelly, Bill Kidd, Rachael Langford, John O'Brien, Alain Pagès, Pamela Pilbeam, Keith Reader, Adrian Rifkin, Helen Roberts, Hugh Roberts, Michael Sheringham, Penny Sewell, Rebecca Spang, Nick White and Geoff Woollen, as well as the staff at the Bibliothèque historique de la Ville de Paris, the Bibliothèque nationale de France, the British Library, the Institut

Acknowledgements

de France, the Institut français in London, the Musée Carnavalet (Catherine Tambrun and Christiane Dole), the Musée d'Art et d'histoire at Saint-Denis (Sylvie Gonzales and Laurence Goux), the Musée d'Orsay (Quentin Bajac), the National Museum of Photography, and the Victoria and Albert Museum (Martin Barnes, Mark Haworth-Booth, Ulrich Lehmann and Rosie Miles). Finally, the writing of this book would have been an almost impossible task without the unfailing support and encouragement of my husband Alasdair. This is one of many reasons that I dedicate this book to him.

I dedicate this book to Alasdair

Chronology of key events 1870–80

1870	July	War with Prussia.
	August	Invasion of France.
	1 September	Napoleon III surrenders at Sedan.
	4 September	Republic declared. Government of National Defence.
	19 September	Paris besieged by Prussians
	October	Insurrection in Paris and failed attempts to launch the Commune.
1871	28 January	Armistice.
	8 February	Election of National Assembly. Theirs · government.
	18 March	Government troops attempt and fail to capture city cannon in Montmartre. Popular uprising. Insurgents capture and execute generals Thomas and Lecomte. Revolutionary crowd descends on the Hôtel de Ville (City Hall).
	26 March	Election of new municipal council, the Central Committee of the National Guard.
	28 March	Commune proclaimed.
	April	Government troops (Versaillais) bombard Neuilly and Courbevoie.
	16 May	Commune pull down Vendôme Column.
	21–8 May	*La Semaine sanglant* (Bloody Week) in Paris. Communards and Versaillais burn parts of

		the city. Communards execute members of the clergy and other hostages.
	28 May	End of Commune. Executions, trials, deportations continue until 1875.
1873	May	Thiers resigns. Succeeded by MacMahon and *l'Ordre moral*.
1876	February, March	Republican electoral victories in Chamber of Deputies.
1877	16 May	MacMahon's attempted *coup d'état* ('la crise du 16 mai). Further republican electoral victory.
1878	May	Opening of *Exposition universelle* (World Fair).
	30 June	National holiday (*La Fête du 30 juin*).
1879	30 January	Mac Mahon resigns. Grévy elected President of the Republic.
	31 January	Gambetta elected President of the Chamber of Deputies.
1880	11 July	Amnesty granted to ex-Communards
	14 July	Annual national holiday established.

1

Introduction

> You must close the book on these last ten years, you must place the tomb-
> stone of oblivion over the crimes and vestiges of the Commune, and you
> must tell everyone – those whose absence we deplore and those whose con-
> trary views and disagreements we sometimes regret, that there is but one
> France and one Republic.
>
> (Léon Gambetta, 21 June 1880)[1]

On 21 June 1880, Léon Gambetta, the recently appointed President
of the Chamber of Deputies, and *de facto* 'Republican party' leader,
stood up to make what would prove to be a landmark speech in favour
of granting all ex-Communards amnesty. With his renowned eloquence,
he exhorted his fellow members of the government, regardless of their
political affiliation (Legitimist, Orléanist, Bonapartist or republican) to
put aside their differences and to 'place the tombstone of oblivion' over
the previous ten years in order to unite the nation and consolidate the
Republic.[2] The process of state obliteration of the memory of the Commune, however, had arguably begun much earlier, straight after the
final, bloody repression of the city at the end of May 1871 when some
20,000 (perhaps many more) men, women and children were killed by
the 'regular' troops of the French army in just the final week of the
conflict, which became known as *la Semaine sanglante* (Bloody Week).
Some 43,500 people were taken prisoner, and the trials, executions
and deportations continued until 1875–76. It has been estimated that
Paris lost approximately 100,000 of its workers – one-seventh of its
adult male working population – and the electoral registers after the
conflict recorded a loss of some 90,000 voters, all male since women
did not have the vote.[3] Of all the fratricidal conflicts of the nineteenth

century, the repression of the Commune was by far the bloodiest in Europe and second only perhaps to that of the American Civil War (1861–65), which just predated it, and during which 620,000 people lost their lives.[4] In the twentieth century, the Commune was to find its echo in the Russian Revolution (1917), the Spanish Civil War (1936–39), the Franco-Algerian conflict (1954–62), and the genocides in the former Yugoslavia and Rwanda in the 1990s. The Commune, like all of these wars, and so many others down the centuries, continues to be shrouded in myths, conflicting memories, and taboos.

In the following chapters I wish to demonstrate two things: firstly, how the governments of the early Third Republic attempted to efface the memory of May 1871 by means of strict censorship in all matters concerning the Commune and through the reinvention of Paris as a modern, healthy, hygienic and regenerated metropolis during the 1878 *Exposition universelle* (World Fair) and the *Fête du 30 juin* (Festival of 30 June); and, secondly, how close readings of a number of representative case studies reveal that, while writers, artists and photographers were often apparently willing to conform to the officially promoted view of the city, the memory of the recent past could not be so easily erased. In so doing, however, it is my aim, when assessing the memorialist aspects of the Paris Commune, to counter the tendency in French literary and cultural studies to concentrate on writers and artists who were either Communards themselves, such as Jules Vallès and Gustave Courbet, or at least sympathetic to the Communard cause, such as Arthur Rimbaud and Edouard Manet.[5] The focus will instead be on the ways in which broadly conservative, counter-revolutionary and reactionary collective memories and myths of this traumatic period in French history manifested themselves in a wide range of cultural production drawn from the illustrated press, socio-historical texts, memoirs, literary fiction and photography.

It has often been necessary in the analyses that follow to assume a certain amount of prior knowledge on the part of readers about the circumstances surrounding the outbreak of the Franco-Prussian War, the fall of the Second Empire, the rise and fall of the Commune and the complex political machinations of the early Third Republic. It may be useful therefore to begin by giving a very brief account of this turbulent period in French history. Readers may also wish to refer to the chronology on pp. xii–xiii and to the special section of the Bibliography, which lists a number of texts on the history, representation and interpretation of the Commune.

The Paris Commune 1871

The Paris Commune of 1871 refers to the revolutionary government
that was established by the people of Paris to administer their own city
following the end of the Franco-Prussian War (1870–71). The Commune lasted only 72 days, from 18 March to 28 May 1871. It was not a
planned or organized revolution and it had no one clear leader. The
causes of the revolt that led to its establishment can partly be attributed
to the anger and exasperation felt by many Parisians to the humiliating
capitulation of the city to the Prussians on 28 January 1871, by the
veteran politician Adolphe Thiers and the newly formed Third Republic, and partly to a number of unresolved social and political grievances
dating back to the previous revolutions of 1830 and 1848 and which
intensified during the Second Empire under Napoleon III.[6]

The Second Empire lasted from 2 December 1852 until 4 September
1870, when Napoleon III was forced to abdicate following his defeat by
the Prussians at Sedan in north-east France. On 4 September 1870 the
republicans effected a bloodless revolution in Paris, setting up a Government of National Defence with the aim of continuing the war against
Prussia. It is important to note at this point, however, that those I have
labelled 'republicans' were not a united political faction. While there
were many in France at the time who believed in the re-establishment of
a republican form of government, there was by no means any consensus
as to exactly how such a government should be constituted. These republicans consisted of a mixture of conservatives, progressives, centrists
or centre-Left moderates, and a number of utopian socialist radicals,
who mostly renounced violence as a way of effecting change, as well as a
few revolutionary republicans and extremists.[7] Many conservatives, led
by Thiers, wished to bring the disastrous war against Prussia to an end
as quickly as possible. To complicate matters further the monarchists,
themselves a mixture of absolutists (Legitimists) and constitutionalists
(Orléanists), hoped, in vain as it would turn out, that Thiers would
help them bring the absolutist pretender the Comte de Chambord to
the throne, to be succeeded in due course by the Orléanist Comte
de Paris. The republican moderates on the centre-Left, led by Léon
Gambetta, on the other hand, wished to continue the war in order to
restore France's honour and promptly set about mobilizing the half-
million or more troops at their disposal into the city's National Guard
in anticipation of an imminent Prussian attack on the capital. Many on
the far Left also wished to continue the war but, in addition, were very

eager to take the opportunity of Napoleon III's fall to establish a whole new social order. There was, however, little clear idea or agreement among them on exactly how this might be achieved in practice.

As the Prussians reached the outskirts of Paris and began to lay siege to the city on 19 September, the Government of National Defence opened negotiations with the enemy but refused their proposed conditions, which included the loss of the north-eastern provinces of Alsace and Lorraine. The National Guard, meanwhile, began to move further to the Left politically as some of its more moderate leaders were replaced by revolutionary republicans, men like Gustave Flourens whose life, as I will discuss later in Chapter 4, would inspire Emile Zola's portrayal of the utopian revolutionary Florent in *Le Ventre de Paris*. On 5 October, Flourens and other radicals marched on the Hôtel de Ville (City Hall) in a bid to force the government into continuing the fight against the Prussians. On 7 October, Gambetta, head of the Ministry of the Interior, controversially also assumed the role of Minister of War and left Paris to take charge of the provinces, all the time seeking to relieve the city and to continue the war to the bitter end.[8] Then on 31 October, after news finally reached Paris that the army had surrendered at Metz, Flourens, the veteran revolutionary Auguste Blanqui, and others marched once more on Paris in a further attempt to establish a new government for the city, but this early attempt to launch the Commune was quickly foiled and a negotiated settlement put an end to the insurrection.

By early November, all men between the ages of twenty and forty had been mobilized and the Parisian National Guard reorganized into active units, as the Prussians continued to shell the walls and outskirts of city. Those Parisians who were obliged to stay in the city suffered starvation and terrible hardship aggravated by an exceptionally harsh winter. Then, after a siege that had lasted four months, Thiers's government finally agreed, on 28 January 1871, to an armistice for all but the east of the country and to the capitulation of Paris with a provision for an immediate war indemnity of 200 million francs to be paid for by the city itself. The general election held on 8 February resulted in a monarchist majority in the National Assembly in favour of peace at any price. This was not a surprising outcome given that, save for radical cities like Lyons, Toulouse and Marseilles, the provinces remained deeply conservative. On his election as leader of the National Assembly, but significantly not President of the Republic, Thiers agreed to the annexation by Prussia of Alsace and Lorraine, with the attendant loss of that region's valuable coal, iron and salt mines, and to an indemnity of 5,000 million francs.

The restoration of the monarchy was now a real possibility. This fact, coupled with Thiers's acceptance of the punitive peace terms and his bungled attempt, on 18 March 1871, to disarm the National Guard by sending in troops to recapture the city cannon stationed on the Butte Montmartre (the hilltop working-class district in the north of the city), proved to be the final straw for the people of Paris, resulting in a spontaneous popular uprising against the national government. The initially peaceful protest saw the women of Montmartre preventing the soldiers from taking control of the cannon and pleading with them to join in their common cause against a government they regarded as cowardly, treacherous and unpatriotic. Many of the soldiers, themselves Parisians, fraternized with the crowd that quickly gathered about them. Events then took on a violent turn as some of the soldiers, egged on by the crowd, turned on their own officers, capturing and executing two unpopular generals, Clément Thomas and Claude Lecomte. The crowd then proceeded to march to the Hôtel de Ville.

A proletarian government was established for the city shortly afterwards and on 26 March a new municipal council, the Central Committee of the National Guard, was duly elected. Two days later the Commune, named in memory of the Commune of 10 August 1792, was inaugurated outside the Hôtel de Ville. Thiers, who had recalled the government troops back to Versailles, where the National Assembly had moved during the last stages of the war with Prussia, abandoned the city to its fate. The choice of Versailles as the nation's new capital was deeply symbolic, given the town's royalist associations. It is estimated that some 300,000 men and women supported the Commune, but there were plenty of other Parisians who were either indifferent or even hostile to it and, as the revolution progressed, many more would also turn against it.[9]

The seventy-nine elected members of the Commune consisted of veterans who had fought during the 1848 Revolution, labour militants, a few radical intellectuals, writers and journalists, and several National Guardsmen or *fédérés* as they became known, again in memory of 1792. The Commune also numbered among its supporters the writers and feminists Louise Michel, Paule Mink, Elizabeth Dmitrieff and André Léo. A few women like Michel also took up arms and fought on the barricades while thousands of others came out in support of the *fédérés*, providing food and first aid for them.[10] For many of their detractors, all Communards were considered to be the 'descendants' of the revolutionaries of Robespierre's 'Reign of Terror' (1792–93), when tens of thousands of people opposed to his dictatorship were executed, but it was the women in particular who were demonized by the right-wing press and in government propaganda, which represented them as savage whores and inebriated *pétroleuses* (female incendiaries) setting the city alight during the *Semaine sanglante*. Hundreds of women were shot or deported to the penal colonies in Cayenne and New Caledonia, many for simply being out in the street poorly dressed or for carrying a milk bottle thought to be filled with paraffin.[11] The image of the *pétroleuse* so captured the bourgeois imagination that the Commune itself came to be thought of metaphorically as a diseased prostitute, an aspect that I shall explore further in chapter 3.

While many workers had become politicized in the 1830s and 1840s and had supported the 1848 Revolution, the majority of the Commune's supporters were not activists but ordinary working-class men and women who had suffered the effects of economic growth and recession for years and who had bravely undergone all the privations of the Prussian war and siege while proudly defending their city against the foreign invader. And, for a short while at least, before Thiers finally sent in the government troops (the Versaillais) to recapture the city, an atmosphere of relief, jollity and carnival prevailed. With Paris cut off from the rest of the country, it felt as if the city was living in a time outside of ordinary time, it was 'Le Temps des cerises' (Cherry time), after a popular song written by Jean-Baptiste Clément in 1867.[12]

Because of its importance as the nation's capital, Paris had traditionally been administered by the national government and, regardless of the political regime in power during the nineteenth century, the city had consistently been denied any form of municipal government of its own.[13] The Commune has typically been seen, therefore, as the first real attempt by the people of Paris to reclaim their city after many had been forced out of the city centre into the urban wastelands on the periphery as a result of Baron Haussmann's building schemes of the 1850s and 1860s.[14] The general assumption that the Communards were all Parisians returning to the city centre to reclaim 'their space', however, has been challenged by Robert Tombs, who argues that there is little hard evidence to suggest that Communards from the *faubourgs* actually were returning exiles. There is reason to believe that some were just visiting sightseers, while most *fédérés* were in fact migrants to the city with little or no memory of pre-Haussmann Paris.[15] William Serman also draws attention to the fact that only fourteen of the seventy-nine elected members of the Commune were actually born in Paris.[16] It is perhaps not surprising that in Zola's novel *L'Assommoir* (also to be discussed in

Chapter 4), only two people among the rowdy, carnivaleque wedding party that descends on the city centre from the heights of Montmartre, in what turns out to be a coded parody of the Commune, have ever been to the centre of Paris before; the bridegroom Coupeau and his neighbour Madinier. The only times the bride and heroine, Gervaise, a 'naturalized' Parisian originally from Provence, leaves her *quartier* are on her wedding day and, many years later, to visit Coupeau at the hospital at Sainte-Anne. From the point of view of the social history of the period, this is consistent with the habits of many working-class Parisians, the majority of whom lived, worked, and sought their entertainment almost exclusively within their own neighbourhood.[17]

Nevertheless, whether the *fédérés* were, strictly speaking, returning Parisians or not, there is still much to be said for Henri Lefebvre's contention that the Commune cannot be explained merely in socio-historical terms as the result of the patriotism of the urban masses and an apparently corresponding unpatriotic reaction on the part of the ruling class. Haussmannization did indeed result in the segregation of social groups and it did mark the contrast between the bourgeois city centre and its working-class periphery. As Lefebvre has argued, urban space is far from geographically and geometrically neutral; it is a setting for confrontation where competing social and political strategies are deployed and played out.[18] Haussmann's demolition of many slum areas may have opened up the city and turned the west, and particularly the centre, of Paris into a new bourgeois residential and entertainment space but, as David Harvey suggests, the more city space was opened up physically, the more it had to be partitioned and closed off through social practice.[19] For example, in *L'Assommoir* again, much is made of the social and cultural difference between the working-class characters and the smart bourgeois Parisians they encounter on their way into the city. And, as we shall see in Chapter 2, some of the articles and illustrations which appeared in the illustrated weekly journal *Le Monde illustré* during the Commune highlight the fact that the Parisian bourgeoisie were greatly angered by, and fearful of, the invasion of 'their' city by what they considered to be working-class undesirables. The consequences of such policies and attitudes to the partitioning of urban space can be seen to persist into the twenty-first century, as evidenced by the riots that erupted in the Parisian *banlieues* in 2005–6.

The Commune, therefore, can be interpreted as an attempt to break down existing hierarchies and social barriers and to improve the lot of the working classes. Once in power, its leaders proceeded to propose a number of measures for the benefit of the Parisian workforce, including, for example: the reimbursement of debts; the free return of pawned goods; the promotion of workers' co-operatives; financial support for orphans and all women, whether married or not, whose partners had been killed fighting for the National Guard and the defence of Paris; the provision of a state education for women and children; and the separation of church and state. Before many of these measures could be brought into effect, however, Thiers decided the time was right to suppress the revolt. For six weeks, starting on 2 April, Paris was bombarded yet again, this time by the Versaillais. The city's defences were finally breached in early May 1871 and from 21 to 28 May, *la Semaine sanglante*, the Versaillais repression became increasingly savage. Before being beaten into submission, the retreating Communards burned parts of the city and some public buildings, including two Renaissance gems: the Tuileries Palace, the city residence of kings and emperors, and the Hôtel de Ville. They also executed some 150 members of the clergy whom they had taken hostage, including Darboy, the Archbishop of Paris. These killings, together with those earlier of the generals Thomas and Lecomte, and the destruction of the city including the ritualized demolition of the Vendôme Column and Thiers's own house, were to form the basis of the justification of the repression, with writers such as Maxime Du Camp ready to cast the blame for all the slaughter on to the Communards themselves. Thus was born the so-called 'bourgeois' memory and myth of the Commune. The term 'bourgeois' was used by Communards at the time to describe anyone who opposed them, whatever their political affiliation – Legitimist, Orléanist, Bonapartist or republican – and is still used today by members of Les Amis de la Commune, the organization founded in 1882 by those Communards who returned to France from exile after the amnesty of 1880.[20]

The period that followed *la Semaine sanglante* was one of unmitigated political, social, cultural and artistic repression and censorship. The trials, deportations and executions of the Communards, and anyone else suspected of having supported them, continued under Marshal MacMahon's government of Moral Order (*l'Ordre moral*), which took over in 1873 after Thiers was forced to resign from office, having lost the support of the monarchists. The monarchists, however, though still in the majority in the National Assembly, had become a spent force by 1874, having made themselves increasingly unpopular with the general population on several counts.[21] There was, firstly, their campaign in favour of the absolutist Comte de Chambord, who refused to accept the *tricolore* flag and insisted instead on the royal *fleur de lys* as the nation's emblem; secondly, their close identification with the Catholic Church; and, finally, their worrying talk of declaring war on Italy in order to restore papal control. MacMahon therefore found himself losing ground to the Bonapartists, who were growing in number in the National Assembly and, with a potential new leader in the Prince Imperial, Napoleon III's son, were emerging as a potential right-wing alternative to *l'Ordre moral*, going on to enjoy a certain amount of electoral success in 1874 and 1875. Despite passing a number of measures to counter both the Bonapartist and republican threats, the monarchists were further weakened by the republican victories in the election of Deputies in 1876. MacMahon's *coup d'état* on 16 May 1877 ('la crise du 16 mai'), a desperate bid to ensure that only those Deputies who supported him would be returned to office in that year's elections, nevertheless still resulted in a further victory for the republicans, after which they came to be recognized as potentially capable of uniting and leading the country. With the differences between all political factions, and within the divided republican camp itself, temporarily put to one side during the successful staging of the *Exposition universelle* and the *Fête du 30 juin* in 1878, thousands of Parisians came out on to the streets to show their overwhelming support for the Republic.

Now surrounded by republicans, and perhaps fearing impeachment following the fallout from his failed *coup d'état*, MacMahon took the decision not to see out his full seven-year term in office and tendered his resignation on 30 January 1879. The Senate duly elected the moderate republican Jules Grévy as President of the Republic. Gambetta's election as President of the Chamber of Deputies took place the next day, 31 January. On 10 February 1879, the republican daily newspaper *Le Siècle* triumphantly announced the return of the National Assembly to Paris, the harsh winter of 1878–79 having dealt a fatal blow to the provincial capital of Versailles ('Le retour [du gouvernement] à Paris est décidé. L'hiver 1878–1879, avec ses neiges et ses frimas, a porté le coup mortel à la capitale rurale.')

The inauguration of the 'republican' Republic following the demise of *l'Ordre moral* thus brings us back full-circle to Gambetta's speech of reconciliation and forgetting on 21 June 1880. His oratory finally convinced the Chamber of Deputies to approve the amnesty bill, which was eventually passed on 11 July 1880 after the Senate had insisted on an amendment denying amnesty to anyone found guilty of arson or assassination.[22] The official adoption in 1879 of *La Marseillaise* as the national anthem followed, in 1880, by the Communard amnesty, the adoption of the *tricolore* flag as the national emblem, and the inauguration of the 14 July (Bastille Day) as an annual national holiday, together put the final seal on the new Third Republic but, in the process, condemned the memory of the Commune to oblivion.[23]

Remembering and forgetting the Commune

Since the 1980s and the rise in Holocaust studies in particular, much critical attention has focused on the problematic relationship between the past and the present.[24] In the 1990s there then followed what has been described by Susannah Radstone as 'an explosion of interest in memory studies' across a wide range of disciplines as commentators tried to understand how memory is *produced* or *(re)constructed* by both individuals and societies; how memory is continually open to contestation; how there are always a multiplicity of 'memories' of events; how the importance or usefulness of different versions of memory shift and change over time; and how sometimes it is perhaps better just to forget and let go of the past.[25] This book was born out of this persisting and widening interest in social or cultural memory studies and finds its basis in such debates.

As I embarked on my research and proceeded to analyse a range of cultural production to discover the ways in which 'bourgeois' (anti-Communard) memories of Paris and the Commune were constructed, transmitted, remembered and, over time, discarded or obliterated, I soon realized that it was important to begin by considering the main nineteenth-century theories of memory. It was a common belief during this period that the experiences and memories acquired by an individual are somehow inscribed within or on the surface of his or her body in the same way that, for example, a monument can be physically inscribed. Such theories of so-called 'organic memory' (advanced, for example, by Jean Baptiste Lamarck, Théodule Ribot and Valentin Magnan) also suggest that acquired experiences can be 'inherited' by future generations just like physical and behavioural characteristics and that as a consequence, there can be a transfer of collective human memory and history from one generation to the next.[26] An understanding of the pervasive importance of 'organic', 'generational' or 'inherited' memory theories is central to any analysis of the reaction of the contemporary dominant classes in France to the people and events of the Commune. Such theories formed an integral part of the language and rhetoric of all sorts of texts, not just medical treaties but also novels and articles in popular newspapers, reflecting the widespread preoccupation with the perceived degeneration and decadence of the human race.[27] Nineteenth-century theories of organic memory, therefore, go some way to help explain why the majority of bourgeois Parisians appeared so ready to accept the Versaillais repression of the Commune, for the insurgents and their supporters were routinely perceived as the inheritors of the 'revolutionary temperament' of their putative ancestors, the men and women of the Terror.

It is Nietzsche, however, who, perhaps better than any other contemporary commentator, encapsulates the political, historical, philosophical and physiological aspects of memory and forgetting in the wake of the Franco-Prussian War (in which he himself participated) and the Paris Commune.[28] Marc Sautet, for example, has shown how Nietzsche was influenced by both these events in his early work, *The Birth of Tragedy*.[29] Sautet argues that Nietzsche's hostility to the Commune was based on a pre-existing fear of, and general hostility towards, worker emancipation and a belief in a feudal, aristocratic system where slavery and exploitation of those on the bottom rungs of society was the mark of a civilized society (pp. 14–17). Though not born out of any corresponding support for bourgeois capitalism on his part, Nietzsche's condemnation of the Commune on the grounds that it represented a terrible, barbarous threat to the established order resonates throughout anti-Communard discourse. Nietzsche's assessment of the Judeo-Christian view of justice and punishment and the way this manifests itself in the form of cruelty, torture, spectacle and theatricality also provides a theoretical context for the hostile representation of Paris and the Commune. His argument in favour of the deliberate forgetting of those elements of an individual's or a nation's past that are deemed contrary to the interests of the present and what he calls the 'hygiene of life', meanwhile, provides an intellectual framework for interpreting the reconstruction and reinvention of Paris during the 1878 *Exposition universelle*, and echoes also Gambetta's Amnesty speech of 1880.[30] It is thus not my intention to discuss Nietzsche at a philological level in this book, but instead to historicize him and to use him as a model for understanding the post-Commune universe inhabited by Zola, Maxime Du Camp and their contemporaries.

Nietzsche contends that the ability to forget is an active phenomenon that is necessary to the proper functioning of the body; what is required in human beings as well as in nations is a '*tabula rasa* of consciousness, making room for the new', for without such 'active forgetfulness' there can be no present.[31] However, he also states that humans, unlike the 'beasts in the field', are psychologically incapable of forgetting and are forever chained to the past: 'however far and fast [Man] may run, this chain runs with him.'[32] For Nietzsche, this inherent human propensity for memory is the result of 'an active will not to let go', and there is, he claims, 'perhaps nothing more frightening and more sinister in the whole prehistory of man than his *technique for remembering things*'.[33] In terms that find their sinister echo in the Versaillais repression of the Commune and its long-drawn-out aftermath under *l'Ordre moral*, as well as in the fundamentalism of the Roman Catholic revival of the period, Nietzsche describes how, historically and psychologically, human beings have been conditioned to remember by means of the infliction of physical and mental pain:

> 'Something is branded in, so that it stays in the memory: only that which *hurts* incessantly is remembered' . . . Things never proceeded without blood, torture, and victims, when man thought it necessary to forge a memory for himself. The most horrifying sacrifices and offerings . . . the most repulsive mutilations . . . , the cruellest rituals of all religious cults (and all religions are at their deepest foundations systems of cruelty) – all these things originate from that instinct which guessed that the most powerful aid to memory was pain. (pp. 42–3)

This passage exemplifies the paradox of life under the early Third Republic. On the one hand, the reprisals against the Communards and the working-class people of Paris were so terrible that no one who experienced or witnessed them could possibly forget them and, therefore, would be actively discouraged from fomenting revolution ever again. Thus, the repression ensured that the memory was not only inscribed in stone in the form of the Sacré-Cœur Basilica, built specifically to expiate the 'sins' of the nation, but that it was also branded into the minds, and often on to the bodies, of those who had supported, or been suspected of supporting, the Commune. Such a memory of events could then be passed on to future generations. On the other hand, the Republic after 1879 practised a form of 'active forgetfulness' where the material city – and, by extension, the consciousness of the nation itself – was indeed turned into a *tabula rasa* for the physical and moral good health of all. This process was facilitated by the *Exposition universelle* in 1878 and, as I will argue in Chapter 5, found its sublime expression in Charles Marville's photographic exhibition, *Travaux* (Public Works). Both Du Camp and Zola, however, as we shall see in Chapters 3 and 4, are unwilling to, or incapable of shaking off the chains that bind them to the past. At the same time, however, certainly in Zola's case generally and in aspects of Du Camp's *Paris: Ses organes, ses fonctions et sa vie dans la seconde moitié du dix-neuvième siècle* (1875), a brave effort is nevertheless often made to try to forget the past and move on.

The Du Camp of *Les Convulsions de Paris* (1878–80), by contrast, epitomizes the desire on the part of the reactionaries of *l'Ordre moral* to remember the Commune 'out of anger at harm done' to society (to borrow Nietzsche's words), a crime for which those who are held to be responsible must be made to repay their debt to society (p. 45). This helps to explain why the granting of amnesty to ex-Communards was so completely out of the question for Du Camp and many others. As Nietzsche goes on to observe, again with relevance to the reactionary governments of Thiers and MacMahon, 'each weakening and deeper endangering of the community brings the return of harsher forms' (p. 53).

In order to explain fully how counter-revolutionary memories of Paris and the Commune were initially constructed, however, we need to take account also of theories that see memory as an external, material and socially based phenomenon. This tradition goes back to Aristotle by way of Saint Augustine, Spinoza, Montesquieu, Leibniz, Auguste Comte, Nietzsche (again) and Emile Durkheim, finding its modern expression in the writings on memory by the French social scientist Maurice Halbwachs.[34]

Halbwachs, like his teacher Durkheim, maintains that all memory has a social foundation. All memories, recent or distant, are thus evoked through the use of a stable structural mechanism which he calls the 'cadres sociaux de la mémoire' (social frameworks of memory). These frameworks are situated in *collective* time and space, and subject to *present circumstances*, and they conform to a given social group's own internal logic and vision of the world.[35] They serve to unify certain general patterns of thought, beliefs and core values and are representative of how the group perceives its own past (pp. 141–2). For Halbwachs, it follows that these social frameworks on which memory depends are representative only of the memory of the dominant social class. Furthermore, the dominant class only assimilates, and thus 'remembers', what it considers to be relevant and useful to itself within the context of the present. In this respect, therefore, Halbwachs's theories recall those of Nietzsche on active forgetting and the 'usefulness' of history for present generations. The passage of time and rapidly changing circumstances inevitably consign much of the past to oblivion. Individuals, however, according to Halbwachs, are still able to reconstruct the past by 'borrowing' material and cultural data from the present; in other words, from other people, the social milieu, language, objects, artefacts and, with particular relevance to the focus of this book, from place (*le lieu*). This concept is further developed in Pierre Nora's vast project on the construction of French collective memory and identity, *Les Lieux de mémoire*.[36]

Halbwachs is not concerned, like those believers in organic memory, with actually *locating* memory in the brain or indeed anywhere else in the body: nor, like his contemporary Henri Bergson, does he hold that memory is a 're-living' of images from the past that lie buried within the individual.[37] On the contrary, he rejects Bergson's view of memory as subject to a Cartesian mind/body distinction and instead posits that memory is at once image *and* reason. Memory for Halbwachs is always a rational, if involuntary, reconstruction of the past based on those elements and mechanisms that are to be found within the consciousness of the social group, to which every individual is in some way connected. For Halbwachs, much like his other contemporary Marcel Proust, memory can be aroused by a material object or, more precisely, by the involuntary sensation that the object arouses.[38] But whereas Bergson and Proust are primarily concerned with the memory of the individual, Halbwachs takes account of the reconstruction of memory by both the individual and the whole social group, since he believes that it is through their interaction with others that individuals acquire their memories, remember them, and locate them.[39]

The term 'mémoire collective' (collective memory) was first coined by Halbwachs in *Les Cadres sociaux de la mémoire* but its full definition appears in his later work *La Mémoire collective*. Halbwachs argues that collective memory is not the same as history. Whereas history only needs to be recorded when tradition ends and the social memory is fading or breaking up, collective memory manifests itself as a continuous current of thought that remains in the consciousness of a given group and is, by definition, only of relevance to that group. So long as there are people within that group to whom such memories are significant in some way, then those memories will continue to be preserved. Once they are no longer deemed worthy of remembrance, because they are no longer considered relevant or useful to present-day life, they will be forgotten.[40] The other key difference between history and the collective memory identified by Halbwachs is that history is unitary, whereas there are multiple collective memories (p. 137). For Halbwachs, the sort of history which is recorded in history books is an external, artificial construct that is a function of the ruling class's representation of events and which, therefore, stands in opposition to history as it is interpreted by the working class.

Halbwachs himself, growing up in the decades following the Commune, had personal experience of the effects of the deliberate denial of working-class memories of the Commune in favour of an alternative, overriding history created by the ruling class. While preparing the fourth manuscript of *La Mémoire collective* between 1943 and 1944, he was also living in Paris under the German occupation, and thus whereas in *Les Cadres sociaux de la mémoire* the socialist and republican Halbwachs argues in favour of one unifying collective memory which embraces all classes, in the later work he becomes acutely aware of the dangers of the establishment of one universal history, and argues instead for the preservation of the past in spite of the present, and for the right to the existence of multiple collective memories. Halbwachs's recognition, under a totalitarian regime, of the importance of the preservation of multiple collective memories has its obvious parallels with the denial of pro-Commune memory in the 1870s by Thiers, MacMahon and Gambetta, each according to his own political agenda. It is this recognition of the need for multiple collective memories that ensures that Halbwachs's work continues to resonate.[41] For, as Paul Connerton also reminds us, 'the mental enslavement of the subjects of a totalitarian regime begins when their memories are taken away'.[42]

While certainly retaining a keen awareness of the existence and importance of the multiple collective memories, myths and interpretations of the Commune, my concern in this book is with those of the dominant social group of the 1870s, the anti-Communard bourgeoisie. For it was this group's 'memory' of Paris and the Commune which was to crystallize into the accepted 'history' of this event as exemplified by Du Camp's *Les Convulsions de Paris*, and which was to have the longest-lasting influence on how the French establishment continued to perceive this period well into the twentieth century, with the result that, even today, the subject remains contentious.[43] And, most importantly, it was this dominant group that was responsible for the reconstruction of Paris in a concerted effort to efface all material traces of the Commune. So effective was this effacement that – with the notable exception of the *Mur des fédérés* with its simple plaque erected in 1909 and inscribed 'Aux morts de la Commune 21–28 mai 1871' ('To the dead of the Commune 21–28 May 1871') and now the Place de la Commune inaugurated

in 2000 in the Butte aux Cailles, and the Square Louise Michel opposite
the Sacré-Cœur in 2004 – the city centre's topography displays virtually
no trace of what took place there between 18 March and 28 May 1871,
at least for the uninitiated.[44]

The case studies

Choosing case studies and using them to interpret historical events is
always problematic. In making my selection, I asked myself several questions. For example, are these texts and images exemplary of conservative
and reactionary thought in the aftermath of the Commune, or are they
only isolated instances, or indeed are they actually only the tip of a very
large iceberg? How is it possible, for example, to assess something as
vast as the press, or even just one illustrated weekly newspaper? Clearly,
this was an impossibly large project for one person to undertake. Each
year, for example, just one edition of *Le Monde illustré* comprised about
500 illustrations and double or treble that amount of texts of various
kinds, figures that would need to be multiplied over and over again to
cover all the years from 1871 to 1878. Obviously, decisions had to be
made in relation to the years and months studied and the specific editions, articles and illustrations to be included for detailed examination.
Choices had to be made too regarding the fictional and historical texts
and photographs to include over and above my initial decision to concentrate on broadly conservative, anti-Communard texts and images.
Which writers appeared best to represent the conservative or reactionary position and, of those writers, which of their texts were the most
appropriate?

As far as the photographic representation of the Commune was
concerned, again I had to be selective but in focusing on images of the
city, rather than on portraits, the choice was immediately narrowed
down. In opting to analyse only certain photographers and by focusing
on the years 1871 to 1878, the choice was narrowed down still further.
Nevertheless, as in all undertakings of this kind, limits had to be set and
reset throughout my research.

The representative cross-section of cultural production on which I
finally settled comprises: *Le Monde illustré*, an ostensibly non-political,
conservative, and family-orientated weekly illustrated journal; Maxime
Du Camp's monumental *Paris: Ses organes, ses fonctions et sa vie dans la
seconde moitié du dix-neuvième siècle* (1869–75) and his reactionary history of the Commune, *Les Convulsions de Paris* (1878–80);[45] three novels

by Emile Zola, *Le Ventre de Paris* (1873), *L'Assommoir* (1877) and *Une page d'amour* (1878);[46] and selected images from four photographic collections, Charles Soulier's *Paris incendié: mai 1871* (1871), Edouard-Denis Baldus's album of heliogravures, *Les Principaux Monuments de France* (1875), and Charles Marville's *Album du vieux Paris* and *Travaux*, which were displayed at the *Exposition universelle* in 1878.

Perhaps the best way to describe my project is to take a cue from Du Camp, Zola and the rest, and to employ a medical metaphor. I like to think of all these individual texts, illustrations and photographs as akin to the multiple pictures or 'slices' of a body taken from all angles by a magnetic resonance imaging (MRI) scanner. Such slices, when assembled together by a computer program, create a three-dimensional screen image of the body under examination that can be rotated in all directions to reveal the organs and soft tissues contained within it. Like the results of an MRI scan, an analysis of these case studies similarly reveals a picture that is greater than the sum of its parts.

The inclusion of a newspaper, especially an illustrated journal, is relevant because of the prime role of the press in the nineteenth century in the dispersal of news and information, the promulgation of official propaganda, and the reflection of readers' opinions, all of which contributed to the creation and transference of public memories and gave rise to what Matt Matsuda calls a 'typographic memory of events'.[47] For many people in the nineteenth century, the newspaper was their education. Improvements in paper production, composition and printing techniques, as well as advances in telecommunications and transportation, had rendered newspapers relatively cheap and widely available. Newspapers thus helped many people to learn to read and to form their view of the world. This is the case, for example, with several of Zola's working-class characters: for example, Lantier in *L'Assommoir* and his son, Etienne, in the later novel *Germinal*. Marcel Proust (at first sight perhaps an unlikely commentator in this respect), writing with specific reference to the Third Republic, and significantly after the implementation of the freedom of the press laws and educational reforms of 1881, goes further and suggests not only that newspapers were more influential than the education system, but that they were also even more important than the Church in their insidious promulgation of official ideology.[48] Maurice Mouillaud goes further still and suggests that there exists a tripartite relationship evoked by the name of a given newspaper, which acts as an inspirational touchstone for the reader or an all-seeing eye placed on high surveying all that is said in its name: that of its founder (God the Father), its director or editor-in-chief (Christ the Son), and the 'person' of the paper itself (the Holy Ghost).[49] For Mouillaud, it is through this all-seeing 'eye', which after the Revolution of 1789 is deemed to be the 'eye of Reason' (rather than of God), that the reader is made to see and interpret the world.

Du Camp, writing in 1855, was perhaps one of the first to recognize the modern reader's preference for the newspaper over the novel which, he claimed, was no longer capable of offering anything new and original, just boring reworkings of outworn ideas and useless nonsense, whereas the newspaper could offer everything and anything from the morning's headline news to tales of the previous night's back-street murders.[50] The reading public, according to Du Camp, is neither ungrateful nor indifferent, it simply asks to be informed and entertained.

The art historian Tom Gretton also compares newspapers to cities, pointing out that they have a topography and that they invite the reader, like the *flâneur*, to indulge in random encounters, take numerous different pathways, and leaf his or her way through fragments gathered from the outside world.[51] For Mouillaud, the newspaper is thus even more Bakhtinian than the novel, reflecting a world which has lost its central unifying core, if it ever possessed one in the first place.[52] It is this inherently random, unstable, fragmentary, polyphonic and polymorphous nature of the newspaper which in the nineteenth-century is the key difference between the newspaper and the novel.[53] This not only helps to explain the popularity and proliferation of newspapers and journals in this period but also the ambiguities and conflicts of interest or point of view that surface over and over again in their coverage of events.

There are several reasons for deciding to focus on *Le Monde illustré* rather than one of the other popular illustrated journals of the period. As part of the Paul Dalloz empire, which also owned *Le Moniteur universel*, the government's quasi-official newspaper, *Le Monde illustré*, can be taken as a good barometer of the establishment view but unlike *L'Illustration*, its major rival in the conservative quality press, however, *Le Monde illustré* was not officially classified as a political journal, a fact that, as we shall see in Chapter 2, did not prevent its contributors from engaging with political issues. As a consequence of its 'apolitical' status, and much to the annoyance of *L'Illustration*, *Le Monde illustré* was spared the payment of the special government levy applied to the political press, thus enabling the journal to keep its cover charge relatively low.[54] In 1871 *Le Monde illustré* sold for 35 centimes per copy in Paris and 40 centimes at railway stations, rising to 50 centimes by 1878. *L'Illustration*, however, was obliged to charge 75 centimes per copy during the same period. Quality daily broadsheets without any illustrations sold for between 10 and 20 centimes, and the satirical *Le Charivari*, which typically carried only one illustration, charged 25 centimes while, at the other end of the scale, the 'canards' or penny-dreadfuls sold for 5 centimes a copy. To put this apparently low sum into its period context, 5 centimes already represented some 12.5 per cent of the price of a kilo of bread, or 17 per cent of the price of a litre of milk. Thus newspapers were a relative luxury for some and usually shared between readers or, more commonly, rented by the hour in the *cabinets de lecture* where they reached a far wider and socially diverse audience.[55]

Surprisingly, given the fact that the illustrations that appeared in the *Le Monde illustré* form part of a well-known general corpus of Franco-Prussian-War and Commune imagery, commentators have invariably divorced these images from their accompanying texts, thus overlooking the potential for further interpretative analysis.[56] Indeed, neither *Le Monde illustré* nor any other French illustrated newspaper has yet been the subject of a detailed analysis, or at least not within the context of the representation of Paris and the collective memory of the Commune. The majority of both contemporary and modern scholars who have taken an interest in the press of the Third Republic have tended, on the whole, to produce general histories, or else have concentrated on the Communard, the reactionary right wing or the satirical press.[57]

Tom Gretton is perhaps the only commentator to have focused specifically on text and image relations in the illustrated weekly press, taking *Le Monde illustré* as a model, but he has done so in order to position the illustrated weekly as a genre within the hierarchy of the visual arts, and not to examine the political or memorialist implications of the articles and illustrations published by the journal.[58] Even Paul Lidsky's dissection of the hostile reaction of many French writers to the events of 1871 stops short of analysing the work of jobbing journalists, preferring instead to focus mainly on canonical names.[59] The historian J.M. Roberts, whilst he examines how the Right has mythologized the Commune, does not nevertheless discuss the role of the conservative illustrated press in perpetuating these same myths.[60] Adrian Rifkin, on the other hand, certainly does acknowledge the importance of popular prints and the press as an influence on, and reflection of, public opinion, but limits his analysis mainly to the Second Empire and the period of the Commune itself.[61] Matsuda, meanwhile, highlights the importance of the press and the function of the written text in general as a key factor in the creation and transference of public memories, but again does not go on to analyse the actual contribution of press articles to the transference of memory in the early Third Republic.[62] Chapter 2, therefore, aims to provide the fullest analysis to date of the relationship between text and image in a contemporary newspaper. The choice of key texts and illustrations is taken from a selection that appeared in *Le Monde illustré* in the months following the *Semaine sanglante*. These posthumous articles on the Commune and early responses to its demise are then compared and contrasted with a representative selection of texts and illustrations appearing in the journal during the *Exposition universelle, Fête du 30 juin*, and other festivities hosted by the city in 1878. In so doing, I seek to demonstrate how, by drawing on the shared cultural heritage of its intended bourgeois readers, *Le Monde illustré* was very well placed to help lay the foundations, along with anti-Communard histories such as that by Du Camp, of the collective memory and myth of the events of Paris and the Commune.

Du Camp's extensive body of work, though often cited, has not to date commanded much critical attention in its own right either. And yet, while his friend Gustave Flaubert was still struggling to make a name for himself, Du Camp was already a very well-known and popular poet, novelist and journalist before then going on to undertake, among many other projects, a series of social-historical studies of Paris and its institutions, an account of the Commune, and a number of volumes of literary history and memoirs.[63] Modern scholars are typically apt to accuse him of being envious of Flaubert and to dismiss him as being a mendacious, malicious, upper-class reactionary who was deeply hostile to the Commune, a view which even the revival of interest in his work as a pioneering photographer of Egypt in the 1840s and Gérard de Senneville's highly sympathetic biography have done little to change.[64]

For Lidsky, Du Camp is an *arriviste* and *Les Convulsions de Paris* are 'la bible de la littérature anticommunarde' (the 'Bible' of anti-Communard literature).[65] There is certainly no disputing the fact that *Les Convulsions* exemplifies the reaction against the Commune and was a key text in the construction and promulgation of the reactionary memory of the Commune. In fact, the work was so in tune with the conservative establishment's conception of the Commune that Du Camp was elected to the Académie française in December 1880 on the strength of it. As further proof of Du Camp's contemporary popularity, both *Paris: ses organes* and *Les Convulsions* remained in print until 1905 and later accounts of the Commune, such as those by Lucien Nass (1914) and Henri D'Alméras (1927), clearly owe a debt to his tendentious interpretation of events.[66] Writing from a different political perspective in 1936, and significantly during the Spanish Civil War, Frank Jellinek describes *Les Convulsions de Paris* as one of the most important reactionary histories of the Commune and warns his readers that it 'must be used with extreme caution'.[67]

Rather than just dismiss Du Camp as the archetypal reactionary and enemy of the Commune, therefore, I would like instead to re-evaluate *Les Convulsions*, as well as his earlier *Paris: ses organes* – a work which is too often read merely as a nostalgic evocation of 'le vieux Paris' (bygone Paris) – as part of a much wider political, historical and memorialist discourse on the Commune and its aftermath. In so doing, my focus will be specifically on reinterpreting the definitive 1876 edition of *Paris: ses organes*, and volume VI in particular, as a potentially politically subversive text which on the one hand attempts to reconstitute the textual and topographical archive of pre-Communard Paris and to preserve the memory of the Second Empire but which, on the other hand, also provides an unexpectedly ironic commentary on *l'Ordre moral* and the political preoccupations of the period. Taken together, *Paris: ses organes* and *Les Convulsions* provide a useful touchstone for the reinterpretation of Zola's literary representations of Paris and their Commune subtext.

The most obvious of Zola's novels to examine in a book on the memory of the Commune would have been *La Débâcle* (1892), the penultimate volume of the *Rougon-Macquart* and effectively the cycle's conclusion in terms of its great social and political themes.[68] However, apart from the fact that *La Débâcle* was written outside of the self-imposed timeframe of this book, the choice of this novel would have been too limiting. Better, I thought, to select novels that on the surface at least do not purport to engage with the memory of 1871 and to see how the themes and imagery that characterize the later novel were in fact already covertly present in Zola's Paris-set novels of the 1870s. The three novels I chose to examine were selected primarily because each one was written and published at a significant moment in the city's history; the immediate aftermath of the Commune in *Le Ventre de Paris*, the period when *l'Ordre moral* was unravelling in *L'Assommoir*, and during the 1878 festivities in *Une page d'amour*.

The initial serializations of Zola's novels in influential, though low-circulation, newspapers guaranteed him a degree of notoriety but, as has often been noted, it was *L'Assommoir* that placed him on the best-seller list (*RM*, II, 1534–5, 1558–68). This success did much to stimulate sales of his earlier novels and created an eager audience for the future volumes of *Les Rougon-Macquart*. However, despite the undoubted popularity of the serializations, which no doubt broadened his audience base, there is strong evidence to suggest that Zola was not much read by the working and lower middle classes, and even less so by women in these groups.[69] The core of his readership in the 1870s consisted primarily of other writers and intellectuals and, importantly, the bourgeoisie; people who had the education, money and spare time required to read novels.[70] This is not to deny Zola's later popularity among some sections of the working classes and the members of the Socialist and Communist parties, and the success of *Germinal* in particular among these groups but, as Anne-Marie Thiesse shows in her study of the reading of popular literature during the Belle Epoque, it was *bourgeois* rather than working-class readers of the period who appear to have been the more profoundly influenced by the novels they read in terms of their own personal development and in the adoption of their ideological stance (p. 55). An appreciation of the importance of Zola's influence on his middle-class readers, particularly in his depiction of the working classes, therefore, is of some importance. As Nelly Wolf argues, so successful was Zola's mid-nineteenth-century bourgeois conception of the working class in *L'Assommoir* and *Germinal* as alcohol-sodden, violent, degenerate, exhausted and starving, that it greatly influenced many other writers after him.[71] A careful reading of his novels of the 1870s, particularly those which are not overtly political such as *L'Assommoir* and *Une page d'amour*, therefore, not only enhances our understanding of Zola's own reaction to the events of May 1871 but also highlights the ways in which he was both influenced by, and a promulgator of, collective memories of Paris during the Commune. Zola was certainly not alone among writers in his adoption of the Commune as an intertext, but the unique blending in his novels of the pedagogical with the 'lisible' (readerly) and the 'scriptible' (writerly), to borrow the terms coined by Roland Barthes,[72] ensured that they endured the test of time whereas the literary fiction of most of his counter-revolutionary contemporaries such as Pierre Zaccone, Pierre Bion, and Elémir Bourges, for example, did not.[73]

In Chapter 5, I go on to trace how some of the same themes and images discussed in relation to *Le Monde illustré* and the Du Camp and Zola texts were interpreted through the medium of contemporary photography. The thousands of photographs taken in the aftermath of the Commune only became the focus of serious critical analysis during the 1970s. Jean-Claude Gautrand's analysis, written not long after May 1968 and the centenary of the Commune (and very much of its time), was perhaps the first real attempt to identify and discuss the subject in any detail; though his somewhat uncritical assessment of the photographer Bruno Braquehais as pro-Communard, on the basis that he produced several close-up shots of Communards posing alongside the Vendôme Column or on barricades, has subsequently been challenged by Linda Nochlin, who points out that Braquehais also photographed Versaillais soldiers.[74]

Building on Gautrand's early work, Donald English's perceptive 1981 study remains the best introduction yet to the whole subject of photography and the Commune, since it draws particular attention to the wider political, social, commercial, cultural and aesthetic contexts in which these photographs were produced and circulated.[75] Christine Lapostolle has also attempted to classify photographs taken during the Commune and its aftermath according to subject matter and ideological viewpoint (pro- or anti-Communard). In so doing, she questions the received opinion that Ernest Eugène Appert's photomontages, for example, were just anti-Communard propaganda and argues, convincingly, that such images should be reinterpreted within the context of contemporary notions of photography and 'reality' and what was deemed acceptable as a 'historical document'.[76] Elsewhere, Lapostolle has also highlighted the extensive use of the ruin as a photographic theme in line with contemporary political and literary discourse.[77] Alisa Luxenberg has taken up and developed this line of argument, citing Jules Claretie's descriptions in *L'Illustration* and Théophile Gautier's *Tableaux de sièges: Paris, 1870–1871* (1871) as the textual equivalents of Jules Andrieu's album 'Désastres de guerre'.[78] Luxenberg, however, like English and Lapostolle, stops short of any detailed comparative analysis between the photographic image of the ruin and contemporary discourse. My aim, therefore, is to focus on Charles Soulier's representation of the Tuileries Palace ruins, in order to explore the full ideological, symbolic, cultural and aesthetic purchase of the ruin at this particularly significant historical moment.

To date, commentators have tended to focus on the images produced by Braquehais, Andrieu, Appert, and Alphonse Justin Liébert. By contrast, the albums and collections produced in the 1870s by Soulier, Edouard-Denis Baldus and Charles Marville, all recognized as important Second Empire photographers, have escaped full analysis within the context of the production and consumption of images of Paris after the Commune. My aim is to redress the balance by looking at some of the political and memorialist implications of their images and to argue that their representations of Paris, each in their own way, in fact exemplify the collective political and aesthetic response of the conservative bourgeoisie – the intended purchasers of their photographs – to the demise of the Second Empire and the repression of Commune. Contrary to received opinion, Baldus's post-Commune vision of Paris, for example, is far from free of political or ideological bias, as the analysis in Chapter 5 will show.[79]

The full political implications of Marville's officially commissioned displays of photographs depicting the old, pre-Haussmann Paris set alongside the new Paris of the early Third Republic for the 1878 *Exposition universelle* have similarly not been much discussed by commentators. This exhibit, as I will demonstrate, effectively created a new photographic 'art of memory' designed to reflect the healthy and hygienic Paris of the new Republic, a Paris which had been suitably purged of both its Second Empire and Communard past. While Marie de Thézy draws attention to the inclusion of Marville's photographs in the 1878 *Exposition*, and while she sheds much light on his contribution to the documentation of the building projects of the Third Republic, she tends to see these projects as a straightforward continuation of Second Empire Haussmannization. In her comprehensive catalogue of Marville's œuvre, Thézy makes only a passing reference to the Commune and no mention at all of the ideological and political agenda that underpinned the reconstruction of the city during the Third Republic.[80] The same holds true of a piece which appeared in the journal *Foncier mensuel*. Marville's photographs of the reconstruction of the Vendôme Column are seen featured alongside interviews with Thézy and the photographer Tom Drahos about his own series of photographs entitled 'La Colonne Vendôme', but the political and memorialist significance of this monument are again left unexplored.[81] Instead, it is left to Jean-Pierre Dufreigne, in his review of Thézy's book on Marville, to politicize the photographer's work of the 1870s. For Dufreigne, Marville depicts the bourgeois, absolutist 'Paris du Thiers-Etat' (a quibble on the Third Estate (Government) and the name of its leader, Adolphe Thiers).[82] Dufreigne, however, goes no further with this provocative line of argument. A reappraisal of Marville's work within the context of post-Commune Paris and the 1878 *Exposition* would therefore seem to be overdue.

Necessarily limited as this choice of case studies is, it did however reveal to me a number of memorialist constructs based on a consistent set of cultural values and assumptions on behalf of the writers, artists and photographers in question. Many of the materials studied, for example, share the same obsession with decadence and attempt to explain the destruction of the city as a form of divine retribution. There is dependence also on a shared literary canon consisting principally of the Bible, Shakespeare, Corneille, Voltaire, and Victor Hugo, all of which are plundered in order to find ways to come to terms with the horror of the *Semaine sanglante* and to describe events deemed to be indescribable. The shared imagery, language, rhetoric, and narrative form are all put to work in order to rationalize and excuse or at least legitimize the repression of the Commune and to suppress the cruelty of the Versaillais and the suffering of their victims.

Now that I have outlined the aims and scope of this book, it is perhaps useful to end this general introduction by noting briefly what I have specifically *not* aimed to do. It has not been my intention to write another history of the Commune and the early Third Republic or to offer another history of nineteenth-century photography or the 'golden age' of the French press. Also, it has not been my intention to provide a further analysis of Zola's politics or another general study of Paris within *Les Rougon-Macquart*. Still less have I aimed to provide a critical philosophical or theoretical assessment of memory theory. What I have tried to do throughout, however, is to remain very closely focused on a selection of case studies in order to explore the ways in which memories of Paris and the Commune were constructed and repressed in the 1870s. In drawing comparisons between different forms and genres of texts and images I have tried to shed new light on our understanding of a particular flashpoint in French history.

Notes

1 Extract from the speech delivered to the French National Assembly translated by J.P.T. Bury in *Gambetta's Final Years: 'The Era of Difficulties' 1877–1882* (London and New York: Longman, 1982), p. 167. Throughout this book all translations into English, unless otherwise attributed, are my own, and reference is given to the original text. Further references to a cited text will appear in brackets after quotations; passages without page reference are from the last-cited page. Unless otherwise noted, all italics are the author's and all ellipses mine.

2 For a comprehensive account of the political machinations surrounding the granting of the amnesty and Gambetta's involvement see Bury, *Gambetta's Final Years*, ch. 8, and Jean T. Joughin, 'The Paris Commune in French Politics 1871–1880', *The Johns Hopkins University Studies in Historical and Political Science*, 73: 1 (1955).

3 Jacques Rougerie, *La Commune de 1871* (Paris: Presses universitaires de France, 1988), pp. 117–19.

4 Robert Cook, *Civil War America: Making a Nation 1848–1877* (London: Pearson Longman, 2003), p. 114. On the parallels between the two conflicts see Wolfgang Schivelbusche, *The Culture of Defeat: On National Trauma, Mourning, and Recovery*, trans. by Jefferson Chase (London: Granta Books, 2003).

5 For example: Walter Redfern, *Feet First: Jules Vallès* (Glasgow: University of Glasgow French and German Publications, 1992); Rachael Langford, *Jules Vallès and the Narration of History: Contesting the French Third Republic in the 'Jacques Vingtras' Trilogy* (Bern: Lang, 1999); Kristin Ross, *The Emergence of Social Space: Rimbaud and the Paris Commune* (Minneapolis: University of Minnesota Press, 1988); Jane Mayo Roos, 'Within the "Zone of Silence": Monet and Manet in 1878', *Art History*, 11: 3 (September 1988), 374–407 and *Early Impressionism and the French State (1866–1874)* (Cambridge and New York: Cambridge University Press, 1996), chs 9, 10; Jacquelynn Baas, 'Edouard Manet and *Civil War*', and Ronda Kasl, 'Edouard Manet's "Rue Mosnier": Le pauvre-a-t-il une patrie?', in *Art Journal*, 45: 1 (spring, 1985), 36–42 and 49–58; Jean Péridier, *La Commune et les artistes: Pottier-Courbet-Vallès-J.-B. Clément* (Paris: Nouvelles éditions latines, 1980); Albert Boime, *Art and the French Commune: Imagining Paris after War and Revolution* (Princeton, NJ: Princeton University Press, 1995); and John House, *Impressionism, Paint and Politics* (New Haven, CT, and London: Yale University Press, 2004). A notable exception is Paul Lidsky's *Les Ecrivains contre la Commune*, 2nd edn (Paris: La Découverte, 1999), but even he concentrates mainly on canonical names. See also J.M. Roberts, 'La Commune considérée par la droite: dimensions d'une mythologie', *Revue d'histoire moderne et contemporaine*, 19 (1972), 187–205.

6 See David A. Shafer, *The Paris Commune: French Politics, Culture, and Society at the Crossroads of the Revolutionary Tradition and Revolutionary Socialism* (New York and Basingstoke: Palgrave Macmillan, 2005), chs 1–2.

7 See Pamela M. Pilbeam, *Republicanism in Nineteenth-Century France* (London: Macmillan, 1995), p. 19, for an analysis of the different republican factions and the often blurred distinctions between conservative republicans and liberal monarchists.

8 See J.P.T. Bury, *Gambetta and the Making of the Third Republic* (London: Longman, 1973), p. 7.

9 William Serman, *La Commune de Paris (1871)* (Paris: Fayard, 1986), p. 281; Rougerie, *La Commune de 1871*, p. 62.

10 See Edith Thomas, *Les Pétroleuses* (Paris: Gallimard, 1963); Gay L. Gullickson, *Unruly Women of Paris: Images of the Commune* (Ithaca, NY, and London: Cornell University Press, 1996); and Carolyn J. Eichner, *Surmounting the Barricades: Women in the Paris Commune* (Bloomington: Indiana University Press, 2004).

11 Maxime Du Camp, *Paris: ses organes, ses fonctions et sa vie dans la seconde moitié du XIXe siècle*, 6 vols (Paris: Hachette, 1884–95), VI, p. 318.

12 Henri Lefebvre, *La Proclamation de la Commune* (Paris: Gallimard, 1965), p. 133.

13 David Harvey, *Consciousness and the Urban Experience* (Oxford: Blackwell, 1985), pp. 205–29.

14 See Lefebvre, *La Proclamation de la Commune*, p. 133.

15 Robert Tombs, *The Paris Commune, 1871* (London: Longman, 2000), p. 106.

16 Serman, p. 277.

17 David H. Pinkney, *Napoleon III and the Rebuilding of Paris* (Princeton, NJ: Princeton University Press, 1958), p. 17.

18 Lefebvre, 'La Classe ouvrière et l'espace' (1972), in *Espace et politique*, 2nd edn (Paris: Anthropos, 2000), pp. 168–9. Lefebvre develops this theme in greater detail in *La Production de l'espace* (Paris: Anthropos, 1974).

19 Harvey, pp. 205–29.

20 For details of the campaigning activities and documentation provided by Les Amis de la Commune, visit the group's website at < http://lacomune.club.fr> [accessed 7 April 2006].

21 For a concise history of this period see Keith Randell, *France: The Third Republic 1870–1914* (London: Edward Arnold, 1986), pp. 27–34.

22 See Bury, *Gambetta's Final Years*, p. 167.

23 See Stéphane Gacon, 'L'Oubli institutionnel', in *Oublier nos crimes: L'Amnésie nationale: une spécificité française?*, ed. by Dimitri Nicolaïdis (Paris: Editions Autrement, 1994), pp. 98–111 (p. 105).

24 See, for example, Fredric Jameson, *The Political Unconscious: Narrative as a Socially Symbolic Act* (Ithaca, NY: Cornell University Press, 1981); Pierre Nora, ed., *Les Lieux de mémoire*, 3 vols (Paris: Gallimard, 1984–93); Andreas Huyssen, *Twilight Memories: Marking time in a Culture of Amnesia* (New York and London: Routledge, 1995) and *Present Pasts: Urban Palimpsests and the Politics of Memory* (Stanford, CA: Stanford University Press, 2003); and Edward S. Casey, *Remembering: A Phenomenological Study*, 2nd edn (Bloomington and Indianapolis: Indiana University Press, 2000). For an introduction to the whole subject of cultural memory see Susannah Radstone, ed., *Memory and Methodology* (Oxford: Berg, 2000); Susannah Radstone and Katherine Hodgkin, eds, *Regimes of Memory* (London: Routledge, 2003); Noel Packard and Christopher Chen, 'From Medieval Mnemonics to a Social Construction of Memory', *American Behavioral Scientist*, 48: 10 (June 2005), 1297–319; and J. Candau, *Anthropologie de la mémoire* (Paris: Presses universitaires de France, 1996).

25 Radstone, *Memory and Methodology*, p. 1.

26 For a discussion of Lamark's *Recherches sur l'organisation des corps vivants* (1802), Ribot's *L'Hérédité: Etude psychologique sur ses phénomènes, ses lois, ses causes, ses conséquences* (1873), and *Les Maladies de la mémoire* (1881),

and for an introduction to the whole concept of organic memory theory, see Laura Otis, *Organic Memory: History and the Body in the Late Nineteenth and Early Twentieth Century* (Lincoln, NE, and London: University of Nebraska Press, 1994).

27 Matt Matsuda, *The Memory of the Modern* (New York: Oxford University Press, 1996), pp. 9–10.

28 The seminal texts are Nietzsche, 'On the Uses and Disadvantages of History for Life', in *Untimely Meditations* (1874), ed. by J.P. Stern and trans. by R.J. Hollingdale (Cambridge: Cambridge University Press, 1983) and *On the Genealogy of Morals* (1887), ed. and trans. by Douglas Smith (Oxford and New York: Oxford University Press, 1996), essays 1 and 2.

29 Marc Sautet, *Nietzsche et la Commune* (Paris: Le Sycomore, 1981).

30 See Nietzsche, 'On the Uses and Disadvantages of History for Life', and *On the Genealogy of Morals*, essays 1 and 2.

31 Nietzsche, *On the Genealogy of Morals*, p. 39.

32 Nietzsche, 'On the Uses and Disadvantages of History for Life', pp. 60–1.

33 Nietzsche, *On the Genealogy of Morals*, pp. 40, 42.

34 The seminal texts are Maurice Halbwachs, *Les Cadres sociaux de la mémoire* (1925), ed. by Gérard Namer (Paris: Albin Michel, 1997), and *La Mémoire collective* (1950), ed. by Gérard Namer (Paris: Albin Michel, 1997).

35 Halbwachs, *Les Cadres*, p. vi.

36 'Les lieux de mémoire ne sont pas *ce* dont on se souvient, mais *là* où la mémoire travaille; non la tradition elle-même, mais son laboratoire'. Nora, *Les Lieux de mémoire*, vol. 2. (1986), *La Nation*, I, vii–x. The concept of the 'lieu de mémoire' (site/locus of memory) – which holds that memory is spatially created and can be ascribed to, or inscribed on, a space or place – goes back to antiquity. See Frances Yates, *The Art of Memory* (London: Routledge & Paul Kegan, 1966).

37 Henri Bergson, *Matière et mémoire: essaie sur la relation du corps à l'esprit* (Paris: Quadrige/Presses universitaires de France, 1997).

38 Halbwachs, *La Mémoire collective*, p. 244. For an account of the development of Halbwachs's thought see also Namer's 'Postface' to *Les Cadres*; Laurent Mucchielli, 'Pour une psychologie collective: l'héritage durkheimien d'Halbwachs et sa rivalité avec Blondel durant l'entre-deux guerres', *Revue d'histoire des sciences humaines*, 1 (1999), pp. 103–41; and one of Halbwachs's own source texts, Emile Durkheim, 'Représentations individuelles et représentations collectives', in *Sociologie et philosophie* (Paris: Presses universitaires de France, 1967), pp. 1–38.

39 Halbwachs, *Les Cadres*, p. vi.

40 Halbwachs, *La Mémoire collective*, pp. 131–2.

41 Halbwachs, *Les Cadres*, pp. 300, 367.

42 Paul Connerton, *How Societies Remember* (Cambridge: Cambridge University Press, 1989), p. 14.

43 See Gacon, for example. Evidence of the Commune's continuing capacity to provoke strong feelings was provided by the controversy that surrounded the showing on French television of the film *La Commune* (1999) by the British filmmaker Peter Watkins. See his website <www.mnsi.net/~pwatkins> [accessed 7 April, 2006]. See also Shafer, p. 186.

44 Other official references to the Commune include the metro station 'Louise Michel' (originally called Vallier and renamed on 1 May 1946) and a number of streets named after other Commune leaders between 1882 and 1930. For a complete list of these see Jean Braire, *Sur les traces des Communards: Enquête dans les rues de Paris d'aujourd'hui* (Paris: Editions Amis de la Commune, 1988), p. 224. Braire (p. 182) also highlights the fact that the bas-relief by Paul Moreau-Vauthier entitled 'Aux Victimes des Révolutions' and situated in the Square Gambetta adjacent to Père Lachaise, and often mistaken for the *Mur des fédérés*, is in fact an inclusive memorial which pays tribute not only to the Parisians who died during the Commune but equally to the hundred or so Versaillais who also died in the combat. On the mythology of the *Mur* see Tombs, *The Paris Commune*, p. 195, and Madeleine Rebérioux, 'Le Mur des fédérés' in Nora, *Les Lieux de mémoire*, vol. 1 (1984), *La République*, pp. 619–49.

45 Hereafter referred to in the body of the text as *Paris: ses organes* and *Les Convulsions* respectively. All interpolated references giving volume and page number are abbreviated to *PSO* and *LC* and unless otherwise stated are taken from *Paris: ses organes, ses fonctions et sa vie dans la seconde moitié du XIXe siècle*, 6 vols (Paris: Hachette, 1884–95), I (1893), II (1883), III (1895), IV (1894), V (1884), VI (1884), and *Les Convulsions de Paris*, 4 vols, 5th edn (Paris: Hachette, 1881).

46 Unless otherwise stated, all references to these novels, giving volume and page number, are taken from the *La Pléiade* edition, *Les Rougon-Macquart*, ed. by Henri Mitterand, 5 vols (Paris: Gallimard, 1960–67), which is abbreviated to *RM*.

47 Matsuda, pp. 13, 88.

48 See Michael Sprinker, *History and Ideology in Proust: A la recherche du temps perdu and the Third French Republic* (Cambridge: Cambridge University Press, 1994), pp. 36–47.

49 Mouillaud, 'Le Journal: un texte sous tension', in *Textologie du journal*, ed. by Pierre Rétat (Paris: Minard, 1990), p. 154.

50 Du Camp, *Les Chants modernes*, 2nd edn (Paris: Librairie nouvelle, 1860), p. 4.

51 Gretton, 'Difference and Competition: the Imitation and Reproduction of Fine Art in a Nineteenth-century Illustrated Weekly News Magazine', *Oxford Art Journal*, 23: 2 (2000), pp. 143–62.

52 Mouillaud, p. 155. On Mikhail Bakhtin see Sue Vice, *Introducing Bakhtin* (Manchester and New York: Manchester University Press, 1997).

53 *Polyphonic text*: a text in which several voices or points of view interact on more or less equal terms. The term is used by Bakhtin in *Problems of Dostoevsky's Poetics* (1929) as an equivalent to *dialogic* and refers to the responsive nature of dialogue as opposed to the single-mindedness of monologue.

54 See Jean-Noël Marchandiau, *L'Illustration 1843–1944: Vie et mort d'un journal* (Toulouse: Editions Privat, 1987), pp. 52, 108, 115, 332.

55 Anne-Marie Thiesse, *Le Roman du quotidien: lecteurs et lectures populaires à la Belle Epoque* (Paris: Seuil, 2000), pp. 10–11; and Richard Terdiman, *Discourse/Counter-Discourse: Theory and Practice of Symbolic Resistance in Nineteenth-Century France* (Ithaca, NY, and London: Cornell University Press, 1985), ch. 2.

56 For example Boime; Roos, 'Within the "Zone of Silence"'; John Milner, *Art, War and Revolution in France 1870–1871: Myth, Reportage and Reality* (New Haven, CT, and London: Yale University Press, 2000); and James A. Leith, ed., *Images of the Commune* (Montreal and London: McGill-Queen's University Press, 1978).

57 For contemporary accounts of the press see, for example, Eugène Dubief, *Le Journalisme* (Paris: Hachette, 1892). The most comprehensive modern survey of the press during the Second Empire, Commune and the Third Republic is Claude Bellanger et al., *Histoire générale de la presse française*, 4 vols (Paris: Presses Universitaires de France, 1972), II and III. On the press and the law see Irene Collins, *The Government and the Newspaper Press in France, 1814–1881* (London: Oxford University Press, 1959); and Robert Justin Goldstein, *Censorship of Political Caricature in Nineteenth-century France* (Kent, OH: Kent State University Press, 1989). On the press and the Commune, see Aimé Dupuy, *1870–1871: La Guerre, la Commune et la presse* (Paris: Armand Colin, 1959). On the illustrated press in general, see Louis Guéry, *Visages de la presse: La Présentation des journaux des origines à nos jours* (Paris: Editions du Centre de formation et de perfectionnement des journalistes, 1997), and Jean Watelet, *La Presse illustrée en France, 1814–1914*, 11 vols (unpublished doctoral dissertation, Université Panthéon-Assas, Paris II, 17 January 1998), III. On the satirical press, see Philippe Régnier, ed., *La Caricature entre République et censure: L'Imagerie satirique en France de 1830–1880: un discours de résistance?* (Lyons: Presses universitaires de Lyon, 1996); and Philippe Roberts-Jones, *La Presse satirique illustrée entre 1860 et 1890* (Paris: Institut français de la presse, 1956), and *De Daumier à Lautrec: Essai sur l'histoire de la caricature française* (Paris: Les Beaux Arts, 1960).

58 Gretton, 'Difference and Competition'.

59 Lidsky, *Les Ecrivains contre la Commune*.

60 Roberts, 'La Commune considérée par la droite'.

61 See Rifkin, 'No Particular Thing to Mean', *Block*, 8 (1983), pp. 36–45; 'Well Formed Phrases: Some Limits of Meaning in Political Print at the End of the Second Empire', *The Oxford Art Journal*, 8: 1 (1985), pp. 20–8; and

also 'Cultural Movement and the Paris Commune', *Art History*, 2 (1979), pp. 51–61.

62 Matsuda, pp. 13, 88.

63 See Emile Zola, *Œuvres complètes*, ed. by Henri Mitterand, 15 vols (Paris: Cercle du livre précieux, 1966–69), XI, p. 141; and Enid Starkie, *Flaubert: The Making of the Master* (London: Weidenfeld & Nicolson, 1967), pp. 234, 237–8.

64 See Michel Dewachter, Daniel Oster and Jean Leclant, eds, *Le Nil*, in *Un Voyageur en Egypte vers 1850: 'Le Nil' de Maxime Du Camp* (n.p.: Sand/Coni, 1987); Sylvie Aubenas and Jacques Lacarrière, *Voyage en Orient* (Paris: Hazan, 1999); and Senneville, *Maxime Du Camp: Un spectateur engagé du XIXe siècle* (Paris: Editions Stock, 1996).

65 Lidsky, p. 57.

66 Lucien Nass, *Le Siège de Paris et la Commune* (Paris: Plon, 1914); Henri D'Alméras, *La Vie parisienne pendant le Siège et sous la Commune* (Paris: Albin Michel, 1927).

67 Jellinek, *The Paris Commune* (London: Victor Gollancz, 1937), pp. 425–6.

68 See Robert Lethbridge's introduction to Zola, *La Débâcle*, trans. by Elinor Dorday (Oxford: Oxford University Press, 2000), pp. vii–xxviii (p. xii). See also Zola himself on *La Débâcle*: 'Mon plan à toujours été d'aller jusqu'à la Commune, car je considère la Commune comme une conséquence immédiate de la chute de l'empire et la guerre' (*RM*, V, 1416).

69 Thiesse, pp. 38, 70–1.

70 See Paule Lejeune, *'Germinal': un roman antipeuple* (Paris: Nizet, 1978), pp. 33–4; Edouard Rod, *A Propos de 'L'Assommoir'* (Paris: Marpon & Flammarion, 1879); Emile Faguet, *Propos littéraires*, 5 vols (Paris: Société française d'imprimerie et de librairie, 1902–9), III (1905), pp. 247, 271–2; and Colette Becker, 'L'Audience d'Emile Zola', *Les Cahiers naturalistes*, 47 (1974), pp. 40–69.

71 Nelly Wolf, *Le Peuple dans le roman français de Zola à Céline* (Paris: Presses universitaires de France, 1990), pp. 15, 264.

72 See Barthes, *S/Z* (Paris: Seuil, 1970), p. 265. *Lisible/Scriptible*: *lisible* denotes texts, typically popular novels (one might say 'airport novels'), written in a realist style that involves little participation/interpretative analysis from the reader other than the consumption of a fixed meaning, whereas *scriptible* refers to, usually, Modernist texts that challenge the reader to produce his/her own meaning from a choice of possibilities.

73 On the Commune in literature see Roger Bellet and Philippe Régnier, eds, *Ecrire la Commune: Témoignages, récits et romans (1871–1931)* (Tusson, Charente: Editions du Lérot, 1994); and Madeleine Rebérioux, 'Roman, théâtre et chanson: quelle Commune?', and Anne Roche and Gérard Delfau, 'La Commune et le roman français', both in *Le Mouvement social*, 79 (April/June 1972), pp. 273–92, 293–318.

74 Claude Gautrand, '1870–1871: Les Photographes et la Commune', *Photo-Ciné-Revue* (February 1972), pp. 53–63; John Wiener, 'Paris Commune Photos at a New York Gallery: An Interview with Linda Nochlin', *Radical History Review*, 32 (1985), pp. 59–70. Daryl Lee's 'Braquehais: photographie, ruines, Paris', in *Bruno Braquehais, un photographe de la Commune. Exposition du 9 mars au 19 juin 2000, Musée d'art et d'histoire, Saint-Denis*, ed. by Sylvie Gonzalez (Saint-Denis: n.pub., 2000), pp. 3–5, does not take account of Nochlin and also automatically assumes that Braquehais 'demeure sympathique aux communards'.

75 Donald E. English, *Political Uses of Photography in the Third French Republic, 1871–1914* (Ann Arbor: University of Michigan Research Press, 1981), chs 1–2. For an account of the use of photographs of the Commune by the state and the police, see also Pierre Gaudin and Claire Revercheron, 'Une image renversée: Les Photographies des barricades de la Commune', in *La Barricade*, ed. by Alain Corbin and Jean-Marie Mayeur (Paris: La Presse de la Sorbonne, 1997), pp. 337–40.

76 Christine Lapostolle, 'Plus vrai que le vrai: stratégie photographique et Commune de Paris', *Actes de la recherche en sciences sociales*, 73 (June 1988), pp. 67–76.

77 Christine Lapostolle, 'De la barricade à la ruine', *La Recherche photographique*, 6 (June 1989), pp. 20–8.

78 Alisa Luxenberg, 'Creating *Désastres*: Andrieu's Photographs of Urban Ruins in the Paris of 1871', *Art Bulletin*, 80: 1 (March 1998), pp. 113–36. See also Luxenberg's 'Le spectacle des ruines', in Quentin Bajac, ed., *La Commune photographiée* (Paris: Editions de la Réunion des musées nationaux, 2000), pp. 25–36.

79 See Malcolm Daniel in *Edouard Baldus, photographe*, ed. by Phyllis Lambert (New York, Montreal, Paris: Reunion des Musées nationaux, 1994), p. 96.

80 Marie de Thézy, *Marville. Paris* (Paris: Hazan, 1994), pp. 26–36, 121–7.

81 'Photographies capitales: Charles Marville, Tom Drahos', *Foncier mensuel* (November 1994), pp. 1–4.

82 Pierre Dufreigne, 'Images d'un Paris perdu', *L'Express*, 17 November 1994, pp. 120–2.

2

Le Monde illustré: images between the lines

In the preface which opens *Les Cadres sociaux de la mémoire*, Maurice Halbwachs recounts a story that he claims to have read in a copy of an old illustrated journal entitled *Le Magasin pittoresque*, of an amnesiac 'Eskimo girl' who, when she was shown a number of pictures depicting aspects of the different countries in which she had lived, miraculously regained her memory. By means of this conceit Halbwachs immediately stakes his claim that an individual's memories are usually evoked by means of external, social triggers.[1] His choice of anecdote is particularly apt involving, in effect, two newspapers: one in which the girl's story, which may or may not be true, was first recorded and the other in which the story was subsequently reproduced and discussed. For not only does the story highlight the self-referential and intertextual nature of the newspaper as a medium of communication and its role in the construction and promulgation of memories and myths, but it also stresses the importance of the pictorial image in mental recall and the interpretation of that image based on collective social criteria. Furthermore, it is through the use of language, a key social framework (*cadre social*), that the meaning of the verbal, visual or auditory image is forcibly articulated. This is not, of course, to deny the power of the pictorial image in itself as a conveyor of meaning or the scientifically proven fact that pictures are a more powerful aid to mental recall than the written text but, as psychologists have also demonstrated, this so-called 'picture superiority effect' is much enhanced when pictures are combined with *concrete* – rather than abstract – *words*.[2] As the analysis of the articles and illustrations in this chapter will highlight, it is the textual frames in all their varied forms (articles, reports, poems, titles, captions) that often act as

'moral labels', guiding the reader/viewer towards a particular interpretation of the accompanying illustrations. Left to themselves the illustrations
would be rather ambiguous. These accompanying texts go a long way to
ensuring that the events depicted by the illustrations are 'remembered'
in a particular way by the intended reader/viewer. The same holds true
of many of the captioned photographic representations of the aftermath
of the Commune that I shall discuss later in Chapter 5.

Since very little background information or critical scholarship exists
on *Le Monde illustré*, particularly in English, it may prove useful before
going on to analyse the representative articles and illustrations in detail
to pause a little first in order to place the journal in its historical, social,
political and aesthetic context and generally to position the illustrated
newspaper as a specific genre.

An illustrated world view

Le Monde illustré was launched by Archille Bourdilliat on 18 April 1857
as a direct competitor to *L'Illustration*, which, since its founding in 1843
on the model set by the *Illustrated London News*, had enjoyed a virtually
unchallenged position at the top of the market for the high-quality,
illustrated, family-orientated journal. Bourdilliat initially appointed
Edmond Pointel to run the paper, which he continued to do for some
ten years. In 1862, Bourdillait sold the paper to Michel Lévy, who in
turn sold it to Paul Dalloz. *Le Monde illustré* thus acquired a highly
prestigious sister paper in the form of *Le Moniteur universel*, the Second
Empire's quasi-official newspaper. Dalloz had owned and managed *Le
Moniteur universel* since Louis Napoleon's *coup d'état* of 2 December
1851, and until 1869 the newspaper held the monopoly for the publication of official reports.[3] As a general rule the political views expressed in
Le Moniteur universel were reflected to a greater or lesser degree in all
the other papers in the Dalloz group, even in those purporting to be
non-political publications such as *Le Monde illustré*. All were conservative and generally supportive of the legally elected regime, and needless
to say *Le Monde illustré*, just like *Le Moniteur universel*, was profoundly
anti-Communard.[4] *Le Moniteur universel*, however, adopted a very reserved stance in all matters concerning the possibility of a restoration of
the monarchy.[5] *Le Monde illustré*, while also remaining reticent on the
restoration, was nevertheless generally highly supportive of both Church
and State throughout the 1870s. By 5 January 1878, however, the journal was gently calling for reconciliation between Left and Right for

the benefit of the nation as a whole and, significantly, by 6 July was placing the *Fête du 30 juin*, which had been very publicly boycotted by MacMahon, prominently on its front page. The origins of this gradual move by the journal towards the centre ground can be traced back to the crucial election of Deputies in 1877.

During the political crisis that followed MacMahon's dissolution of the Chamber of Deputies on 16 May 1877, Dalloz was awarded the contract to publish and distribute the vast quantities of official propaganda produced in the run up to the elections. Despite MacMahon's attempt to ruin their chances of success, the republicans emerged victorious. By campaigning on issues of parliamentary government and amnesty for ex-Communards, they held on to the majority they had gained in February and March 1876, losing only very few seats in the Chamber. By 18 October 1877, therefore, it comes as no surprise to learn that *Le Moniteur universel* was rallying to the republican cause (p. 164); and where *Le Moniteur universel* led, *Le Monde illustré* was sure to follow.

Le Monde illustré's first editor-in-chief, Alphonse Hermant, was succeeded, in 1870, by Edouard Hubert, who successfully managed to continue publishing the journal throughout the Franco-Prussian war and during the Commune, unlike the twenty-eight Parisian newspapers that were forced to cease publication for having collectively published a text protesting against the city's new revolutionary regime (p. 375). The sub-editors, journalists and other contributors to the journal were typical of the period in that they usually also wrote for other papers in order to supplement their living as novelists, playwrights or poets. These included, at various times and among many others, Baudelaire, Alexandre Dumas père, Paul Férval, George Sand, Pierre Véron, Charles Monselet and François Coppée.[6] The many artists, engravers and caricaturists who, over time, worked for *Le Monde illustré* included Daubigny, Gavarni, Daumier, Edmond Morin, Cham, Bertall, François Chifflart, Albert Robida, Henry Scott, Daniel Vierge and Jules Férat.

With the exception of only a short temporary interruption from June 1940 to June 1945, *Le Monde illustré* continued publication until 25 December 1948, when the journal was finally absorbed by its rival *France-Illustration* (previously *L'Illustration*), which itself ceased publication not long afterwards, the market for such papers having severely declined.

In its heyday *Le Monde illustré*, like *L'Illustration*, took great pride in the quality and accuracy of its illustrations, many of which, in a bid to compete with photography, were designated as 'après nature' (after nature/eye-witness account) or specifically dated as a validation of their authenticity.[7] Despite its reputation, *Le Monde illustré* was in practice no different from other newspapers, contemporary or modern, in its dissemination of ideas and the promulgation of ideologies.[8] However, if official ideologies can be promulgated via newspapers, so can unofficial, counter-ideologies. Unlike novels, which are generally read in private, typically within the home, newspapers form part of the public sphere and belong to that potentially dangerous and subversive world of 'the street' and the café. And cafés, of course, along with cafés-concerts and dancehalls were the main public spaces where people were perceived by the authorities to congregate and foment moral, political and artistic revolution. Throughout the Second Empire, therefore, the press had been one of the main targets of Napoleon III's strict censorship controls and, recognizing the special power of the visual image, the illustrated press was subject to even stricter monitoring. Article 22 of the Decree of 17 April 1852 specifically stated that anyone wishing to print or sell newspapers, books, or illustrations and photographs of any kind was first required to register these with the Ministry of the Interior or Prefect of Police. For the illustrated press this restriction effectively amounted to a form of direct censorship. For Thiers, and later MacMahon, the role played by the left-wing radical-revolutionary press during the Commune served to confirm the perceived causal link between newspapers and insurrection and heightened pre-existing government paranoia regarding the press.

Nevertheless, as a recognition of the support that the republican press at least had lent to the overthrow of the Empire by the new regime, and for its almost unanimous acceptance of the bloodless revolution of 4 September 1870 and the continuation of the war against Prussia, the Government of National Defence initially took the decision to declare the press officially free.[9] The government did not, however, decide to repeal Article 22 of the 1852 Decree. During the two Paris sieges, the ordinance was not enforced and consequently no newspaper felt the need to register, but within days of the end of the *Semaine sanglante*, the Decree of 1852 was revived and rigorously enforced in a bid by the new regime to quell the overwhelming free circulation and trade in thousands of images connected with the Commune.[10] This action, together with the passing of the Decree of 28 December 1871 by General Ladmiraut (the military governor of Paris and one of those responsible for re-taking the city in May 1871), can be seen as the first official act of suppression of the memory of the Commune by the Third Republic. The Decree, initially only applicable to Paris, banned all representations of the Commune which the censors deemed to be 'de nature à troubler l'ordre public' (of the sort to upset public order).[11] In November 1872 the Decree was extended to apply across France.

All representations, but especially visual ones, deemed to be sympathetic to the Commune were obviously unacceptable and could result in the execution or imprisonment of their creator or disseminator. However, all hostile representations of the Commune were equally proscribed on the basis that they might provoke further violent reactions from the Parisian populace. Composite photographs of Communard prisoners, especially women, awaiting trial and of Communards killing priests, however, seem to have evaded censorship, at least until about 1873, and the apparent lack of a political message in aesthetic illustrations of Paris in flames or in ruins meant that such representations also apparently escaped censorship.[12] Such depictions of the city were far from ideologically innocent, particularly when accompanied by tendentious captions but by the end of 1871 such aesthetic, apocalyptic representations of the city came to be accepted as a valid expression of the collective memory of the Commune, apparently with the full support of Thiers's censors.

During the period 1873–75, the pro-republican press and any other critics of *l'Ordre moral* became the principal victims of government censorship. It was impossible, legally, to caricature or even appear to caricature MacMahon, for example, and the Commune more than ever remained a highly contentious subject. In 1875 the censors banned a total of 225 illustrations. The temporary relaxation of censorship in 1876, reflecting the appointment of new censors after the republican electoral victory, led to the banning of only 100 illustrations. However, following MacMahon *coup d'état* of 16 May 1877, there was a predictable return to a high level of government censorship.[13] Consequently, 1877 saw a total of 2,500 press prosecutions and the banning of 243 illustrations in the third quarter of the year alone. Censorship was again relaxed during the spring and summer of 1878 as the government was more preoccupied with the *Exposition universelle*.

In terms of its form, structure and editorial content, *Le Monde illustré* is practically identical to its rival *L'Illustration*. Both journals carry a title in the same capitalized font but whereas *L'Illustration*'s subtitle is 'Journal Universel', *Le Monde illustré* styles itself as 'Journal Hebdomadaire' (Weekly Journal). Both subtitles are, again, composed in the same size and font, with the only difference being that in *L'Illustration* the text is shadowed.[14] Both journals have a similar illustration under the main title followed by the date, price and the editorial address. Both journals typically consist of sixteen large-format pages (365 × 265 cm), with an average of eight pages comprised solely of close text without any significant titles (a common feature of all newspapers of the period), and the rest given over to some thirty high-quality reproductions of wood-block engravings, photo-engravings and lithographs. While still of high quality, the paper used by *Le Monde illustré* does not quite match that used by *L'Illustration*, which is very fine indeed for a newspaper. The centre-fold pages of both journals often carry large illustrations with the verso side left deliberately blank so that these may be removed for mounting in their own right.[15] Some editions of both journals carry extra long fold-out illustrated pages, which again could be detached and framed. Such illustrations were also often reproduced and sold specifically as prints. One page in each issue of both journals is typically given over to cartoons, usually by Cham, and the last one or two pages are dedicated to crosswords, games and advertisements. The articles in *Le Monde illustré* consist of regular features such as *Le Courrier de Paris*, *A Travers Paris*, *Revue des théâtres*, *Courrier du Palais*, a *roman-feuilleton* (serialized novel) and occasional poems, as well as national and international news items, with equivalents of all of these also to be found in *L'Illustration*. The focus throughout *Le Monde illustré*, however, is very much on its illustrations, and the tone of the journal is generally lighter than that of *L'Illustration* which, while still not a seriously intellectual journal, nevertheless liked to include features on scientific and technological innovations and processes, voyages of discovery and accounts of the diverse mores and cultures of France's colonies. *Le Monde illustré*, on the other hand, tended to be more technically innovative than *L'Illustration* and editor-in-chief Edouard Hubert, for example, was responsible for publishing the first photomechanical reproduction in the journal on 10 March 1877 (of the polar explorer Nordenskjöld), and the first real press photographs on the occasion of Victor Hugo's funeral in 1885.[16]

Le Monde illustré and *L'Illustration* were not mass-market publications. They, along with their cheaper rivals *Le Journal illustré* and *l'Univers illustré*, as their generic names suggest, formed a distinctive sub-genre aimed at a well-heeled, educated, bourgeois audience. Table 1 gives an indication of the number of copies sold by each of these journals, but the number of readers is impossible to determine.

Annually, each of these titles published bound volumes of all their fifty-two issues, which in the case of *Le Monde illustré* contained some 500 printed illustrations.[17] Newspapers are generally considered ephemera, but these fully indexed editions were in fact conceived and

Le Monde illustré

Table 1 Estimated average annual sales figures for the quality illustrated press

Title	Sales
Le Journal illustré	105,000 copies (50,000 in 1869)[a]
Le Monde illustré	33,000 copies (rising to 40,000 in 1876[b] and 100,000 in 1892[c])
L'Univers illustré[d]	15,400 copies
L'Illustration	18,000 copies

Source, unless otherwise indicated: Guéry, p. 86.

[a] As noted in Bellanger, II, 356. Le Journal illustré was acquired by the Girardin group in 1873.
[b] As noted in the journal itself.
[c] As noted in Dubief, p. 232.
[d] L'Univers illustré reproduced illustrations which had already appeared in the Illustrated London News and L'Illustrierte Zeitung with the result that it mostly covered British and German events and news. See Guéry, p. 86.

marketed as collectors' items of historic and pedagogical interest and destined to become valuable additions to the bourgeois subscriber's family library. The ephemeral thus took on the function and format of an encyclopaedic reference book. In addition, special one-off editions comprising guides to exhibitions or covering important events, such as the destruction of Paris in 1871, were also published. On 19 August 1871, for example, Le Monde illustré proudly carried an advertisement for an illustrated, eye-witness, day-by-day 'History of Paris' ('Histoire illustrée de Paris: prise sur le fait et au jour le jour'), covering all the trials and tribulations borne by this 'great and unhappy city' including the War (against Prussia), the Siege of Paris, the Commune, the conflagrations and the city's 'deliverance' (the religious connotations are worth noting). The whole 'histoire douloureuse' (painful story) could thus be enjoyed in its entirety in this special two-volume edition. Each volume sold for eleven francs and comprised 410 pages and over 300 illustrations. The Commune, it would seem, had been turned into a commercial opportunity to be exploited by Le Monde illustré no less than by all the other newspapers of the period as well as the large numbers of photographers who descended on the city to record the spectacle of its ruins for posterity and their own material gain.

The positioning of an illustration within the structural hierarchy of modern newspapers and magazines is always important, the key placements being the front and back pages or what Mouillaud terms the 'pages "exposées"', while the principal inside pages or 'pages "couvertes"', are those forming the centrefold.[18] The front page is likened by Mouillaud to a skin or membrane which is in direct contact with the outside world and therefore open to any news item considered worthy of the status, while the information treated on the internal pages is generally ordered according to theme, geography (international, national, local), or perceived level of importance. The centre is in fact the 'periphery', the area where the news is bedded down, while the front page is the part of the newspaper that is the most affected and 'shaped' by external events. That is not to say, however, that the occurrence of some momentous event might not completely upset the pre-set order. The juxtaposition of one illustration to another is also frequently used to reinforce the power of the images, while captions invariably predispose the reader/viewer to a particular ideological interpretation of what is being shown or described.

In the case of the nineteenth-century illustrated journal, as Gretton points out, the demands of page-layout and of the different impression-quality achieved in printing the recto and verso sides often resulted in the splitting of texts from their associated images, and the larger in size the illustrations became, the more this problem was intensified.[19] The separation of the text from its associated image became a practical solution to the problems of page layout but it also promoted the privileging of the more spectacular illustrations. Furthermore, according to Gretton, 'images dealing with widely different topics in different ways must sit promiscuously together, stripped of their textual marks of distinction, on the same page or opening'. Gretton's assessment notwithstanding, the rules that govern modern newspaper layout did still generally apply and it is interesting to note that certain juxtapositions between texts or between texts and images in *Le Monde illustré*, whether intentional or not, do often result, as we shall see, in particular subjective readings. Let us turn now to some specific examples from the first issues of *Le Monde illustré* to appear after the *Semaine sanglante* and then later in 1871, before considering the articles and illustrations covering the festivities of 1878.

Language and icons, memories and myths

On 27 May 1871 Belleville, the working-class suburb and Communard stronghold in the north-east of Paris, fell to the Versaillais. By 29 May the last pockets of Communard resistance in the cemetery of Père-Lachaise and elsewhere had been brutally squashed, and the Fort at Vincennes been made to surrender. The Commune had thus finally been destroyed. The first edition of *Le Monde illustré* to be published after the demise of the Commune, however, is dated 27 May. The edition contains a mixture of articles clearly written before the Versaillais repression and more up-to-date news. On the front page, for example, is an illustration of the demolition of Thiers's house, an event which actually took place on 11 May and was consequently 'old news', while Charles Monselet's *Courrier de Paris* reflects on the battle at Père-Lachaise, which had only just been fought before the journal went to press. The full story of the so-called 'purging' of the cemetery by Thiers's troops with a front page illustration to accompany it, appears later, however, in the edition dated 24 June 1871. Over the coming weeks and months there are several such temporal dislocations in *Le Monde illustré*'s coverage of events as the journal, like the city, struggled to return to its former routine.

Edouard Hubert's piece entitled 'Aux Tuileries' ('At the Tuileries') in the edition dated 27 May is one such retrospective account of life under the Commune. The piece, and its accompanying illustration by Jules Noël (Figure 1), is of particular interest not only because of the anger it expresses on behalf of bourgeois Parisians at the invasion of 'their' city by working-class Communards, but also for the further resonance that Hubert's nostalgic hankering after the long-lost days of the Empire would have acquired by the time the journal actually reached his readers. If Hubert's longed-for 'triumph of good over evil', in the form of the Versaillais victory had indeed come to pass by then, and if the children would indeed come back to play in the Tuileries gardens, they would do so only in the shadow of the palace ruins. For while the Tuileries was finally re-appropriated by the bourgeoisie, this was only after it had been set alight by the Communards. For many conservatives and reactionaries these ruins, along with those of the Hôtel de Ville and other important buildings destroyed in the conflagrations, quickly became symbolic of the Commune's 'crimes' against the nation, with some wishing to see them left untouched as a perpetual reminder of the horrors of popular revolution.[20] As a result, the Tuileries palace ruins were left standing for twelve years because no consensus could be reached as to what to do about them.[21]

Hubert's piece begins with an ironic, contrived description of the scene in the gardens outside the Tuileries palace during the Commune

Figure 1 'PARIS-COMMUNE – Aux Tuileries – Rapprochements et contrastes – (Dessin de M. Jules Noël)' *Le Monde illustré*, 27 May 1871. (© British Library Board. All Rights Reserved. Shelfmark F23)

where, as the civil war rages close by in the Champs-Elysées and around the Arc de Triomphe, innocent (bourgeois) children are seen at play, pretending to be Communards or, as Hubert would have it, 'le chef jureur', 'le soldat aviné' and 'la cantinière *Commune* ou la femme à 15 sous' (the chief blasphemer, the drunken soldier and the whores who supply their food).[22] He asks rhetorically, who are these sinister-looking men guarding the entrance to the Tuileries palace and sprawled out all over its noble steps, shouting and cursing and reeking of tobacco?

Ces gens-là seraient-il nos maîtres, qu'ils usurpent ainsi la place de ceux que nous nous donnons! Quelles sont ces femmes avinées qui viennent s'abriter sous nos lambris dorés? Quelles sont ces quêteuses noires avec leurs petites boîtes à croix rouge? Hélas! tout cela ne nous rappelle que trop le despotisme de la canaille et la guerre civile.

[Do these people think they are our masters; that they can usurp the place of those that we have elected for ourselves? Who are these drunken women who come sheltering under our gold panelling? Who are these black-clad women on the lookout with their Red Cross tins? Alas, all this serves only too well to remind us of the tyranny of the rabble and the civil war!]

Hubert's use of the plural possessive pronoun and the first person plural is not just an example of patriarchal discourse, but also serves to highlight a collective complicity in the authenticity of what is being described.

We should note also the fact that the women conform to the usual anti-Communard stereotype in that they are automatically assumed to be inebriated and/or prostitutes. By the time Hubert's article went to press all the women associated with the Commune, indeed all working-class women in general, were being vilified as a *pétroleuses*.[23] In Jules Noël's illustration, which is no less contrived than Hubert's article, we see these Communard women depicted as masculine in demeanour and, by the conventions of the day, ugly, in contrast to their feminine bourgeois counterparts on the right of the picture. The attitude of the bourgeois group resembles that of a *fête galante* in paintings such as *Fêtes Vénitiennes* (1718–19) by Jean-Antoine Watteau, with the Communard group on the left as its grotesque parody. The Communards appear strong and defiant and the woman in the foreground on the left is not afraid of looking straight at the bourgeois group. No one in that group returns her gaze, however, for to ignore the other is obviously to attempt to deny their existence. The physical distance between the two opposing groups also serves to emphasize the social and, by extension, perceived moral gulf between the them, as implied by the quibble in the subtitle to Noël's illustration, 'Rapprochements et contrastes'. As discussed earlier in the general introduction, the assumption that the Commune was indeed a concerted attempt to reappropriate the city after its *embourgeoisement* by Haussmann is considered rather simplistic today, but certainly for Hubert and his bourgeois readers in 1871, the sight of vast crowds of working-class Communards descending on the city, taking full possession of the Tuileries palace and its genteel gardens and turning both into the focal point for their fund-raising and Sunday concerts was a source of great anger and fear.

Despite the fact that the Tuileries palace features prominently in Hubert's text, Noël's illustration does not depict the palace side of the Tuileries gardens, but instead looks in the other direction, towards the Obelisk of Luxor in the Place de la Concorde with the Arc de Triomphe just visible in the distance. The two blurred monuments, seen through the flocks of white clouds and the dust raised by the shelling taking place in the Champs-Elysées, appear to hover in mid-air above an indistinct mass of people, presumably Communards. The threat to the Arc de Triomphe, which along with the Vendôme Column was such a potent symbol of France's earlier victories over Prussia, was to disturb and horrify not only republicans and Bonapartists but also monarchists. The harsh sound of the shelling around the Champs-Elysées was also to remain a traumatic memory for many people, finding its sinister echo in the sound of the fireworks let off during the 1878 celebrations.

It is obviously difficult at a distance of over 130 years to establish why *Le Monde illustré* chose Noël's view towards the Arc de Triomphe and the Obelisk as an accompaniment to Hubert's text, rather than an illustration that takes in the façade of the Tuileries palace. Research to date has also not revealed whether the illustration was included for publication before or after the palace had been burnt down. However, one could speculate that the Arc de Triomphe, associated with Napoleon I and the symbol of France's glory and national identity, was a better choice than the Tuileries palace on the basis that the latter was closely associated with Napoleon III and thus France's humiliation. Any threat to the Arc de Triomphe, therefore, would certainly have horrified republicans and Bonapartists but also Orléanists, since the monument had after all been constructed under Louis-Philippe and consecrated in 1840 when Napoleon's ashes were transferred there from Saint Helena by François, Prince de Joinville, the Citizen King's third son, who, it is worth noting, had been elected to the National Assembly in February 1871. In what perhaps could be perceived as a calculated move to endear itself to the Orléanists, *Le Monde illustré* carried a piece on the Prince de Joinville in its edition dated 27 June, in which it reminded its readers of his distinguished naval career and his retrieval of the Emperor's ashes.

The Obelisk of Luxor, meanwhile, received as a gift by Louis-Philippe from Mohammed Ali, the Pacha of Egypt, and erected in the Place de la Concorde as a way of purifying one of the most important sites associated with 1789, can either be seen as a politically neutral monument or again, in 1871, as a symbol of tacit support on the part of *Le Monde illustré* for the Orléanist cause. However, this interpretation should be counter-balanced by the knowledge that the Place de la Concorde was equally the site where on 24 February 1848 Louis-Philippe famously made his humiliating escape from the revolutionary mob before seeking exile in England.

Another posthumous article in the edition of the journal dated 27 May 1871 is V.-F. Maisonneufve's 'Démolition de la Colonne Vendôme'.[24] The title appears straightforward and neutral enough with no indication of the position the author will adopt in his account of the event. That task is left to the caption which accompanies the eyewitness illustration

Figure 2 'LES ŒUVRES DE LA COMMUNE – La colonne aussitôt
après sa chute – Fédérés et faux marins plantant le drapeau rouge sur
son socle – (D'après nature, par M. Lançon)' *Le Monde illustré*,
27 May 1871. (© British Library Board. All Rights Reserved. Shelfmark F23)

by Lançon of the fallen Column with the *fédérés* and 'faux marins' (literally 'fake sailors') erecting a red flag on its base (Figure 2), and which
appears two pages before the text.[25] The statement 'Les œuvres de la
Commune', followed by the derogatory description of the Communard
volunteers (Maisonneufve refers to them as 'pseudo-marins') already
predisposes the reader/viewer to a negative interpretation of the event.
In other words, the only 'œuvres' or acts the Communards are capable
of are destructive ones and they themselves are no more than impostors,
illegitimate usurpers of power and, by implication, barbarians. Furthermore, for *Le Monde illustré*'s typical audience of educated middle-class
readers influenced by the latest Darwinian theories of race and evo-
lution, this picture of musket-brandishing *fédérés* and their frenzied
arm-waving supporters, triumphant at having destroyed one of the most
revered of icons of 'civilized' France, would no doubt have been perceived as a terrifying image of sub-human savages. This is clearly the
view expressed by Du Camp in a characteristically racist description of
the Communards and their destruction of the Column:

C'était bien là en effet l'égalité rêvée par ces hommes qui, mieux que les dissertations des naturalistes, ont moralement prouvé l'excellence des théories de Darwin et démontré, par leur exemple, que si l'homme descend des orang-outangs, il ne demande qu'à retourner à ses ancêtres. ... Sous le rapport des fantaisies du pouvoir sans contrôle, la Commune ressemble à ces cours de rois nègres dont les voyageurs nous ont conté l'histoire. (*LC*, II, 114–15)

[This act, which represented the equality that these men dreamed of acquiring, served only to prove, more effectively than the dissertations of any naturalists, the excellence of Darwin's theories and demonstrated that if Man is descended from the orang-outangs, he asks no more than to return to his ancestors. ... As for its fanciful desire for power without control, the Commune resembles the courts of those Negro monarchs described in the stories told to us by travellers.]

The use of the plural possessive pronoun is again worth noting.

The intended meaning of Lançon's illustration, in contrast to Maisonneufve's anti-Communard text, is less clear-cut, however. For without the framing text which predisposes the reader to an anti-Communard reading of the depicted event, those who supported the Commune (like Lançon himself, for example, who was almost executed by the Versaillais), could easily interpret the illustration as a celebratory record of the Column's destruction. It is also ironic to think that the Communard Lançon's sketches of the Franco-Prussian war so impressed the anti-Communard Théophile Gautier, who claimed that the artist could always be trusted to render accurately what he witnessed with his own eyes.[26]

The other illustration which accompanies Maisonneufve's text, again executed 'après nature', but this time by François Chifflart (whose name is correctly spelt 'Chifflard'), bears the caption: 'PARIS-COMMUNE. – La colonne avant sa chute. – Moyen de la détruire' ('PARIS-COMMUNE. – The Column before its fall. – Method used to destroy it') (Figure 3).[27] Again, it is not known whether or not this caption was added retrospectively after the defeat of the Commune and just before *Le Monde illustré* went to press but, on the surface at least, it would appear to be an objective description of what is actually being depicted. On closer examination, however, the choice of the verb *détruire* (to destroy), rather than the *demolition* of the accompanying article, is quite revealing. If both terms can obviously be used interchangeably, *détruire* also implies the *renversement* (toppling) not just of an edifice but also of an entire established social, moral and political order. In effect, the

Figure 3 'PARIS-COMMUNE – La colonne avant sa chute – Moyen employé
pour la détruire. (D'après nature, par M. Chifflard [*sic*])' *Le Monde illustré*,
27 May 1871. (© British Library Board. All Rights Reserved. Shelfmark F23)

Commune's aim was precisely that, to overturn the imperial establishment and to destroy all the illusions and pretensions of military glory on which it had been founded. But *détruire* also, significantly, carries with it some particularly violent connotations as some of the verb's standard French dictionary synonyms would suggest: *brûler, incendier (cf. réduire en cendres), exterminer, massacrer, anéantir* (to burn, to set fire to something (cf. to reduce to ashes), to exterminate, to massacre, to annihilate). Therefore, from the anti-Communard perspective, the caption emphasizes the apocalyptic, destructive nature of the Commune. As for the Commune itself, it used the more neutral *demolir* (to demolish) in its edict of 12 April 1871.[28]

It is also interesting to compare Chifflart's depiction of the Column awaiting its destruction with contemporary photographs taken from the same angle showing the Column and statue from the back, looking towards the rue de Castiglione, such as that reproduced in the collection edited by Bernard Noël and Jean-Claude Gautrand from an anonymous print held by the Bibliothèque nationale.[29] As is to be expected of a nineteenth-century professional photograph, the perspective is virtually perfect with the Column placed firmly in the centre of the shot. This lends a classical orderliness to the photograph, an aesthetic value that is enhanced by the fact that the Place Vendôme is deserted. With nothing to distract it, the eye is naturally drawn to the noble Column with the buildings on either side of it retreating towards a natural central vanishing point. In the photograph the Column appears indomitable, despite the scaffolding and supports attached to it and the fact that anyone looking at this photograph would have known that it would soon be demolished. Chifflart's drawing by contrast places the Column off-centre, causing the viewer to focus initially on the dark barricade in the foreground. The barricade effectively forms a barrier between the Column and the viewer. The dark outlines of the *fédérés* also add a further sense of foreboding.

In Chifflart's illustration the viewer is not welcome in this space. The addition of the ropes attaching the Column to the buildings at either side of it serve to emphasize the monument's instability, making it look as if it were already shaking and about to fall. The stark, dark outline of the Column is silhouetted against a pale sky in both Chifflart's drawing and in the photograph, but the artist has also decided to add some swirling clouds. By the time this edition of *Le Monde illustré* reached its readers, the Commune and the *Semaine sanglante* were of course over and in the light of that knowledge these clouds, particularly above the buildings on the right-hand side, take on the appearance of smoke and flames. Directly behind the Column, just to the left above the top of Napoleon's statue, Chifflart has also included three birds flying upwards into a clear, open sky. These birds can be read as symbolic of the Commune's bid for freedom from oppression, for Chifflart, like Lançon, is known to have been a Communard. Certainly Chifflart's birds are not like the ominous dark ravens in Romantic print such as Charles Meryon's *Le Vampire* (1853). From the anti-Communard perspective, however, these birds rising phoenix-like into the sky exemplify nature's regenerative optimism in the face of human folly and barbarism and as such are at one with nineteenth-century discourse on the decline, fall and rebirth of states and empires. The use of birds as a metaphor for purification and regeneration is found throughout the literature of the period, for example at the end of Zola's *Une page d'amour* and *La Débâcle*. The title of Elémir Bourges's novel, *Les Oiseaux s'envolent et les fleurs tombent* is another case in point.

Maisonneufve's accompanying textual account, meanwhile, also emphasizes what he believes to be the senselessness of this act of destruction. While the Vendôme Column may not be to everyone's taste aesthetically, he argues, it is nevertheless a perfectly acceptable monument from all points of view. The journalist no doubt spoke here not just for other bourgeois republicans like himself but also for monarchists and Bonapartists who were all equally outraged by the destruction of the monument.[30]

The Column, modelled on Trajan's Column in Rome, had been erected in 1810 to commemorate Napoleon's victory at the battle of Austerlitz in 1805 and was covered with a bronze shell made from the actual cannon captured from the Austrians and Russians. As such, it was both the material and symbolic embodiment of France's glory.[31] Thus, with the Prussians on the doorstep, Maisonneufve like many of his contemporaries believes that the Commune's destruction of this 'sacred icon' is the ultimate betrayal of all those Frenchmen who had fought and died for their country. For Maisonneufve, if anything could have helped him and his fellow Frenchmen to forget the humiliation of Sedan and Metz it would have to be the past victory against the Prussians at Iéna. Du Camp puts forward much the same argument (*LC*, II, 188), as does Zola in *La Débâcle* (*RM*, V, 875). All that would have been required in order to rid the Column of its unpleasant associations therefore, claims Maisonneufve, would have been the removal of Napoleon's statue.[32] As Victor Hugo's poem quoted at the end of Maisonnneufve's piece makes clear, ultimately it is only Paris and France that count, not the memory of some upstart emperor:[33]

> Justice! Otez de là César, mettez-y Rome.
> Qu'on voie à cette cime un peuple et non un homme.
>
> [O Justice! Remove Cæsar from there, replace him with Rome itself.
> Let a nation not a mere man be seen on that summit.]

Maisonneufve ends his piece by suggesting that Hugo's eloquence even surpasses that of Pierre Corneille, the great seventeenth-century French dramatist. Surely no one other than an Hugo, he opines, could so eloquently have condemned this odious and unpatriotic act carried out by these modern-day iconoclasts who want to erase history and destroy the nation's memories: 'Comme si on pouvait détruire la patrie, surtout quand elle s'appelle la France!' (As if it were even possible to destroy the nation/fatherland, especially when that nation/fatherland goes by the name of France!)

For Maisonneufve and many of his contemporaries, however, the demolition of the Column is not just an unacceptable affront to the memory of the veterans of the Grande Armée and a denial of France's history, it is also an act of vandalism against an aesthetic object and consequently also an affront to the artists who created it. Such sentiments may have contributed to the decision to replace the destroyed monument with an exact replica of the original, rather than with a Column surmounted by a statue of France (that is, a republican symbol), which, as Maisonneufve's reports, is what the National Assembly was in fact considering in May 1871. He does not mention, however, that some members of the Commune would similarly have been quite happy to replace the Column with a statue representing the Republic and that this suggestion was debated twice, on 25 April and 18 May 1871.[34] In fact, the Column was ultimately restored by *l'Ordre moral* complete with Napoleon's statue between December 1875 and January 1876.[35] This decision is not as bizarre as it might at first appear for it not only helped restore French military pride but it also helped consolidate the denial of the memory of May 1871, with the result that many of the visitors who crowd into the fashionable Place Vendôme today remain unaware of the Column's history and of the fact that only the base and plaque celebrating Napoleon I's 1805 victory are in fact original.

Charles Monselet's piece for the regular feature *Courrier de Paris*, written after the Versaillais victory but which also appeared in the retrospective 27 May edition of *Le Monde illustré*, picks up on some of the rhetoric in the articles by Hubert and Maisonneufve and rehearses virtually all the counter-revolutionary myths and obsessions which were to dominate anti-Communard discourse for decades to come.[36] For example, the Commune is to be compared with the Terror; the Commune is a saturnalia, a carnival ('une saturnale, un branle-bas, une Courtille!') typified by its stupidity, mendacity and violence. Its leaders are no more than Punch and Judy puppets ('ces législateurs fantoches, ces gouvernants sortis de la baraque de Guignol'), mindlessly spouting the same old clichés of 1793 (see also Du Camp, *LC*, I, 218, 222, 286). Were he to live to be a hundred, Monselet declares, he would always remember those days during May 1871 that made the June Days of 1848 look like mere child's play.

The destruction of Paris is also compared to that of London during the Great Fire of 1666. Both events are perceived as apocalyptic, but the comparison with London specifically would also have reminded Monselet's contemporaries, including any self-satisfied and moralizing Englishmen of the sort later singled out by Du Camp (*PSO*, VI, 288), that Britain's own glorious capital city had a similar long tradition of violent and bloody civil unrest and that only recently, in the 1860s, many anti-government riots had broken out on its streets. Futhermore, in 1871, as readers of the *Le Monde illustré* would be reminded in the 24 June edition of the journal, Britain also had a civil war of her own to worry about in Ireland.

Monselet's other comparison is with the sacking and burning of a decadent imperial Rome by the barbarians. For Monselet, like many of his generation, the destruction of Paris in 1871 came as no real surprise. On the contrary, it was perceived as the fulfilment of a number of apocalyptic 'prophecies' that had haunted the collective French literary, artistic, historical and philosophical imagination for over a century. In Louis-Sébastien Mercier's *Le Tableau de Paris* (1788), for example, the fate of the ruined cities of antiquity foreshadowed the destruction of Paris. In the Comte de Volney's *Les Ruines, ou méditation sur les révolutions des empires*, written in the aftermath of 1789, the reduction of the city to ruins was not to be seen as part of any natural phenomenon or cycle of life and death, but as the direct consequence of human pride, greed and stupidity. The same theory holds true not just for Monselet but also for Maisonneufve, who, in the 3 June 1871 edition of the journal, declares that Paris was destined to have its own Nero or Herostratos and that, like Rome or Alexandria, the city would necessarily be destroyed by fire.

For Catulle Mendès, too, Paris after the fall of the Empire and the Commune is akin to Rome under Tiberius or after the barbarians had sacked it.[37] This leitmotif is found again in Théophile Gautier's *Tableaux de siège*.[38]

Monselet then goes on to relate how he quoted Shakespeare to himself ('Horrible! Horrible!'), as he witnessed the devastation of the centre of Paris and how, finally, the whole monstrous 'drama' came to an end in a cemetery, just like the final act of *Hamlet*. Monselet's reference to *Hamlet* is particularly apposite since this tragedy deals with many of the same moral issues raised by the repression of the Commune: fratricide, national pride and honour, revenge, and political order.[39] Shakespeare's protagonist, since he is presented as a sympathetic character, is not perceived by the audience at the end of the play as having committed any crime. If he is to be blamed for anything, it is that he should have taken control of the situation and exacted revenge sooner, thereby avoiding so many unnecessary deaths. The parallel, oblique as it may at first appear, is with Thiers, who, whilst the majority of the bourgeoisie supported him, was nevertheless criticized by Du Camp, among others, for his retreat from Paris and his failure to deal effectively with the insurrection early on (*LC*, II, 11, 348).

Monselet's overt literary references may be to Shakespeare but his declamatory, poetic prose with its personification of death and extensive use of anaphora and alliteration, brings it closer to the rhetoric of Corneille. Thus Monselet declares melodramatically:

> Ô mort! voilà bientôt dix mois que tu t'es abattue sur la France; voilà bientôt dix mois que ta large faux n'a cessé de se promener sur nos champs. Tantôt tu nous apparais, guerrière farouche, coiffée du casque de l'invasion; tantôt furie de faubourg, cachant dans un cabas fétide l'essence incendiaire; tantôt enfin, justicière implacable, fusillant contre un mur de pâles troupeaux de fédérés.

> [O Death! Soon it will be ten months that you have been raining down on France; soon it will be ten months that you have been continuously wielding your scythe across our lands. Now in the guise of a fierce warrior bearing the invader's helmet; now in the guise of a working-class harpy with paraffin hidden in her filthy sack; now in the guise of an implacable Justice, firing on herds of whey-faced *fédérés* lined up against a wall.]

In this representative extract, Monselet makes profitable use of the fact that Death – *la mort* – is a feminine noun. The personification of Death as the working-class harpy and *pétroleuse* is predictable but

Monselet also manages, by extension, to feminize the usually male figure of the Grim Reaper as well as the male Prussian invader. The feminine is to be wholly associated with all that is evil and negative. Even the normally positive identification of the feminine with Justice is rendered ambiguous, as Death and Justice become one to mete out punishment by execution to the *fédérés* who, stereotypically again, are described as 'pâles troupeaux', that is to say cowardly, ignorant and bestial. By appealing in this way to the political and cultural values of his implied readers and especially by employing a language and idiom (one of Halbwachs's *cadres sociaux*) that recalls a long-established literary tradition, Monselet would have invoked a whole series of shared associations and memories in his reader's mind, and thereby procedes to create a myth which rationalizes and justifies the Versaillais repression.

Corneille's tragedies *Horace*, *Cinna* and *Polyeucte* were all much performed as the decade progressed. *Horace* in particular had long been exploited by the state because of its depiction of the subordination of self-interest to the demands of *la patrie* (the fatherland/nation), as witnessed in Jacques-Louis David's epic painting *Le Serment des Horace* (1785). The play raises many of the same moral and political issues facing France in 1871, with Paris like classical Rome, having suffered at the hands of her internal and external enemies.[40]

Shakespearean allusions and Cornelian-style rhetoric are put to much the same myth-making use in a piece to accompany a full front-page illustration by Albert Robida, which appeared a few weeks later in the 24 June 1871 edition of the journal, under the unattributable and most probably shared pseudonym of Léo de Bernard.[41] The article purports to give an account of the 'last stand' of the *fédérés* against the Versaillais at Père-Lachaise ('La Dernière Etape des fédérés au Père-Lachaise').[42] In the same theatrical and tragic vein as Monselet's earlier article, Bernard proceeds to gloss over the full horror of the massacre that took place in the cemetery. As contemporary and modern historians have noted, however, the final engagements actually took place the next day on 28 May 1871, with the Versaillais returning repeatedly to Père-Lachaise on 29 May with groups of between 150 and 300 captured *fédérés*, most of whom had already surrendered, as well as civilians including women and children. After lining their hostages up against the northern wall of the cemetery, the Mur de Charonne (today's Mur des fédérés) the troops executed them. Their bodies were soon piled high in the long, deep ditch that had been specially dug for the purpose in front of the wall. Those who were not killed outright were finished off in the ditch itself.[43]

Their task over, the soldiers hastily buried the corpses. The total number of people killed is not known. The scene was later immortalized by Ernest Pichio in his anti-Versaillais painting, *Le Triomphe de l'ordre* (c.1872).[44]

The perceived cathartic nature of the Versaillais repression is evident in the caption to Robida's illustration, 'L'AGONIE DE LA COMMUNE. – Marins, infanterie de marine et 74° de ligne purgeant le Père-Lachaise des derniers insurgés, le samedi 27 mai à 8 heures du soir' ('THE AGONY OF THE COMMUNE. – Sailors, the Marine Light Infantry and the 74th Line Infantry purging Père-Lachaise Cemetery of the remaining insurgents on Saturday 27 May at 8 o'clock in the evening') (Figure 4). The notion of purgation announces the ideological interpretation to be placed on the event in the accompanying written account, which is structured like a five-act tragedy. The first few paragraphs of the text provide the exposition of the 'drama', introduce the 'characters', and culminate in the customary note of suspense and expectation as, we are told, the whole of Paris waited with bated breath to hear of the outcome to the bombardment of the city. During the second 'act', played out through the night, the attack and counterattack presage the final bloody outcome. The third 'act' is punctuated by the desertion of some of the Communards. Then, as befits a true classical tragedy, the fourth part of the text reports on the struggle and ultimate defeat by the Versaillais of the 'groupe de forcenés' (frenzied group), which is to be heard emitting its final 'cri de haine' (cry of hatred) amid the tombs of Charles Nodier, Emile Souvestre and Balzac. The reference to these three great French men of letters serves to underline the difference between cultured, 'civilized' France and the 'barbaric' Communards who are, significantly, led by an unnamed Polish, rather than French, colonel, suggesting to the reader that the Commune was a foreign-backed socialist conspiracy. The republican but anti-Communard newspaper *Le Siècle*, for example, declared in an equally melodramatic and xenophobic fashion on 30 May 1871 that this whole lamentable drama and the attempt to destroy Paris had been conceived by a band of 'scélérats cosmopolites' (wicked foreigners). Europe should be made aware, the newspaper fulminated, that the barbarians who instigated the destruction of 'our' monuments were not Frenchmen (noted in *LC*, II, 306–7). For Du Camp, however, it was not 'foreigners' who were to blame for the insurrection, but 'l'écume de la province' (provincial scum). This is another stereotype also shared by Zola, whose own would-be revolutionaries are similarly from the provinces: for example, Silvère in *La Fortune des Rougon*, Florent in *Le Ventre*

LE MONDE ILLUSTRÉ

JOURNAL HEBDOMADAIRE

ABONNEMENTS POUR PARIS ET LES DÉPARTEMENTS
Un an, 11 francs; — Six mois, 11 francs; — Trois mois, 6 francs.
Le numéro : 25 c. à Paris — 40 c. dans les gares des chemins de fer.
Tout numéro demandé quatre semaines après son apparition sera rendu 40 c.
Le volume semestriel : 11 fr. broché. — 16 fr. relié et doré sur tranche.
LA COLLECTION DES 27 VOLUMES : 212 FRANCS.
Directeur, M. PAUL DALLOZ.

BUREAUX DE VENTE ET D'ABONNEMENT
9, RUE DROUOT, OU 13, QUAI VOLTAIRE
15e Année. No 741. — 24 Juin 1871.

DIRECTION ET ADMINISTRATION
13, QUAI VOLTAIRE
Toute demande d'abonnement non accompagnée d'un bon sur Paris ou par la poste, sera considérée comme non avenue. — Toute réclamation, toute demande de changement d'adresse doit être accompagnée d'une bande imprimée. — On ne répond pas des manuscrits envoyés.
Administrateur, M. BOURDILLIAT.

L'AGONIE DE LA COMMUNE. — Marins, infanterie de marine et 74e de ligne purgeant le Père-Lachaise des derniers insurgés, le samedi 27 mai à 8 heures du soir.
(D'après le croquis de M. Robida.)

Figure 4 'L'AGONIE DE LA COMMUNE – Marins, infanterie de marine et 74º de ligne purgeant le Père-Lachaise des derniers insurgés, le samedi 27 mai à 8 heures du soir. (D'après le croquis de M. Robida.)' *Le Monde illustré*, 24 June 1871. (© British Library Board. All Rights Reserved. Shelfmark F23)

de Paris, Lantier in *L'Assommoir*, Etienne Lantier in *Germinal*, and Maurice in *La Débâcle*. Sigismond in *L'Argent*, a Jew of German origin, is the exception, bringing Karl Marx to mind instead.

The slaughter of the Communards in Bernard's account, unsurprisingly, takes place 'off-stage'. We only have the writer's sanitized version of what happens: 'le vraisemblable', or the artistic illusion of truth of French seventeenth-century classical tragedy, as opposed to 'le vrai', or realistic representation. Robida's illustration, on the other hand, focuses on the fighting *fédérés* themselves, and nothing at all is shown of the subsequent massacres which had certainly taken place well before this edition of the journal went to press. The suppression of the full story could be seen as an attempt by *Le Monde illustré* to protect the delicate sensibilities of its readers or, more likely, as a form of self-censorship and as an early attempt at revisionism in line with official propaganda. However, taken purely on its own merits (that is, without Bernard's gloss), Robida's illustration shows the *fédérés* in a positive light, unlike the impression he is apt to give in the majority of his other sketches of the period, which depict the Communards as drunken, lazy, and undisciplined soldiers.[45] Like most of the writers and artists of the period, Robida was unsympathetic to the Commune but no less appalled and sickened by the indiscriminate slaughter by the Versaillais of so many innocent people once the armed struggle was over. This may have had a bearing on the way he chose to represent the Communards in this particular illustration, as his *fédérés*, particularly the central figure, appear strong and heroic, quite unlike the frenzied group described in the text.

'Act five' of the tragedy opens with a description of the dawn breaking after the final agony:

> Le ciel était bleu; les arbustes et les plantes exhalaient leurs parfums du matin et leur feuillage printanier semblait plus verdoyant sous les rayons d'un soleil éclatant. La nature souriait au milieu des tombes et la faux de la mort, toute ensanglantée, se reposait un moment.

> [The sky was blue; the shrubs and plants perfumed the morning air and their spring foliage looked even greener under the sun's brilliant rays. Nature smiled among the gravestones and Death's bloody scythe rested awhile.] (Cf. Monselet's imagery above)

The corpses, still covered in their tattered uniforms, are buried in the communal ditch and the contemporary bourgeois reader would have been left in no doubt that the Communards, guilty of hubris, had brought about their own downfall. Captured still brandishing their weapons, they were made to submit to the Versaillais. According to Bernard the dead numbered some 1,600. This total figure may well be fairly accurate but he significantly fails to mention the summary executions against the same wall on 29 May, and the implication is that all those who died did so as a result of armed combat, which was not the case. Later, Alphonse Daudet in his fictional account, 'La Bataille du Père-Lachaise' (1872), published in his collection entitled *Les Contes du lundi*, even goes so far as to deny that any battle at all took place at Père-Lachaise, claiming that the whole story was made up by the newspapers and that the *fédérés* executed against the wall totalled only 147 and consisted only of those rounded-up 'criminals' who had spent the previous night imprisoned at La Roquette. Later still, in *Les Convulsions de Paris* Du Camp states, 'with certainty', that the total number of Communards shot at Père-Lachaise on the morning of 28 May was a mere forty-eight. Both Daudet and Du Camp also ignore the massacres that followed, with Du Camp swiftly shifting the emphasis in his account from the executions carried out by the Versaillais to those carried out by the Commune. Not far from where the bodies of the insurgents fell into the communal ditch, he is quick to note, lie the graves of Monsignor Darboy, Louis Bonjean (President of the Supreme Court of Appeal), and three other hostages killed by the Commune (*LC*, II, 301).

In Bernard's account, the reader's pity is to be aroused finally not by the spectacle of the dead *fédérés* but by the grief-stricken women and children they leave behind. There is catharsis at last as he delivers the (reactionary) moral:

> Et les oiseaux se poursuivaient de branche en branche, gazouillant leurs petits cris joyeux. Ah ! que les horreurs de la guerre civile sont atroces devant ce calme inconscient de la nature, devant cette imperturbable sérénité de la création, qui ne semble si puissante que lorsqu'elle accuse l'inanité humaine.

> [And the birds chased each other from branch to branch, happily chirping away. Oh how heinous are the horrors of civil war compared with nature's innocence; compared with the peaceful serenity of creation that seems to be so powerful when it points the finger at human folly!]

As Lidsky observes, it is difficult to produce a counter-revolutionary epic of the Commune when the 'heroes', Thiers and the Versaillais, are such unromantic and unsympathetic characters.[46] And yet, by its appropriation of the high genre of classical French tragedy, Bernard's account of the final triumph of the Versaillais over the doomed *fédérés* achieves just that. The article is effectively a minor epic that manages to aestheticize and legitimize the brutality of the Versaillais reaction. Robert Tombs's judgement of *La Débâcle* would seem to be equally applicable in this case: 'the Commune ceases to be a political conflict and becomes an allegory. This permitted an optimistic conclusion round the themes of redemption and renewal.'[47]

The conclusion to Bernard's account, much like that of Monselet's earlier piece, is fully consistent with the conservative bourgeois mood of the time, which sought a rapid return to a sense of political and social stability, and, if this meant supporting Thiers and thus apparently condoning his violent suppression of the Commune then so be it. The belief that life must and will go on is further reinforced, intentionally or not, by the fact that Bernard's theatrical account of the defeat of the Commune is followed by something as banal as Monselet's serialized novel, which appears on the same page and contains a review of a Marivauesque comedy at the Comédie française entitled, *Venez, je m'ennuie! (Come on, I'm bored!)* This unfortunate juxtaposition may well have been the result of editorial and page layout constraints, but it is telling nonetheless.

The fire in the sky: the memory of the image

Between June and September 1871 *Le Monde illustré* continued to carry a large number of illustrations associated with the Prussian siege and the destruction of Paris during the Commune. These illustrations consist mainly of engravings reproduced from the thousands of photographs of the city in ruins taken during this period. By the end of the year, however, we witness a change in the journal's overall perception of Paris and the Commune. Amid increasing government censorship, aesthetic representations of the Commune such as François Chifflart's Romantic and apocalyptic visions of the city begin to take precedence over reportage-style images. Similarly, there is a marked shift away from the 'factual' reporting of the events surrounding the Commune towards the evocation of the sheer, dramatic beauty of the city in flames as in the piece entitled 'Les Journées de mai: Paris en feu' ('The Days of May: Paris on fire'), which appeared in the 7 October 1871 edition of the journal signed with the initials 'M.V.' (that is, Maxime Vauvert, another unattributable pseudonym).[48] In the same sort of melodramatic, cliché-ridden rhetoric used by Monselet and the pseudonymous Léo de Bernard (perhaps all three are one and the same person), the spectacle of Paris on fire is described in artistic terms as 'horriblement grand et pittoresque' (horribly great and picturesque) and as surpassing anything that a painter-poet could ever have imagined. Paris is turned into a stage setting for a Manichean battle between good and evil. The fact that the city's churches and those buildings representative of French civilization, such as the Louvre and the Institut de France, have survived the 'foudres lancés par les génies de la destruction' (the thunderbolts hurled at them by the genies of destruction), while those associated with the 'decadent' Second Empire, such as the Tuileries, have been destroyed is seen (unsurprisingly) as the result of divine intervention. What else other than a miracle, Vauvert asks, could have spared such sacred religious and artistic relics as the Sainte Chapelle, Saint-Germain-l'Auxerrois, Saint-Gervais and Notre-Dame from the flames?

Vauvert's vision of the future, again like that of Monselet and Léo de Bernard, is optimistic. His (or her) version of apocalypse is more in keeping with the New rather than the Old Testament, with the Revelation rather than with the burning of Sodom and Gomorrah. Those destructive genies (a symbolic allusion in Vauvert's case to Napoleon III and the Communards), have been overthrown and the underlying message is clear: Paris like Rome will be saved by its return to God and the Catholic Church.

The piece concludes with a description of Chifflart's accompanying illustration entitled, 'HISTOIRE DE PARIS. – LES NUITS DE MAI' ('HISTORY OF PARIS. – THE NIGHTS OF MAY') (Figure 5), which he says allows one to re-experience the actual witnessed event. Should some other witness claim that the picture does not do full justice to the scale and colour of the real spectacle, one would reply that in order to render such events in a painting one would need a canvas the size of the sky and Satan's own palette ('il faudrait pour toile l'étendue du ciel et pour couleur la palette de Satan'). Given the undoubted dramatic impact of Chifflart's illustration, it is surprising that few modern commentators have discussed it in any detail, and that it is typically reproduced in miniature;[49] in its setting in the centrefold of the large-format *Le Monde illustré* it is truly impressive. The power of this image is heightened by the intensity of the black and white reproduction, which serves to strengthen the symbolic charge of the flames and swirling clouds of smoke, rendering these even more fantastical. By contrast, the Louvre, the twin towers of Notre-Dame, and the spires and domes of the churches are silhouetted against a clear, white horizon while the burning buildings representative of the Second Empire are seen to disappear beneath

Figure 5 'HISTOIRE DE PARIS – LES NUITS DE MAI. (Dessin de M. Chifflard [*sic*])' *Le Monde illustré*, 7 October 1871. (© British Library Board. All Rights Reserved. Shelfmark F23)

the dark billowing clouds that veil two barely discernible, winged Medusa-like figures that Vauvert calls 'genies of destruction' (detail, Figure 6). The illustration's impact is further heightened, however, by the fact that the following pages carry the journal's usual banal, lightweight items.

Figure 6 'HISTOIRE DE PARIS – LES NUITS DE MAI. (Dessin de M. Chifflard [*sic*])' *Le Monde illustré*, 7 October 1871. Detail (© British Library Board. All Rights Reserved. Shelfmark F23)

According to Hélène Millot, representations of the Commune such as Chifflart's constitute a denial of history.[50] Certainly, such illustrations with their biblical imagery would have appealed to a humiliated and angry nation seeking redemption for the 'sins' committed by the Empire and 'unpatriotic' revolutionaries. However, one could also argue that rather than a denial of history, the appropriation of Chifflart's illustration by the anti-Communard lobby merely exemplifies the selective use of history by governments of the early Third Republic. It is an example of the Nietzchean/Halbwachian preservation of only those aspects of the past that are considered 'useful' in the present. As Halbwachs reminds us, when a given social group is in the process of creating and establishing its own system of values – be they religious, moral or aesthetic – it will try to diffuse these across all the other social groups that make up the nation.[51] If these values succeed in becoming universally recognized and accepted, then they become an integral part of that nation's identity and consciousness. There is no doubt that images such as Chifflart's 'Histoire de Paris: les nuits de mai' played an important role in such a process in the early years of the Republic. After all, it was not just the reactionaries who sought to deny the political and social grievances that gave rise to the Commune but also many moderate republicans.

Knowing that Chifflart had been a Communard, however, might lead us to question his use of the same apocalyptic and 'apolitical' vision of Paris in May 1871. His inclusion of the two avenging angels or Furies raining fire and brimstone on the city is reminiscent of Monselet's description of Death (personified as a woman) wielding her scythe across 'our lands' and, as such, might appear to be similarly reactionary in tone. In fact Chifflart's use of such imagery is nothing unusual, either in his own art or indeed within the context of the aesthetic standards of the time. His rendering of the reflection of light on the waters of the Seine in 'Histoire de Paris: les nuits de mai' may owe much to Impressionism and his swirling clouds may look forward to Symbolist and Expressionist paintings such as Van Gogh's *The Starry Night* (1889) and Munch's *The Scream* (1895), but his overall vision is nevertheless still a highly Romantic one. In this illustration no less than in his earlier and equally apocalyptic *Cholera sur Paris* (inspired by the 1849 epidemic), we find the same combination of a realistic panoramic view of the city with Notre-Dame on the horizon, offset by fantastical elements reminiscent of the juxtapositions of medieval and modern Paris to be found in Meryon's *Le Vampire*, Alphonse Chigot's *La Bourse* and Felicien Rops's

Satan Sowing Evil Grain over a city that the Church has ceased to control. It is perhaps worth noting also that in Rops's image, the 'evil grain' in question is rendered as naked women. Furthermore, the use of the she-devil, Harpy, Fury or Medusa figure for propaganda and ideological purposes was not the preserve of reactionary anti-Communards but was employed by artists on both sides of the political divide.[52] The monstrous figures in 'Histoire de Paris: les nuits de mai' can therefore be interpreted either as God's avenging angels or as evil destructive genies or she-devils who could be taken to symbolize the Communards or the Versaillais depending on one's own point of view.

The same sense of religious optimism detected in Vauvert's piece finds its poetic expression in François Coppée's poem 'L'an mil huit cent soixante et onze' (The Year Eighteen Hundred and Seventy-One), which appears in *Le Monde illustré*'s final edition of 1871, dated 30 December.[53] Coppée was virtually the only anti-Communard poet to write about the Commune either during April and May 1871 or after *la Semaine sanglante*; for example, his poem *Plus de sang!* (April 1871) and his one-act lyric drama, *Fais ce que dois*. The latter proved to be a great success when it was performed at *L'Odéon* on 21 October 1871 starring Sarah Bernhard, no doubt because it echoed the sentiments of many of his contemporaries.[54]

Coppée's poem for *Le Monde illustré* in December 1871, addressed to the Old Year, provides a summary of all the horrors and humiliation visited upon France from the Prussian defeat to the Commune. Neither is referred to by name but the two episodes are nevertheless inextricably linked. The worst humiliation of all, however, and the one that cannot be put aside and forgotten, is the enormous debt to be paid to Prussia and the loss of Alsace and Lorraine. As if to echo this sentiment, Coppée's poem is situated next to a short piece on *L'Alsace*, a painting by the Alsatian artist Jean-Jacques Henner in which the lost province is personified as a young girl dressed in mourning.

Ultimately, however, in keeping with the reactionary and conservative political and religious rhetoric of the period, Coppée's message (like that of Vauvert) is one of hope for the future:

Avenir incertain de l'année inconnue,
Ramènes-tu l'honneur, le travail, le devoir?
Qui le sait? Ton aurore est du moins un espoir
Viens donc, ô jeune année, ô sois la bien-venue.

[The future uncertainly of an unknown New Year,
Will you bring back honour, work, and duty?
Who can tell? Your dawning at least gives us hope
Come then, we welcome you O New Year.]

The poem expresses much the same sentiments conveyed in Coppée's *Fais ce que dois*; out of chaos, saturnalia and death, it is hoped, will come salvation and regeneration, the New Year being traditionally associated with the confession of sins and purgation in preparation for a new beginning.

Coppée's poem for *Le Monde illustré* is accompanied by a double-page illustration by Edmond Morin to be found on the last but one page of the journal and also entitled: 'L'AN MIL HUIT CENT SOIXANTE ET ONZE! . . .' (Figures 7, 8 detail).[55] The addition of the exclamation mark in the illustration caption, however, betrays a degree of irony that is lacking in the poem. Morin's drawing depicts a very sinister and emaciated Old Father Time flying away from the flames and destruction of France in 1871. Only just visible beneath him, to the left of his feet, Morin has included as grim reminders of the war, the last three letters of the name 'Alsace' and, a little further back, a Prussian helmet. There is none of Coppée's hopefulness for a better future in Morin's illustration. Father Time looks back to the Old Year not forward to the rising moon of 1872 while the inscribed date itself has a question mark after it. What is more, Father Time takes all the baggage of the past with him into the New Year, for bulging out of the sack on his back are to be found the following emotive and ironic slogans and relics of the past: 'Capitulation de Paris', 'Metz' and 'Lauriers Prussiens. Prix: 5 Milliards' (The Prussian Victor's Laurels: Cost 5,000 Million Francs), a reference to the cannon on Montmartre, a toppled Vendôme Column complete with statue of Napoleon under the words 'Gloires nationales', a tattered flag bearing the words 'Guerre civile' (Civil War), and a bottle bearing the label 'Pétrole' (Paraffin). Despite its apparent fantastical nature, which probably enabled it to evade censorship, Morin's drawing is arguably the most 'realist' of all the texts and illustrations of the events of 1871 to appear in *Le Monde illustré* during this period because it is the only representation which admits that the world has changed and that the new regime has still to deal with much unfinished business in a country that has been ravaged, physically and psychologically, by national and civil war. The inclusion of this illustration is evidence that while *Le Monde illustré* was normally quite happy to promote the official line which sought to marginalize the political difficulties of the period, the

Figure 7 'L'AN MIL HUIT CENT SOIXANTE ET ONZE! . . . (Composition de M. Ed. Morin. Texte de M. F. Coppée)' *Le Monde illustré*, 30 December 1871. (© British Library Board. All Rights Reserved. Shelfmark F23)

journal's (republican) editors were in fact capable of engaging with the real issues as well as indulging in a little quiet subversion, thereby once more disrupting the authority of the journal's dominant voice. Morin's image exemplifies all the repressed psychological baggage of 1870–71 that would continue to weigh on the collective unconscious over the coming decades. In the battle of the images surrounding the events of 1871, however, it was Chifflart's representation with its explication (ironi-cally, given his own Communard sympathies) of *la Semaine sanglante* as divine retribution that was to take hold in the collective memory at a conscious level. As J.-J. Frappa was to note in *Le Monde illustré* in a nostalgic piece dated 30 March 1918 recalling the journal's illustrators of the previous generation, Chifflart's chiaroscuro effects and billowing clouds had justifiably earned him a solid reputation as the pre-eminent artist of the great conflagrations of the Paris Commune.

The moral modern metropolis: a walker's guide

Just as Morin's grim 'L'AN MIL HUIT CENT SOIXANTE ET ONZE! . . .' provides a suitable epitaph for 1871, so his illustration entitled, '1878! –

Figure 8 'L'AN MIL HUIT CENT SOIXANTE ET ONZE! . . . (Composition de M. Ed. Morin. Texte de M. F. Coppée)' *Le Monde illustré*, 30 December 1871. Detail. (© British Library Board. All Rights Reserved. Shelfmark F23)

NOTRE OBJECTIF' (1878! – Our Objective) (Figure 9), and reproduced on the front page of *Le Monde illustré* dated 5 January 1878, provides a suitable representation of the optimism mixed with an element of fear for the future at the start of 1878, a year that is expected to be another landmark for Paris and France as a whole. As Jane Mayo Roos points out in her meticulously researched account of the political machinations behind the staging of the *Exposition universelle* and the *Fête du 30 juin*, Morin's illustration with its depiction of two disembodied hands – one labelled 'Gauche' (Left), the other 'Droite' (Right) – is symbolic of the belief among the majority of political moderates that the *Exposition* should be used as a vehicle to heal the breach between the

Figure 9 '1878! – NOTRE OBJECTIF (Composition de M. Ed. Morin)'
Le Monde illustré, 5 January 1878. (© British Library Board. All Rights
Reserved. Shelfmark F23)

nation's warring political factions.[56] Up until this point, *Le Monde illustré* had pursued a broadly pro-Thiers followed by a pro-MacMahon/monarchist line. Now, however, in thus advocating conciliation between the political factions, the journal is itself clearly moving gradually towards the republican middle ground.

This message is also conveyed in the text accompanying Morin's illustration and which appears on page 4 in the form of a greetings card addressed to the journal's readers and signed 'the Editorial Team'. Optimism prevails, just as it did in Coppée's poem in December 1871, and, to an extent, this is justified given the early settlement of the huge financial reparation to Prussia in September 1873 and the subsequent revival of the country's industry and economy.[57] Nevertheless, the text like the illustration is fraught with ambiguities.

The editorial team's stated 'Objectif' is to keep their readers fully informed of all the events taking place around the world and a telling analogy is made between the journal's function and that of photography; both are said to exist in order to record and inform on world events. At one level, this analogy serves to emphasize the journal's modernity and quest for truth, photography being considered in the nineteenth century as the epitome of both these virtues. At another level, however, it also betrays the journal's need to compete with the ubiquitous new medium. At another level still, the image of the photographer in Morin's accompanying illustration recalls the aftermath of the Commune when the photographers were out in force recording the city's humiliation for posterity. Equally, the reference in the text to the impending Spanish Royal marriage is another symbol of reconciliation but it is also an oblique reminder that the dispute over the Spanish succession had been a cause of the Franco-Prussian conflict. The seemingly innocent reference to the *Exposition* and to the return of a festive atmosphere to Paris is also double-edged for it acts as a reminder not just of Napoleon III's notoriously extravagant world fairs but also that this will be the first popular celebration in the city since the 'fête' of the Commune. As if this were not worrying enough, there is also war on the horizon, this time between Russia and Turkey.

The ironic and often ambiguous musings of 'Walker' (an obvious pun on the English for *flâneur*), the journal's pseudonymous roving reporter during the *Exposition universelle*,[58] similarly betray the tensions of the period. On the one hand Walker's accounts conform to the officially promoted view of the city as a modern, healthy and hygienic metropolis born of a collective desire to practise a form of Nietzschean

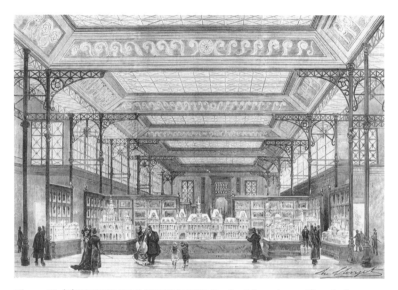

Figure 10 'L'EXPOSITION UNIVERSELLE – Intérieur du pavillon de la
Ville de Paris, situé au centre du Palais du Champ-de-Mars – (Dessin de
M. Clérget, d'après le projet en cours de M. Bouvard, architecte)' *Le Monde
illustré*, 20 April 1878. (© British Library Board. All Rights Reserved.
Shelfmark F23)

'active forgetfulness', while on the other hand, the writer betrays his/her
own inability to break free completely from the memory of the past.[59]

The 20 April 1878 edition of *Le Monde illustré* carries the first of
Walker's articles under the general heading *Nos Gravures* (Our Engravings), and the subtitle 'Promenades à l'Exposition' (Walks through the
Exhibition). The key theme to emerge in this and subsequent articles
over the coming months is the return of the fairytale city of light, made
more resplendent than ever by the extensive use of electric lighting, now
a viable and inexpensive option following recent technological innovations and very much a feature of the 1878 *Exposition*. Unlike the
brightly lit but 'decadent' Paris of the Second Empire, which had also
stereotypically been described as 'féerique', the new fairytale city is now
to be regarded as a paragon of moral order, civilization, progress and
technological achievement as embodied in the architect Joseph Antoine
Bouvard's three-dimensional models on display in the exhibition's
Pavilion de la Ville de Paris.[60] Walker's text, accompanied by Hubert
Clérget's illustration (Figure 10), summarizes the virtues of the city in

which the old quarters and wastelands are to be transformed into airy, light-filled cities and gracious squares. The construction of new hospitals, libraries and schools, the introduction of new methods of teaching and a whole host of other improvements are to ensure the moral and material betterment of the citizens of this great city which prides itself on being at the forefront of progress and which calls itself 'the capital of the civilized world.'

The city's labourers, as Walker informs us at the very beginning of the piece, are being kept busy working through the night like 'gnomes' building the exhibition pavilions with the aid of electric lights as if they were under the orders of a fairy waving her magic wand ('l'ordre magique de la baguette d'une fée)'. The reference to 'l'ordre magique', while maintaining the fairytale theme, reads like a politically subversive allusion on Walker's part to l'Ordre moral; but the likening of the workers to gnomes is similarly heavy with ideological and cultural significance. As Lidsky points out, the maintenance of old superstitions, including a belief in fairies, was to be recommended at the time as a way of instilling respect in the populace for 'ce qui est vieux' (what is old/established), a practice considered by conservatives and reactionaries to be preferable to providing the masses with a 'scientific' (empirically based) education, on the basis that knowledge in the wrong hands, that is in the hands of the working classes and *de facto* potential revolutionaries, invariably leads to trouble.[61]

Cham (pseudonym of Le Comte Amédée de Noé (1818–79)), a regular contributor to *Le Monde illustré*, takes up the fairy motif a few weeks later on 1 June with a cartoon of France personified as a fairy waving her magic wand over the palaces and pavilions of the *Exposition* (Figure 11, top row on the left). An aristocrat and right-wing conservative who was almost as famous for his vaudeville comedies as his cartoons and caricatures, Cham seems to have enjoyed relative immunity from the censors and his grimly humorous depictions of the privations suffered by Paris during the Prussian siege and sardonic gibes against ex-Communards appeared in *Le Monde illustré* as early as 9 September 1871.[62] His stock characters include Polyte and Gugusse, a pair of stereotypical working-class dimwits and a hirsute *chiffonnier* (rag-picker) who after the Commune is transformed into the 'ex-colonnel pétroleur'. The latter makes an appearance in the same group of cartoons that features the wand-waving Fairy (Figure 11, second row on the right) with a caption that makes a direct reference the Commune: 'Nos professeurs de barricades songeant à aller s'établir au Japon' (Our barricade experts

Figure 11 'REVUE COMIQUE, PAR CHAM' *Le Monde illustré*, 1 June 1878.

dreaming of setting themselves up in Japan). What would seem to be merely humorous witticisms by both Walker and Cham, therefore, are in fact heavy with ideological and cultural allusions that would not have been lost on *Le Monde illustré's* contemporary bourgeois audience.

The Commune, of course, had strongly advocated the introduction of free universal secular education together with the separation of Church and State and, ironically, laws enforcing obligatory free, non-denominational education were to be implemented under the Republic in 1882 and 1886. In 1878, however, these two subjects were the cause of much heated debate. Set within this context Walker's praise for the model *Ville de Paris*, with its libraries, schools and new methods of teaching is offset by his/her patronizing description of the workers as 'gnomes'. Not only, it would seem, are these men forced by *l'Ordre moral* to undertake hard labour as a means to survival, they are also being kept in a state of enforced superstitious ignorance. Walker's description of the workers as 'poulpiquets' and 'korrigans' (mischievous, often cruel Breton elves and sprites with a reputation for leading women and children astray), can again be read as an oblique reference to the Communards. Walker is clearly supporting the establishment line but his/her somewhat ironic tone is also reminiscent of some of Zola's less subtle attacks in *La Cloche* (29 September 1872) on *l'Ordre moral* and the cult of miracles that had been sweeping the country since the end of the Commune. However, as with Walker, Zola's position remains ambiguous since he was at the same time highly suspicious of educating the masses beyond the supposed demands of their class and their mental capacity.[63]

If the working classes are nowhere to be seen in Clérget's depiction of the Pavillon de la Ville de Paris, they were certainly out in force in the city's real streets during the spring and summer of 1878. The image of 'la foule' (the crowd, or the more ominous mob) taking to the streets would certainly have evoked memories of May 1871.[64] However, Walker's article of 27 April attempts to allay any fears in the minds of the journal's bourgeois readers that the working-classes may be about to rise up against them again and the initial ominous image of the vast crowd encircling the *Exposition* concourse is soon mitigated by the religious metaphor which accompanies it. The crowd we are told is on an 'Easter pilgrimage', many people having made their way to the *Exposition* on Easter Sunday, a few days before its official opening. The irony, of course, is that this 'pilgrimage' has nothing at all to do with religion and everything to do with making money. It is Walter Benjamin's 'pilgrimage to the commodity fetish' or phantasmagoria serving to distract and alienate people from each other and turning them all into customers for the luxury objects of desire on display.[65] It is far from the missions to rural parishes and pilgrimages to Lourdes organized by the Catholic Church throughout this period as part of its campaign to reassert the rights of God and the monarchy over the nation in an attempt to counter 'anti-Catholic' and 'anti-French' republican values and also to raise funds for the building of the Sacré-Cœur. The excavations for the great basilica, to be built in Château-Landon stone (chosen specifically because it whitens with age), were also currently underway, the monarchists having voted on 24 July 1873 to erect it on the site of the 'red' Commune's origins on the hilltop in Montmartre.[66]

If the Sacré-Cœur was to be the symbol of the nation's return to God then, ironically, the *Palais de l'Exposition* was to be the symbol of its return to the same outright, hard-nosed capitalism championed by the 'evil' Second Empire. Cham's cartoon of a restaurant cook telling the unfortunate chicken he is plucking to console herself with the thought that they will also be fleecing the person who'll be eating her ('Console-toi, pauvre amie! Celui qui te mangera, nous le plumerons aussi!') (Figure 11, bottom row on the right), is no doubt an accurate reflection on the whole enterprise. It is worth noting, however, that despite the record number of visitors to the *Exposition*, the event actually made a loss of 28,704,765 F (over £1 million) owing to the cost of construction of the two exhibition pavilions.[67] This financial loss was nevertheless more than offset by the fact that the *Exposition* returned the capital and the nation to the international stage.

In the 9 November 1878 edition of *Le Monde illustré*, Cham also takes the opportunity to take yet another sardonic swipe at both the proletarian Commune and its pious critics. He depicts his wild-eyed *libre-penseur* (freethinker) in the guise of an old Communard colonel pointing at a huge church organ being gawped at by visitors to the *Exposition*, and proclaiming: 'Je connais bien qu'un orgue qu'a du cœur, l'orgue de Barbarie! Comme moi, il n'entre pas dans les églises!' (I know of only one organ with a heart, the barrel organ! Like me it doesn't go into churches) (Figure 12, third row in the centre). The joke is over the fact that though the organ is the epitome of the Christian church music tradition, the 'orgue de Barbarie' (barrel organ) is an instrument of the people. In another direct jibe at the religious lobby Cham again depicts the same *libre-penseur* and one of his two dimwitted cronies in front of a poster for a performance of Corneille's famous Roman tragedy

Figure 12 'REVUE COMIQUE, PAR CHAM' *Le Monde illustré*, 9 November 1878. (© British Library Board. All Rights Reserved. Shelfmark F23)

Polyeucte, with a caption that reads: 'Paraît qu'il [Polyeucte] finit mal, il se fait chrétien!' (Apparently he [Polyeucte] comes to a bad end, he becomes a Christian!) (Figure 12, top row on the right). As noted earlier, Corneille's plays were particularly popular after the Commune for their promotion of patriotism, monarchy and Christian moral values and *Polyeucte* was currently playing at L'Opéra in an interpretation disparagingly dismissed by Zola as forming part of a hackneyed repertoire staged by clapped-out old actors![68] A further irony underlying all these allusions to the quasi-religious nature of the *Exposition* is to be found in the knowledge that Napoleon III's own great world fairs of 1855 and 1867 had similarly been inspired by both Christian and classical archaeology and iconography, with Rome once again forming the role model for Paris.[69]

Walker's article dated 27 April is accompanied by a centrefold illustration by Jules Férat inspired by Japanese prints (Figure 13),[70] depicting the city's labourers, this time likened to buzzing insects, firmly back in their place, picks and shovels in hand, building the new city under the watchful eyes of their foreman, a gendarme, and their other masters, the bourgeois visitors in their fine clothes and top hats (Figure 14). Coppée's New Year wish in December 1871 for a return of the nation to the values of 'honour, work and duty' thus appears to have been realized. In itself, the raising and enlarging of the Pont d'Iéna can also be interpreted as symbolic of France's own renaissance. An important icon of French national identity, the bridge was built by Napoleon I between 1809 and 1813 to celebrate his victory over the Prussians and as a link between the Champ-de-Mars and the Colline de Chaillot, where he had originally intended to erect an immense palace for his son, the King of Rome. The bridge's Napoleonic associations are played down in Férat's illustration, however, and the giant imperial eagles mounted underneath it as arch supports by Napoleon III are conveniently out of sight. If the *Exposition* was the consolidation of the effacement of Communard Paris, it was also, paradoxically – given the completion of some of Baron Haussmann's stalled schemes during this period – the consolidation of the effacement of Napoleon III's Paris.

Walker's article continues with a discussion of the merits of Rochet's statue of Charlemagne, which was currently being erected temporarily inside the Palais du Camp-de-Mars. The text is accompanied by an illustration dated 13 April by Henry Scott (Figure 15).[71] Scott's imposing double-page illustration does full justice to the vast scale of the Rochet's statue as well as showing just how much the interior of the

Figure 13 'LES GRANDS TRAVAUX DE L'EXPOSITION. – Le Pont d'Iéna surlévé et élargi – (Dessiné le 12 avril par M. Férat)' *Le Monde illustré*, 27 April 1878. (© British Library Board. All Rights Reserved. Shelfmark F23)

Figure 14 'LES GRANDS TRAVAUX DE L'EXPOSITION – Le Pont d'Iéna surlévé et élargi – (Dessiné le 12 avril par M. Férat)' *Le Monde illustré*, 27 April 1878. Detail. (© British Library Board. All Rights Reserved. Shelfmark F23)

Figure 15 'LES GRANDS TRAVAUX DE L'EXPOSITION – Installation sur son piédestal de la statue colossale du CHARLEMAGNE de feu Rochet (Dessiné par M. Scott le 13 avril)' *Le Monde illustré*, 27 April 1878. (© British Library Board. All Rights Reserved. Shelfmark F23)

Palais du Champ-de-Mars resembled that of a medieval cathedral. For Walker, this is the most important bronze monument ever erected to the glory of the nation; in other words it is greater even than the Vendôme Column, so venerated by Maisonneufve, for example, in the 27 May 1871 edition of *Le Monde illustré*. Walker's oblique reference, in 1878, to that other great Napoleonic bronze icon would no doubt have also reminded his/her readers of the Napoleonic associations attached also to Charlemagne's statue. Firstly, Napoleon I had originally planned to have a statue of Charlemagne adorn the summit of the Vendôme Column before being persuaded to dedicate the latter, with a statue of himself on the top instead, to his victory at Austerlitz. Secondly, Rochet's statue was currently the subject of much controversy. Originally commissioned under the Second Empire, it had been greatly praised during the previous *Exposition* in 1867. The Municipal Council of Paris was now being offered the statue in memory of its creator, Rochet, on condition that it paid for its pedestal. The republican Council, who regarded the statue as far too strongly associated with Napoleon III, flatly refused the offer.[72] Walker's hagiography of France's medieval emperor, therefore, only serves to highlight the shortcomings of her two more recent imperial leaders:

Dans l'empereur, on sent le grand souverain, grand guerrier et aussi grand protecteur des lettres, des sciences et des arts, tandis que ses deux compagnons [Roland and Roger] sont bien le type vrai de ces indomptables Francs qui viennent de faire crouler l'empire des Gaules sous le poids de leur épée.

[In the emperor we sense the great sovereign, the great warrior and also the great patron of literature, art and science, while his two companions [Roland and Roger] are typical of those indomitable Franks who had just crushed the Gaulish empire with their heavy swords.]

Walker's praise of Charlemagne is also in line with contemporary discourse which regarded the first Holy Roman Emperor as a representative of the perfect compromise between the royal and religious power bases and whose own strong link with Rome was a powerful reminder that France was very much a Latin country in her language, temperament and most importantly her faith. The first translation into modern French of the *Chanson de Roland*, the epic poem in which the legend of Charlemagne is recounted, appeared in December 1870 with an introduction by Léon Gautier and soon came to be read as a glorification of royalist, Catholic France as well as an allegory of France's defeat by Prussia.[73]

By promoting Charlemagne, the epitome of the 'civilized' French monarch and defender of the Roman Catholic faith, Walker would thus appear to be supporting the Catholic/Monarchist line. In obliquely taking a swipe at the 'barbarous' Prussians, represented by the two Franks, Roland and Roger, however, s/he deviates from the prevailing view of the period, expressed by Léon Gautier and others, which instead sought to turn Roland into a patriotic hero and Christian martyr. As a consequence of this ambiguity, Walker's apparently indignant railing against the decision to place Charlemagne's statue inside the Palais du Champ-de-Mars, instead of being purchased by the Municipal Council of Paris and proudly erected in the centre of the Trocadéro, could be interpreted as yet another ironic and mischievous commentary on current events.[74]

If Charlemagne suffered somewhat from his unfortunate appropriation by the Bonapartes, then Joan of Arc at least provided the perfect symbol for the monarchist, reactionary right. In an anonymous piece dated 8 June 1878, under the title, 'Le Centenaire de Voltaire' (The Voltaire Centenary), which subliminally declares where its real allegiance lies, *Le Monde illustré* covered both the controversial and unofficial festival dedicated to the famous fierce opponent of the Roman Catholic Church, sponsored by the republican Chamber of Deputies, as well as the staging by the religious lobby of a rival, supposedly 'more touching', celebration dedicated to Joan of Arc, that 'heroine of Orleans and Paris' and 'liberator of France'. The text is accompanied by two full-page 'eye-witness' illustrations by Daniel Vierge.[75] The first, on the left-hand page, depicts the silent demonstration that took place in front of Joan's statue in the place des Pyramides on 30 May 1878. Vierge's illustration, with its impressionistic rendering of the rain-wet pavement, fully captures this quiet moment of solemn respect and is particularly interesting for its depiction of women of all classes apparently obeying the appeal issued by Bishop Dupanloup (a key proponent of the cult of Joan of Arc and a leading campaigner for her canonization), for them to assemble and lay flowers at the foot of Frémiet's statue of Joan, located on the site where the future saint was wounded while fighting against the English. Following the involvement of working-class women in the Commune and now, in 1878, at a time when French feminists were actively campaigning for the rights of women, the image of Joan of Arc was being heavily promoted by the religious Right as a counter-model of femininity based on Christian virtue and patriotism. The illustration on the opposite page, meanwhile, depicts the scene at the *Théâtre de la Gaîté* where Victor Hugo is seen making a speech, also on 30 May, to mark the Voltaire centenary. The article stresses the fact that Hugo's speech, which contained an impassioned appeal for amnesty for ex-Communards, was also attended by a large number of women and the two juxtaposed illustrations can be seen as exemplifying the journal's stated aim to unite those on the political Left and Right. However, whether by design or not, the illustrations themselves are 'reversed' with that of Hugo appearing on the right-hand page and that of Joan on the left. The article and Vierge's image of the respect paid to Joan notwithstanding, the bitter arguments between monarchists and republicans over the rival celebrations, together with the apparent ignorance in practice on the part of the Parisian populace over what all the fuss was about, provide Cham (4 May 1878) with another excuse to poke fun at all concerned.[76] In a caricature of Joan's statue seen coming to life and attacking a (presumably republican) bourgeois gentleman with her lance, the caption warns the reader not to go to the Place des Pyramides and start talking about the Voltaire centenary.

The official opening of the *Exposition* was marked on 1 May 1878 by MacMahon amid much pomp and ceremony, and Walker's account of the event (11 May 1878) is filled with much predictable enthusiasm accompanied by an equally predictable sigh of relief, no doubt shared by many contemporary readers, that the celebrations were a great success and that the crowd had behaved itself. Throughout the whole day and part of the night, we are told, a spirit of happiness and goodwill reigned and the opening of the *Exposition* was joyously celebrated without any discordant note upsetting the festivities ('sans qu'aucune note discordante soit venue troubler la fête'). More importantly, the *Exposition* is seen by Walker to mark not the mere regeneration of the nation but, more tellingly and in keeping with the earlier reference to the 'Easter pilgrimage', the resurrection of 'notre belle patrie' (our beautiful nation/fatherland). France now, in accordance with the official rhetoric, 's'impose à l'admiration de tous' (commands everyone's admiration).

The fact that Walker stresses that the *fête* has returned to the streets of Paris is also worth noting for this would again have resonated with contemporary readers. *Fêtes* and carnivals, though very much in the French popular tradition, had always been regarded with suspicion by the upper classes who saw in such events the opportunity for the populace to indulge in drunken and disorderly behaviour, often leading to revolt. Since the Commune, the *fête* had acquired even greater notoriety with many writers – contemporary and modern, and on all sides of the political divide – frequently emphasizing the festive, carnivalesque nature of the insurrection, at least in its early stages.[77] Furthermore, the opening of the *Exposition* was accompanied by a violent thunderstorm. Walker tells us that, all of a sudden, the crowd was caught out by a torrential downpour ('une averse épouvantable, un véritable déluge vient s'abattre sur la foule'). A violent thunderclap followed and one of the pavilions in the Champ-de-Mars was struck by lightning. Like the *fête*, the thunderstorm was also often used metaphorically to describe revolutionary uprisings, a fact that seems to have been overlooked by modern commentators, and yet it is a recurring image in the anti-Communard discourse of the period. Not wanting to alarm his or her readers unduly with these worrying adumbrative reminders of May 1871, however, Walker again offers reassurance, though not without a characteristic touch of irony accompanied by an oblique, but unmistakable, reference to the recent past:

> 'Un Romain eût reculé', mais les Parisiens ne sont pas superstitieux, et, après un moment de désarroi, chacun se retrouve à sa place, trempé jusqu'aux os, les pieds dans la boue, mais prenant fort gaiement cette mésaventure.

> ['A Roman might have drawn back', but Parisians are not superstitious. After a few moments of uncertainty, everyone is back in their appointed places, soaked to the skin, up to the ankles in mud, but taking the mishap with a strong measure of good humour.][78]

Reading between the lines, the Franco-Prussian War and the Commune might have caused 'un Romain' (Emperor Napoleon III) to retreat but Parisians, and by extension all Frenchmen, remain strong. They may have been beaten and humiliated ('après un moment de désarroi'), they may be suffering still ('trempé jusqu'aux os, les pieds dans la boue'), and they may find themselves back where they started, no better off than before ('chacun se retrouve à sa place') but they have weathered the storm and survived. There may still be discontent in some quarters, symbolized by the rain and the odd rumbling of thunder that, we are told, continued for some time, but better times lie ahead signalled by the fact that the sun reappeared as if to welcome the start of the ceremony.

In addition to the usual report on the *Exposition*, Walker's regular Column also carried descriptions of the other *fêtes* taking place in the city that June: *La Kermesse de l'Orangerie, La Fête fédérale de Gymnastique* and *La Fête du 30 juin*. The first of these, *La Kermesse de l'Orangerie*, was a charity event held on behalf of *Les Amis de l'enfance* and organized by several hautes-bourgeoises and attended by Madame MacMahon. Walker's account of the proceedings (15 June 1878) is reminiscent of similar events parodied by Zola in *La Conquête de Plassans*, *Son Excellence Eugène Rougon* (in which a charity event is actually staged in the Orangerie (II, 327–49)), and *L'Argent*, and again in Maupassant's *Bel Ami*. *La Kermesse*, literally 'fête d'église' (church festival), once again brought out the crowds in the Tuileries gardens and the Place de la Concorde, and Walker's piece can almost can be read as a companion to Hubert's 'Aux Tuileries' discussed earlier, resonating at it does with echoes of the Communard invasion of this city space in 1871. But, once again, Walker is quick to allay any latent fears the crowd might pose for his bourgeois readers. Once again, the emphasis is on the fairytale appearance of the electrically lit city as the crowd undertakes yet another 'pilgrimage' and the *Kermesse* acts as proof that Paris and its citizens are capable of enjoying themselves peaceably and soberly.

The emphasis on clean, healthy living is further emphasized in Walker's account of the *Fête de Gymnastique*. Not wanting to be left behind by England and Germany, France is seen to be most concerned with promoting a culture of sport and exercise. And, once more, in spite of the rain and the fact that the Alsace-Lorraine gymnastics team carried a banner draped in black (which an emotional crowd solemnly saluted), this *Fête* proved to be another resounding success.

Walker's account of the *Fête du 30 juin* (dated 6 July 1878) again betrays an ironic sigh of relief that this brilliant, and above all 'spontaneous', celebration also passed without any problems, surpassing even the success of the opening of the *Exposition*. Fearing that the official involvement in the organization of the *Fête* would have resulted in a rather banal display of lights, Walker is pleased to report that, on the contrary, the *Fête* outdid any other festival within living memory (another oblique reference perhaps to the great world fairs of the Second Empire and/or the 'fête' of the Commune). Rather than attempt to describe this marvellous event, which was attended by some two million people, Walker contents him/herself with giving the readers a description of the scene from the Tuileries all the way to the Bois de Boulogne. Walker's choice of route through the city reads like an 'art of memory' of Paris and the Commune. The Tuileries, the Place de la Concorde, the Champs-Elysées and the Bois de Boulogne all saw some of the fiercest fighting between the *fédérés* and the Versaillais but, still in keeping with the fairytale theme, Walker declares that the architect, Adolphe Alphand (who had previously worked for Haussmann), has turned the Place de la Concorde into 'an enchanted garden' and that the silvery glow cast by the electric lights projected over the city from the top of the Arc de Triomphe ('les projections électriques lancées du haut de l'Arc-de-Triomphe') gives the *cafés-concerts*, restaurants and even all the little kiosks along the Champs-Elysées the semblance of fairytale palaces. Walker then goes on to describe the firework display:

> Vers dix heures... boum... boum... les bombes éclatent, semant en l'air leur gerbes de feu qui pâlissent successivement devant les étoiles multicolores des fusées qui sifflent sans interruption. Les cris, les applaudissements se mêlent au fracas des bombes et des coups de feu jusqu'au moment du bouquet. Une immense clameur accueille ce couronnement de la fête, et chacun se précipite vers le point où s'est concentrée la musique qui doit exécuter la retraite aux flambeaux.

> [Getting on for ten o'clock at night, bang, bang, the bangers explode, spraying the sky with sparks which fade in rings, one after the other, amongst the multicoloured stars produced by an endless stream of whistling rockets. Shouts and applause mingle with the noise of the bangers and the shots, until the finale, which is greeted with loud whoops of joy. Everyone then rushes to where the band is preparing to accompany the torchlight procession.]

The language used to describe the scene ('les bombes éclatent', 'gerbes de feu', 'fusées qui sifflent', 'fracas des bombes', 'coups de feu'), is highly evocative and must have recalled memories of the bombardment of the city (particularly heavy around the Arc de Triomphe) and the conflagrations that produced their own 'firework display' at the end of May 1871. At a subliminal level, therefore, the Commune is everywhere present in Walker's descriptions, just as many physical traces of the destruction wrought on the city seven years earlier were still in evidence, such as the ruined Tuileries Palace. Walker's 'promenade' exemplifies Halbwachs's contention that the city – particularly on festive days – enables its present-day observers to recognize and reconstruct the past from what they see and experience in the present.[79] For Walker, like the other writers, artists and photographers discussed in this book, who all actually lived through the events of the Commune, it is hardly surprising that despite the fact that Paris was a very different place by the spring and summer of 1878 from that which it had been in May 1871, repressed memories of that traumatic time invariably resurface in their descriptions of the city by means of Freudian displacement or condensation, or through encounters with the modern city itself. Often it is the juxtapositions between the strange and familiar and the evocation of what is irretrievably lost yet still somehow hauntingly present in the city which, in the various ways suggested by Halbwachs and Michel de Certeau, evoke memories of the past initially in the minds of the writers themselves and then in the minds of their implied co-reminiscers or readers.[80] Walker's descriptions, however, are also very much a product of the present, of the city in 1878. The immediate social impact of past events having been mitigated in the present, it is inevitable that the memory of those events will lose their impact and eventually be confined to oblivion.[81]

The description of the entrance to the Bois de Boulogne, which also forms the focal point of Scott's accompanying illustration (Figure 16), indirectly but no less effectively emphasizes the fact that the *Fête du 30 juin* was very much a successful celebration of the Republic, despite the fact that the celebration was not held on 14 July (the anniversary of the 1789 Revolution) as some republicans had wanted. For the monarchists, the staging of a popular celebration on 14 July would have represented a vindication of the Commune, but equally for the majority of moderate republicans the date was considered to be too contentious. Whilst many agreed that 14 July was the obvious date on which to celebrate the Republic, they did not wish to appear to be condoning the violence of the Revolution (and, by association, the Commune) and, in the event, the politically neutral date of 30 June had been chosen. The *Fête du 30 juin* has been dismissed by some modern commentators as being 'a totally meaningless holiday' and a 'tactical *defeat* for the left',[82] but there is no denying that the event was hugely popular with the majority of Parisians, who adorned the city streets with *tricolore* flags and gathered in the squares to sing the outlawed *Marseillaise* in open defiance of MacMahon.[83] By publicly boycotting the *Fête du 30 juin*, MacMahon and the monarchists arguably rendered themselves even more unpopular with the greater part of the electorate thus precipitating their electoral defeat and MacMahon's own resignation on 5 January 1879, making way for Grévy and Gambetta.

The fact that *Le Monde illustré* carried Scott's jubilant illustration on the front page is a strong indication that the political tide had turned, itself a turning point for the journal which, until now, had been so careful not to offend MacMahon. Both Walker and Scott single out the two 'pyramids' marking the entrance to the Bois de Boulogne, each of which carries 'un énorme soleil' embossed with the initials R.F.

Figure 16 'PARIS LE 30 JUIN 1878 – La Fête de nuit – L'entrée du Bois de Boulogne par la porte Dauphine (Dessin de M. Scott)' *Le Monde illustré*, 6 July 1878. (© British Library Board. All Rights Reserved. Shelfmark F23)

(*République française*), clearly representing the new republican dawn about to break. The *fête* had seemingly finally been sanitized by *l'Ordre moral* and appropriated by the new Republic. The working classes are no longer to be perceived as a threat, on the surface at least, but on the contrary, according to Walker, they are to be found the morning after the night before, 'disséminés à travers le bois [de Boulogne] et dormant, sous le toit du bon Dieu, d'un sommeil réparateur' (lying peacefully asleep all over the Bois de Boulogne with only 'God's ceiling' for cover). Not only was the *Fête du 30 juin* spared any real thunder and lightning but any cloud that might have cast a shadow on the event, invoking memories of the Commune, had been safely blown away by an apparently appeased and benevolent God. Any apocalyptic representations of the city such as those by Chifflart had thus given way to a vision of a moral, ordered and healthy modern metropolis. As the British journalist George Augustus Sala also noted at the time, the same city he had seen ' "knocked into a cocked hat" over and over again – barricaded, bombarded, beleaguered, dragooned, and all but sacked [was] now ' "Paris Herself Again" – comelier, richer, gayer, more fascinating than ever'.[84]

Notes

1 Halbwachs, *Les Cadres*, pp. v, 62–3.
2 See Allan Paivio and Csapo Kalman, 'Picture Superiority in Free Recall: Imagery or Dual Coding?', *Cognitive Psychology*, 5 (1973), pp. 176–206. Also: Allan Paivio, *Mental Representation: A Dual Coding Approach*, 2nd edn (Oxford: Oxford University Press, 1990); Roger N. Shepard, 'Recognition Memory for Words, Sentences, and Pictures', *Journal of Verbal Learning and Verbal Behavior*, 6 (1967), pp. 156–63; and Marilyn Chapnik Smith and Lochlan E. Magee, 'Tracing the Time Course of Picture-Word Processing', *Journal of Experimental Psychology: General*, 109: 4 (December 1980), pp. 373–92.
3 The year 1869 saw the monopoly switch to Emile de Girardin's *Journal officiel*. For more information on Paul Dalloz (1829–87) see Bellanger, II, pp. 163–4.
4 On the anti-Communard views of *Le Moniteur universel*, see Bernard Noël, *Dictionnaire de la Commune*, 2 vols (Paris: Flammarion, 1978), II, pp. 104–5.
5 Bellanger, II, p. 191.
6 See Watelet, III, pp. 291–4.
7 See Dubief, p. 232.
8 Pierre Albert, *La Presse française* (Paris: La Documentation française, 1990), p. 30.
9 See Collins, pp. 164–8.
10 See English, pp. 64–74 and Bertrand Tillier, *La Commune de Paris: Révolution sans images?* (Seyssel: Champ Vallon, 2004).
11 *Archives nationales* reference F18 2363.
12 See English, pp. 67–9.
13 See Goldstein, pp. 198–220, and Collins, pp. 164–8.

14 See Guéry, pp. 86–7.

15 See Gretton, p. 148.

16 See Frizot, *A New History of Photography* (Cologne: Könemann Verlagsgelsellschaft, 1998), p. 361, and Watelet, III, p. 294.

17 Noted in *L'Annuaire de la presse 1881* (Paris: L'Agence télégraphique universelle, 1881).

18 Mouillaud, pp. 147–8.

19 Gretton, p. 149.

20 See, for example, *Correspondance de Berthe Morisot avec sa famille et ses amis*, ed. by Denis Rouart (Paris: Quatre Chemins Editart, 1950), p. 58.

21 On the protracted history of the Tuileries palace ruins see Kirk Varnedoe, 'The Tuileries Museum and the Uses of Art History in the Early Third Republic', in *Saloni, gallerie, musei e loro influenza sullo sviluppo dell-arte dei secoli XIX e XX*, ed. by Francis Haskell (Bologna: CIHA, 1979), pp. 63–8.

22 Cf. also Zola: 'aux Tuileries, les femmes brodant à l'ombre des marronniers, tandis que, là haut, du côté de l'Arc de Triomphe, des obus éclatent.' Quoted in Rougerie, *La Commune de 1871*, p. 88.

23 See further examples in Gullickson.

24 Maisonneufve also contributed to Paul Dalloz's *Petite presse*, a low-circulation daily (c.35,000 copies). Following the Commune he published an account seeking to rehabilitate the reputation of the penal colony of New Caledonia, entitled *La Nouvelle-Calédonie et les îles de déportation* (Paris: Au Bureau de *L'Eclipse*, 1872).

25 Auguste André Lançon (1836–85), a carpenter's son from the Jura, exhibited at the Salon of 1872 and also worked as a book illustrator, for example for Victor Hugo's *Quatre-vingt-seize* in 1877. He contributed illustrations to several newspapers and travelled to the Balkans to cover the war between Russia and Turkey for *L'Illustration*. See the entry in Marcus Osterwalder, ed., *Dictionnaire des illustrateurs, 1800–1914* (Neuchâtel: Ides et Calendes, 1989).

26 Osterwalder, p. 585.

27 Nicholas-François Chifflart (1825–1901), winner of the prestigious Prix de Rome in 1851, contributed a number of illustrations to *Le Monde illustré* throughout this period which were subsequently published in album form by the journal. On his life and work see Valérie Sueur, *François Chifflart graveur et illustrateur* (Paris: Reunion des Musées nationaux, 1994), and Louis Noël, *François Chifflart: peintre et graveur français, 1825–1901* (Lille: Imprimerie Vandroth-Fauconnier, 1902).

28 See Noël, *Dictionnaire de la Commune*, II, pp. 273–4.

29 Bernard Noël and Jean-Claude Gautrand, *La Commune, Paris 1871* (Paris: Nathan Collection Photo Poche, 2000), figure 32.

30 Maisonneufve's praise of the republican journalist, Tony Révillon, in his *La Presse populairie: Tony Révillon* (Paris: Lachaud, 1869), p. 46, can be taken as evidence of his own republican stance.

31 See Roos, *Early Impressionism and the French State*, pp. 147–59, and Matsuda, pp. 19–39.

32 The Commune was not the first regime to remove the Emperor from the top of the Column. In 1814, under the restoration of Louis XVIII, Napoleon's original statue was destroyed and replaced by one of Henry IV. This statue was then in turn also destroyed during the 'cent-jours' when Louis XVIII fled the capital. It was later replaced with a giant Fleur-de-lys. In 1830, Louis-Philippe had this royalist symbol replaced by a new statue of Napoleon, this time dressed in a frockcoat and hat. During the Second Empire when Napoleon III replaced the statue with a new one of his uncle, once more dressed as a Roman Emperor, the Column once again came to stand for Napoleonic imperialism, which is why the Commune voted to demolish it.

33 'La Colonne' (the Column), became a focal point for anti-royalists and a republican icon, immortalized by Hugo in his *Ode à la Colonne Vendôme* (1827).

34 See Maurice Agulhon, *Marianne au combat: l'imagerie et la symbolique républiaines de 1789 à 1880* (Paris: Flammarion, 1979), p. 180.

35 The event was photographed by Marville (see Thézy, pp. 126–7), and covered by *Le Monde illustré* in its edition dated 8 January 1876 with an illustration by Henry Scott.

36 See in particular Lidsky, chs III and IV, Roberts, pp. 189–90, and Catherine Glazer, 'De la Commune comme maladie mentale', *Romantisme*, 48 (1985), pp. 63–70. A prolific writer, Charles Monselet (1825–88) covered a range of genres including poetry, novels, plays, history, theatrical reviews, journalism, and works on gastronomy. He contributed a number of articles, theatre reviews and serialized novels to *Le Monde illustré*, among other newspapers. See André Monselet, *Charles Monselet: sa vie, son œuvre* (Paris: Emile Testard, 1892). Aspects of this section first appeared in my article ' "La Dernière Etape des fédérés au Père-Lachaise": The Contribution of *Le Monde illustré* to the Right-Wing Myth of Paris and the Commune', in *Reading and Writing the Forbidden: Essays in French Studies*, ed. by Bénédicte Facques et al. (Reading: The 2001 Group, 2003), pp. 103–16.

37 Mendès, *Les 73 journées de la Commune (du 18 mars au 20 mai 1871)* (Paris: Lachaud, 1871), p. 327. On the whole subject of the nineteenth-century obsession with decadence see A.E. Carter, *The Idea of Decadence in French Literature: 1830–1900* (Toronto: University of Toronto Press, 1958), and Koenraad W. Swart, *The Sense of Decadence in Nineteenth-Century France* (The Hague: Martinus Nijhoff, 1964).

38 Théophile Gautier, *Tableaux de siège: Paris, 1870–1871*, 2nd edn (Paris: Charpentier, 1895).

39 For further examples of the Commune as Shakespearean tragedy, see Mendès, pp. i–vi.

40 Cf. Camille's speech in *Horace*, IV, 5, pp. 1309–19.

41 On 'Léo de Bernard' see *Dictionnaire des pseudonyms*, ed. by Georges d'Heylli (Geneva: Slatkine reprints, 1971), p. 43. Albert Robida (1848–1926) covered the Prussian Siege of Paris and the Commune for *Le Monde illustré* before subsequently moving to *La Vie parisienne* and, in 1880, founding his own paper, *La Caricature*. See Philippe Brun, *Albert Robida (1848–1926): sa vie, son œuvre suivi d'une bibliographie complète de ses écrits et dessins* (n.p.: Promodis, 1984), and Fred Robida, 'Albert Robida en 1870–71', *Europe*, 19 (1971), pp. 63–75.

42 Père-Lachaise was mythologized as the setting of the last engagement of the civil war by the Commune's detractors as well as by some of its supporters. See Tombs, *The Paris Commune*, p. 195, and Rebérioux, 'Le Mur des fédérés: Rouge, "sang craché"' in Nora, *Les Lieux de mémoire*, vol. 1 (1984), *La République* pp. 619–49.

43 See Serman's account, p. 523.

44 On the censorship of Pichio's painting and the representation of the Mur, see Tillier, pp. 255–65, 417–35.

45 See Robida, *Album du Siège et de la Commune*, ed. by Lucien Scheler, 2 vols (Librairie Historique & Librairie Thomas-Scheler, 1971), I, p. 62 (Robida's diary entry for Friday 26 May 1871), II.

46 Lidsky, pp. 93–4.

47 Tombs, *The Paris Commune*, p. 194. See also Christophe Reffait, 'La renaissance de la nation selon *La Débâcle* de Zola', *Journal of the Society of Dix-Neuviémistes*, 6 (2006), pp. 42–54.

48 Heylli, p. 43.

49 For example, Hélène Millot, 'Une Commune fin de siècle?' in Bellet and Régnier p. 194, and Milner, pp. 172–3.

50 Millot in Bellet and Régnier, p. 195. See also Lidsky, pp. 91–6.

51 Halbwachs, *La Mémoire collective*, pp. 143–92.

52 See William Kidd, 'Marianne: From Medusa to Messalina. Psycho-sexual Imagery and Political Propaganda in France 1789–1945', *Journal of European Studies*, 34: 4, pp. 333–48.

53 François Coppée (1842–1908), whilst not much read today, was in his own time a very well-known and respected Romantic poet and playwright. He was awarded the *Légion d'honneur* in 1876 and elected to the *Académie française* in 1884. During the Dreyfus Affair he joined forces with the anti-Semitic group comprising Henri Rochefort, Edouard Drumont and Maurice Barrès. He was popular throughout the last decades of the nineteenth century and also during the Vichy period. His poetry remained a part of the French secondary-school curriculum well into the 1940s. See Daniel Milo, 'Les Classiques scholaires', in Nora, *Les Lieux de mémoire*, vol. 2, *La Nation*, II (1986), pp. 542–3. For evidence of Coppée's support for MacMahon and his anti-republican sentiments see his letter to his sister Annette dated July 1877 in *François Coppée: Lettres à sa mère et à sa sœur: 1862–1908*, ed. by Jean Monval (Paris: Alphonse Lemerre, 1914), p. 188.

54 See Lidsky, p. 92, and Coppée, *Œuvres: Poèsies II, 1869–1875* (Paris: Alphonse Lemerre, n.d.) and *Œuvres: Théâtre: 1869–72* (Paris: Alphonse Lemerre, n.d.). In 1872, Dalloz's *Le Moniteur universel* published, in serial form, Coppée's novella *Une Idylle pendant le Siège*, an almost documentary account of the fall of the Second Empire, the revolution of September 1870, the Prussian Siege and the Commune.

55 Edmond Morin (1825–82) worked in Paris from 1846 as a *peintre-dessinateur*. He exhibited at the Salon of 1857 and subsequently moved to London, where he founded the short-lived *Pen and Pencil* and worked for a number of British newspapers until 1861. On his return to Paris, he joined *Le Monde illustré* where, until 1879, he was the journal's principal illustrator. He also contributed to *L'Illustration* and *La Vie parisienne*. In 1874 he contributed to *Le Monde illustré*'s *Album du mémorial des deux sièges de Paris*. His work also included book illustrations, notably for Hugo's *Les Misérables*. See Osterwalder, pp. 715–16.

56 Roos, 'Within the "Zone of Silence"', p. 378.

57 See Alistair Horne, *The Fall of Paris: The Siege and the Commune, 1870–71* (London: Macmillan, 1965), p. 427.

58 A similar column to Walker's, entitled 'Impressions d'un flâneur à l'Exposition' and signed by one, 'X Rambler', also appeared in *L'Exposition de Paris (1878)* (Paris: Librairie illustré and Librairie M. Dreyfous, 1878), a special edition weekly published to coincide with the exhibition and edited by Adolphe Bitard.

59 My analysis of Walker's articles, and later also Marville's photographs in Chapter 5, is based on my article 'Memory and the Politics of Forgetting: Paris, the Commune, and the 1878 *Exposition Universelle*', which appeared in the *Journal of European Studies*, 35: 1/2 (2005), pp. 173–89, and I am grateful to Sage Publications for permission to reproduce this material.

60 Improved streetlighting in general also serves a political and moral purpose for Du Camp (*PSO*, V, pp. 271–91) and Vallès, *Le Tableau de Paris* (1882) (Paris: Editions de Delphes, 1964), p. 27.

61 See also Alphonse Daudet's, 'Les Fées de France' in his *Contes du Lundi*: 'la France était bien belle quand elle avait encore ses fées. Nous étions la poésie du pays, sa foi, sa candeur, sa jeunesse . . . nous venons de voir ce que c'est un pays qui n'a pas de fées'. Lidsky, p. 127.

62 See Michel Nathan, 'Cham polemiste', in *La Caricature entre République et censure*, ed. by Philippe Régnier (Lyons: Presses universitaires de Lyon, 1996), pp. 182–91.

63 Lidsky, p. 126.

64 See Glazer, pp. 63–70.

65 Benjamin, *The Arcades Project*, trans. by Howard Eiland and Kevin McLaughlin (Cambridge, MA, and London: Belknap Press of Harvard University Press, 1999), 'Exposé of 1935', pp. 7–8.

66 See Harvey, ch. 4, and Raymond Jonas, *France and the Cult of the Sacred Heart: An Epic Tale for Modern Times* (Berkeley, Los Angeles and London: University of California Press, 2000).

67 See Brigitte Schroder-Gudehus and Anne Rasmussen, *Les Fastes du progrès: le guide des expositions universelles, 1851–1992* (Paris: Flammarion, 1992), p. 96.

68 Cited in Mitterand, *Zola jounaliste: de l'affaire Manet à l'affaire Dreyfus* (Paris: Armand Colin, 1962), p. 197.

69 See Anne Green, 'France Exposed: Madame Bovary and the Exposition Universelle', *The Modern Language Review*, 99: 4 (October 2004), pp. 915–23 (p. 917).

70 Jules Férat (1819–?) was a regular contributor to *Le Monde illustré*, who, since 1866, had also worked for the publishing house of Hachette, contributing to their 'Bibliothèques des Merveilles' editions, and also exhibiting a number of works at the Paris Salon between 1857 and 1878. See, Osterwalder, p. 359.

71 Henry Scott (1849–84), born in Le Havre of English decent, made his debut at the Salon of 1872 after initially training as a theatre stage decorator. See Osterwalder, pp. 971–2.

72 See June Hargrove, 'Les statues de Paris', in Nora, *Les Lieux de mémoire*, vol. 2 (1986), *La Nation*, II, p. 253.

73 See Schivelbusche, pp. 142–7.

74 The statue was finally placed in front of the Cathedral of Notre-Dame at the heart of the medieval city rather than in the modern city centre in 1879, but the Municipal Council of Paris continued to refuse to pay for it until 1896 and only found a suitable pedestal for it in 1908. See Hargrove, 'Les statues de Paris', in Nora, *Les Lieux de mémoire*, vol. 2 (1986), *La Nation*, II, p. 253.

75 On the influential Spanish artist Daniel Vierge (1851–1904) see Osterwalder, pp. 1092–3.

76 On the controversy surrounding the centenaries of both Voltaire and Rousseau see Georges Benrekassa et al., 'Le Premier Centenaire de la mort de Rousseau et de Voltaire: significations d'une commémoration', *Revue d'histoire littéraire de la France*, 79: 2–3 (March–June 1979), pp. 265–95, and Langford, ch. 2. On Joan of Arc, see Charles Wayland Lightbody, *The Judgements of Joan: Joan of Arc, a Study in Cultural History* (London: Allen & Unwin, 1961).

77 See Lefebvre, *La Proclamation de la Commune*, p. 133; Mendès, pp. 21–2; and Du Camp, *LC*, II, 197.

78 I would like to express my gratitude to Penny Sewell at Birkbeck College for her help with the translation of Walker's idiom in this and the next quotation.

79 Halbwachs, *La Mémoire collective*, pp. 116, 188.

80 See Halbwachs, *La Mémoire collective*, pp. 51–3, 188–9, and Michel de Certeau, *L'Invention du quotidien*, 2 vols (Paris: Gallimard, 1994), I, part 3, 'Pratiques de l'espace', II, part 1, 'Les Revenants de la ville'.

81 Halbwachs, *Les Cadres*, pp. 110–11, 130.

82 Boime, pp. 132–5; Roos, 'Within the "Zone of Silence"', p. 389. Care should be exercised in the use of the term 'left' or 'leftist' to describe the republican position. Roos, for example, states that *La République française* carried a series of articles in which the *Fête du 30 juin* 'was lauded as a victory for the radical republic' and that '*Le Siècle* also viewed the event as a demonstration of leftist Republicanism'. *Le Siècle* opposed MacMahon and is described as a left-wing republican newspaper (Bellanger, II, p. 215) but it nevertheless condemned the Commune and supported Thiers, who was responsible for its repression. *La République française* was founded by Gambetta in 1871 in an attempt to rally republicans of all hues to his political party, *l'Union républicaine* (Bellanger, II, pp. 222–4). It is important to distinguish between the broadly centrist republicanism of such newspapers, which had always sought to distance themselves from the Commune, and the more revolutionary form. As Beth Archer Brombert notes, 'what the French call radical republicanism . . . has always been a moderate position in European politics. . . . Today the word *radical* creates an unfortunate confusion with the more common connotation of an extreme ideology': *Edouard Manet: Rebel in a Frock Coat* (Chicago: University of Chicago Press, 1996), p. 290. It is also important to note that ex-Communards such as Louise Michel as well as some moderate republicans such as Zola perceived Gambetta as a tyrant: see Bury, *Gambetta's Final Year*, pp. 221, 223.

83 Kasl, p. 53.

84 George Augustus Sala, *Paris Herself Again 1878–1879* (London: Golden Gallery Press, 1948), p. 13.

3

Du Camp's *Paris*: between history, memory and reportage

Now that I have analysed the contribution made by *Le Monde illustré* to the construction of the collective memory of Paris and the Commune, the aim of this chapter is to look at the representation of Paris in the period from 1872 to 1878 in Du Camp's *Paris: ses organes* and *Les Convulsions*. In this way I hope to establish how these texts also function as narratives of collective memory by rehearsing and developing many of the themes, tropes and stereotypes that have already been identified and which reappear in the subtext to Zola novels, which form the subject of the next chapter.

Du Camp's *Paris: ses organes* is nowadays considered to be a *sui generis* text, since it straddles so many different disciplines and genres: history, geography, urban studies, sociology, politics, economics, journalism, memoir, and good old-fashioned storytelling.[1] For Du Camp's contemporaries, however, this blend of the factual and novelistic would not have seemed in any way untoward. Zola, for example, was particularly impressed with the first volume, noting its anatomical and highly detailed approach to its description of the city. He declared the work to be sharply written and was particularly taken with Du Camp's account of the Paris morgue, which he was later to put to good effect himself in *Thérèse Raquin*.[2] André Finot, writing in the late 1940s, stresses the readability of *Paris: ses organes*, describing it as a well-written and observed text offering the best description of the functioning of the city to have been written for a century.[3] As far as the thoroughness of Du Camp's research is concerned, however, Finot is not quite as impressed as Senneville, Du Camp's more recent biographer, and suggests that the writer should have gone back more to original source documents and archives. This criticism is telling and consistent with the generally held view of Du Camp as an unreliable witness and self-interested manipulator of facts and events, and as someone who easily blurred the distinctions between the fictional and the real.[4]

For the modern reader, Du Camp's writing style, based on storytelling techniques, is surprisingly accessible since it manages to offset close, detailed research and statistical data, with many personal observations, insights and anecdotes. In his own general introduction to *Paris: ses organes*, Du Camp states that it is not his intention to write a monograph on Paris, still less a history of the city (*PSO*, I, 8). Nevertheless, each chapter begins with a historical account of a particular aspect of the city, and Du Camp's point of view, narrative technique, language and rhetoric conform to many of the conventions expected of historical narrative at the time. Nineteenth-century historians such as Prosper de Barante, Jacques Thierry and Hippolyte Taine, following in Aristotle's footsteps, all claimed that historical narrative is close to poetry, a form of free verse which is used to describe past events in a language which is both easy to understand and which does not bore the reader.[5] Hayden White draws attention to the fact that 'realism' in the novel and 'objectivity' in historiography in the nineteenth century developed side by side since both have a shared dependency on a specifically narrative mode of discourse.[6] It is therefore the plot structures, themes, language, rhetorical devices and so on that produce the meaning in both historical and fictional narrative, the explanation of why things happened as they did. If a past event is narrated as a romance, tragedy, comedy or farce in a historical narrative, and readers recognize the 'story' being told as such, then that is how those events will be interpreted and understood. As Barthes points out, the appearance of facts will have just as much 'truth' effect in a narrative as real facts.[7] The recounting of the supposed 'last stand' of the *fédérés* against the Versaillais at the cemetery of Père-Lachaise by Léo de Bernard in *Le Monde illustré* in 1871 as if it were a classical tragedy and Du Camp's account of the Commune as farce are both examples of this. Furthermore, the demand for closure in both historical narrative and, no less, in narrative fiction in the nineteenth century is a demand 'for moral meaning, a demand that sequences of real events be assessed as to their significance as elements of a moral drama', and no historical narrative is ever free of the moral authority of its author.[8] It is difficult, as White suggests, to think of any historical work produced during the nineteenth century, the classic age of historical narrative (but not only during this period, and this book included!) that does not impose a moral judgement on the events it relates.

So much for the relationship between historical narrative and fictional narrative, but how exactly can Du Camp's supposed eyewitness accounts be said to function as examples of discursive reminiscence, as memory narratives? Edward S. Casey's theories on reminiscing and reminding, and memory and place help to provide the answer. For Casey, 'reminiscence' is defined as a *voluntary*, performative act of remembering which draws upon the reminiscer's own lived experience, memory or knowledge.[9] As such, 'reminiscence' finds its counterpart in the French 'remémoration' rather than 'réminiscence', which relates instead to acts of involuntary or unconscious remembering in the ways variously described by Bergson, Proust and Halbwachs, though this may, of course, be the experience engendered in the reader of such texts. Reminiscing, and especially co-reminiscing, or remembering with others, according to Casey, 'involves *resharing of already shared experiences*', and while it is possible to reminisce without the use of words, as when photographs are silently passed around between friends who participated in the scene being depicted, most reminiscing is usually done orally between participants (p. 119). Written forms of 'auto-reminiscing', such as autobiographies and memoirs, have much in common with their oral counterpart. Firstly, words, as Casey points out, 'facilitate' reminiscing by freeing the speaker/writer from any material supports – such as photographs, newspapers and other ephemera – connected with the original scene to be remembered. Echoing Saussure and Derrida, Casey states that 'words, in contrast, are much less perishable because they are not material entities in the first place' (p. 116).[10] And, in a definition that might have been written by Halbwachs, Casey states that 'words' are 'the most effective and enduring form of symbolism which human beings have devised', providing 'a collective and massive framework for communication and expression at many levels' (p. 117).[11] Secondly, according to Casey, words enable 'refinement of expression', an exactitude of reference as well as a subtlety of insight unmatched by nonverbal systems of signification: 'for the most part, *reminiscing is talking the past out*; it is teasing the past into talk, reliving it in and by words.' And finally, reminiscing enables us to 'understand or re-understand' the past, and here Casey draws attention to the etymology of the word 'understand' as the 'standing under', or the gaining of an intimate perspective on something, or to place oneself back inside an experience in order to know it better. Thanks to its discursiveness, reminiscing transforms experiences into articulate and enduring wholes possessing sufficient integrity to be understood in memory.

Thus, our understanding of the past in and through reminiscing occurs, Casey suggests, 'mainly by means of its discursive ex-plication, through its unfolding in fully articulated words. Such articulation is the primary way a past experience comes to be comprehended in reminiscing. The reminiscential return to the past is a return via discourse – via the word, *logos* – and as such it is an *understanding remembering* of it.'

Where written reminiscence differs from oral reminiscence or story-telling is in the reminiscer's (the writer's), express aim to allow their reminiscences to be read by others through publication, at which point the need for accuracy, or at least the semblance of it, comes into play. As an ostensibly eyewitness account of some of the key events of the Commune, therefore, Du Camp's *Les Convulsions* – which he specifically states right on the first page of volume I is *not* a history of the Commune – often functions as a memoir, as a written form of reminiscence, which draws upon what Casey would call 'a commonality of past experience' and/or a 'diffuse commonality of era and ambiance'. Even if Du Camp's readers/co-reminiscers had not themselves actually been present at the scenes he describes, they would nevertheless have been able to share in the experience evoked as though they had in fact been there. Much the same is also true of *Paris: ses organes*, the memorialist intentions of which are acknowledged by Du Camp himself. His descriptions are direct reminders of a shared past, expressly designed to draw his readers back from the edge of oblivion. In contrast, Zola's novels *Le Ventre de Paris*, *L'Assommoir* and *Une page d'amour*, set as they are in a pre-Commune Paris, act, as we shall see in the next chapter, as more subtle or adumbrative reminders of the Commune. The means by which Zola consciously or unconsciously recreates the memory of the Commune is through allusion, evocation or oblique referencing. This is also the case with Walker's articles in *Le Monde illustré*, which describe Paris during the 1878 *Exposition universel* but which also include embedded references to the city in 1871.

What all these 'reminders' have in common, however, is their reliance on place to evoke memory. As Casey would have it, 'memory is naturally place-orientated or at least place-supported' and is in itself 'a place wherein the past can revive and survive'.[12] Whereas 'site' can refer to any given open area and lacks any points of attachment on to which memories can be fixed and subsequently retrieved, 'place' acts as 'a *mise en scène* for remembered events', guarding these and keeping them within its boundaries (p. 189). This intimate relationship between memory and place is made possible at one level through the living body that puts us

in touch with the psychological aspects of remembering and the physical features of place, and through the place-name which evokes 'the
spirit of a place' (pp. 189–96, 197). One need only think here of the
resonant power of Paris as a place name. Paris becomes a topographical
palimpsest or, to borrow Lefebvre's definition, a social text to which
each generation has added its own pages but also in the sense that it
superimposes itself on to actual written accounts, thereby producing
its own interpretation and commentary on the past.[13] Thus the articles
in *Le Monde illustré*, Du Camp's memoir/social-history hybrids and Zola's
novels all ultimately define themselves as narratives of collective memory
primarily by means of the interaction between place and time; Paris
between the years 1871 and 1878.

Reconstructing the archive in *Paris: ses organes*

For Walter Benjamin, writing in the 1930s, *Paris: ses organes* is both a
work of nostalgia for a fast disappearing world as well as an objective
description of the city in the tradition of Jacques Antoine Dulaure's
*Histoire physique, civile et morale de Paris depuis les premiers temps
historiques*, though one would perhaps wish to question Benjamin's apparent acceptance of either Du Camp's or Dulaure's work as 'objective'.[14]
Paris: ses organes does indeed resemble Dulaure's monumental history
of the city in many ways as well as echoing aspects of Mercier's *Tableau
de Paris*, cited as an influence by Du Camp himself, just as *Les Convulsions* can be read as the post-Commune equivalent of Mercier's post-1789
opus, *Paris pendant la revolution (1789–1798) ou Le Nouveau Paris*. Du
Camp's *Paris: ses organes* can thus be considered, at one level, as the
apotheosis of the many scholarly works and guide books by eminent
nineteenth-century journalists and writers documenting and celebrating
virtually every aspect of the city in a tradition stretching back to the
eighteenth century. The *Paris Guide*, published in 1867 to coincide with
the *Exposition universelle* of that year, and to which Du Camp himself
contributed a piece entitled 'Promenades en Paris' as part of the second
volume, is a noteworthy example, as were the famous tourist guides
produced by Adolphe Joanne, such as *Paris illustré en 1870: Guide de
l'étranger et du Parisien* (published in 1871), in which Du Camp is warmly
thanked for his valued contribution. In turn, *Paris: ses organes* was to
exert its own influence on writers as diverse as Edouard Drumont, who
specifically cites Du Camp as an influence in the introduction to his
reactionary *Mon vieux Paris*, and Jules Vallès who, whilst he does not

refer specifically to Du Camp's *Paris: ses organes* as a source of inspiration for *Le Tableau de Paris*, nevertheless still alludes to the earlier work intertextually through his choice of subjects and themes, and particularly in his praise for the modern city, to which he also owed a debt to Zola's Parisian novels.

Flaubert was perhaps the only contemporary critic of *Paris: ses organes* who disapproved of the work. His attitude exemplifies not just the temperamental differences between the two men, but also the marked differences in their whole conception of the nature and purpose of literature itself. Du Camp tells us that for Flaubert the novel was a work of the imagination inspired by reality and as such was the historical document *par excellence*.[15] Flaubert apparently criticized his friend for pulling Paris apart in *Paris: ses organes* in order to describe the way it functions for, in his eyes, this was the work of a mere mechanic and tantamount to committing a criminal offence. Waspishly, Du Camp told his friend that he had firmly decided to be both 'a criminal and a mechanic'.

The content of the six volumes which eventually comprised *Paris: ses organes* was initially published, between January 1867 and April 1874, as a series of articles in *La Revue des deux mondes*, a highly conservative (though, significantly, not pro-royalist), influential and long-running literary and political journal. The articles proved so popular with readers that, even before serialization was complete, Du Camp turned them into chapters for publication by Hachette in volume form with the declared aim to produce the sort of book about Paris that the historians of antiquity had failed to write about their own great cities. Each volume was priced relatively expensively at 7.50 francs (Zola's novels, for example, sold for 3.50 francs), and, as such, the main purchasers would have been libraries and the relatively well off. Table 2 provides estimates of the number of print runs.

The first volume, covering the postal and telegraphic services, the transport system, and the Seine's bridges, islands, navigation system and industries, appeared in 1869, earning its author the admiration of Napoleon III, who invited him to join a commission charged with the task of investigating the possibility of decentralizing the nation's administrative system.[16] Volume II soon followed in February 1870, comprising chapters on tobacco, the mint and the Bank of France, and the production, marketing and consumption of food in the capital, including detailed descriptions of the great market of Les Halles which were to prove invaluable to Zola for *Le Ventre de Paris*. The events of 1870 and 1871 as

Table 2 Paris: ses organes: number of editions and/or reprints of individual volumes

Year of publication or reprint	No. of entries[a]	Vols	Estimated no. of copies based on average print run of 1,000 copies[b]
1869	1	I	1,000
1870	1	II	1,000
1873	5	I	5,000
1874	4	I	4,000
1875	6 or 7	I to VI	1,000 of each vol. plus a further 1,000 of one of the volumes. Or 6,000 or 7,000 copies of each volume in the set.[c]
1876	2	V & VI only or complete set I to VI	1,000 each of vols V and VI. Or 2,000 of each vol. in the set.[d]
1879	2	IV and VI	1,000 of vols IV and VI.
1883	3	I to IV	Possibly 3,000 each of vols I to IV.[e]
1884	2	V and VI	1,000 each
1893	2	I and III	1,000 each[f]
1894	2	II and IV	1,000 each
1898	1	VI	1,000
1905	1	I	1,000

Vol. VI	Total no. of entries	Estimated total based on a print run of 1,000
1875–1905	4	6,000 or 12,000 depending on how the entries are interpreted.

Source: *Bibliographie de la France*

[a] Figures in the 'No. of entries' column represent either the total number of print runs for all the volumes listed or each of the individual volumes published.

[b] The estimate of 1,000 copies per edition (or reprint) is based on Zola's general statement regarding the average print run during the period in *Œuvres complètes*, XI, 221.

[c] The listing under the heading *Géographie* appears to refer to all six volumes but does not indicate whether the seven entries refer to seven re-printings of the total set or one print run of each individual volume plus an extra reprinting of just one of the volumes. The alphabetical listing by author gives six entries.

[d] The listing under the section *Histoire* indicates all six volumes with two entries which would imply two reprintings (estimated 2,000 copies) of each volume in the set, but the alphabetical listing by author only lists volumes V and VI under the same entry references as in the *Histoire* section. Since Du Camp is known to have re-edited the complete set for the 1876 final edition, two reprintings for all six volumes would appear more likely.

[e] It is not clear if the three entries represent three reprintings (estimated 3,000 copies) of each of the first four volumes, or one reprinting of three of the volumes and two reprintings of one of the volumes.

[f] Listed under the abbreviated title *Paris dans la seconde moitié du dix-neuvième siècle*.

well as the need to attend to pressing personal matters, however, caused Du Camp to put *Paris: ses organes* temporarily to one side (pp. 315–23). Volume III – on the police and the criminal justice system – and most of Volume IV – on occult practices, the care of the urban poor, the aged and mentally sick, and the hospitals and orphanages – though both ready at the end of 1870 were not published until 1872 and 1873 respectively. All too aware, like Zola with *Les Rougon-Macquart*, that the defeat of Napoleon III by the Prussians on 1 September 1871 meant that his account of the administrative functioning of Paris under the Second Empire was now mostly only of historical interest, Du Camp nevertheless took the decision not to revise volumes III and IV. In the *Avertissement* (Notice) dated January 1872 which accompanies Volume III, he states that it is his intention only to describe the 'normal' functioning of the city, not its existence under exceptional and morbid circumstances during the recent political upheavals (*PSO*, III, 2). He also admits to the memorialist aspect of his work. He has kept to his original text, he says, addressing his fellow Parisians directly as he does throughout, because it describes the state of the administration of the police force and the criminal justice system at the precise moment when the authoritarian empire gave way to a more liberal imperial regime, when Napoleon III's personal authority gave way to the authority of parliament, thus marking a special date in the city's history.[17]

The new (Third Republic) regime's prevailing strict censorship laws, particularly given the sensitive nature of the subjects covered in Volumes III and IV, and the desire not to delay publication still further may also have influenced his decision.[18] In addition, Du Camp's action is consistent with the desire on the part of many bourgeois conservatives at this time to deny that the Commune, euphemistically referred to by Du Camp as 'nos bouleversements politiques' ('our political upheavals'), ever happened, or at least to reduce it to a morbid aberration in the otherwise 'normal' healthy life of the city. As discussed earlier in relation to Hubert's article 'Aux Tuileries' in *Le Monde illustré* in 1871, Du Camp's use of the plural possessive pronoun, *nos*, is a further example of standard patriarchal rhetoric (Zola makes a similar use of it in his preface to *L'Assommoir* where he refers to 'nos faubourgs' ('our [working-class] suburbs'), but it is also a device which denotes an Orwellian-style collective complicity in the 'truthfulness' of his version of events (see Orwell's *Homage to Catalonia*).

On another level, Du Camp, again like his contemporaries, also feels a strong need to express the anger he felt at the destruction not just of the city but of a whole way of life, to the extent that the very identity of the nation was felt to be at stake. The same sentiments are expressed by Victor Fournel in *Paris et ses ruines en mai 1871* (1872). Thus, despite the threat of censorship, Du Camp cannot resist adding some explanatory notes to the text in order to highlight the irreparable loss to the nation of the police and judicial documents and archives following the 'epileptic attacks' of the Commune (the medical analogy is worth noting as consistent with anti-Communard rhetoric), and which, hitherto, had been cared for religiously (*PSO*, III, 3). The whole of *Paris: ses organes* after 1871 can be read, therefore, as an attempt by Du Camp to reconstruct the archive which, in his view, has been sacrilegiously destroyed in a moment of apparent mental aberration.

Later, in volume VI, he explicitly states that the last normal month in the life of the city was August 1870, and in the chapter on the city's libraries he mourns the loss of the Bibliothèque de Paris housed in the Hôtel de Ville and destroyed during the Commune (*PSO*, VI, 96, 202). This particular collection numbered some 125,000 volumes that lay hidden under the eves above the main galleried reception hall and, rarely consulted, had been left to rot. Du Camp bemoans the ill treatment of all books kept in administrative buildings and states that it is only now that so many books have been destroyed that their value can be fully appreciated. It was this acute sense of what had been lost, Du Camp states, that led to the government's decision, in 1873, to give this great city a library of its own that did it full justice (*PSO*, VI, 204). The new library was housed in the Hôtel Carnavalet in the Marais district, and Du Camp's pride as a Parisian, a pride he clearly shares with his implied reader, is unmistakable as he announces that the library, 'our own library, for us as Parisians', was inaugurated on 1 January 1874.[19] There is Parisian pride too in the wide-ranging influence and importance of the city itself in the arts, sciences, philosophy, and national and international history. But most telling of all is the belief that the city's past and its sense of history and identity resides in its books. 'We must remember our past', he exhorts, and the fact that 'our monuments' have been destroyed is proof that 'we should preserve multiple copies of our documents'; 'the more we have', he goes on, 'the more chance we would have of saving our heritage following any cataclysmic event'. He also reminds his readers of the cost to the nation of what had been lost since 1830 including, for example, the losses incurred during the sacking of the Archbishop's palace, the Palais-Royal and the Tuileries Palace during the Commune and the fact that, were this trend to continue, then in a hundred years' time 'we would no longer be able to provide any authentic proof of our history' (*PSO*, VI, 204–5).

Following the destruction of the Hôtel de Ville's archives and public records of births, deaths and marriages (likened by Du Camp to gold in their preciousness), it was no longer possible for Parisians to provide documentary evidence of their identity: a problem which, in nineteenth-century France, was considered a moral, as well as an administrative, catastrophe. Until the archives could be reconstituted following the laws passed on 10 July, 19 July and 23 August 1871, every Parisian couple was technically cohabiting out of wedlock and its offspring effectively illegitimate, a fact which leaves Du Camp morally outraged (in print, at least) (*PSO*, VI, 66). More worrying still for Du Camp, however, is the thought of a possible recurrence of the nation's misfortunes and that, having been destroyed once already, the nation's archives could be so again. Influenced no doubt by his own (or Flaubert's) reading of Vico and the contemporary belief in the eternal recurrence of cycles of war and peace from which there is no escape, Du Camp concludes, pessimistically, and in anticipation of *Les Convulsions*, that it is highly unlikely that the experience of May 1871 will serve as any lesson at all for the future, human beings, in their mediocrity, being condemned for good or ill to spin forever within the same circle (*PSO*, VI, 72).

As a precaution to guard against another loss of the nation's population archives, Du Camp suggests producing multiple copies of these 'precious documents'. The originals, he thinks, should be kept in local parishes with copies kept by the Ministry of Justice and the Hôtel des Invalides, and in the vaults of the Arc de Triomphe, the enduring strength of which would surely defy any attempt to set it alight by paraffin in the event of the city falling prey to another cataclysm. In this way, all those documents deemed to be indispensable to men living in society would be saved from total destruction (*PSO*, VI, 73). By implication, therefore, the Communards, with their heretical desire to abolish the Christian sacraments, were not fit to be part of civilized society.

The loss of the nation's archives and books – including Adolphe Thiers's own extensive library which was destroyed when his house was deliberately demolished by order of the Commune on 11 May 1871, in retaliation for the taking of the Fort d'Issy by the Versaillais – can be seen, therefore, as one of the root causes of the anger directed at the insurgents by their detractors. It is tempting to speculate that Thiers's over-reaction against the Commune and his ordering of the assault on Paris which led to the whole *Semaine sanglante* episode, was perhaps driven by the need to exact personal revenge for the destruction of his property and most of his life's work. For the ruling class in general, the 'burning of the books' would have been tantamount not just to the effacement of their collective history and sense of national identity, but equally to the destruction of the whole dominant political, social and moral order itself.

In Volume III, written before 1871, Du Camp had already stressed the importance of the archives held by the Palais de Justice, particularly the nation's criminal records, and he asks, rhetorically, whether the Empire should not deliver these up for public scrutiny (*PSO*, III, 191). In his 1872 footnote to this passage, not surprisingly, he blames the 'envious' Communards for the destruction of these archives in an attempt to stem the course of justice with dire consequences for history itself. And he regrets, even more bitterly in hindsight, that all the documents in the custody of the Palais de Justice had not been deposited, as had often been suggested, in the city Archives, where they would no doubt have been spared by the raving madmen of the Commune. In an additional footnote, he expresses the same sense of outrage at the loss of the archives held by the Préfecture de Police. Evidence of whole periods of the nation's history and its most precious secrets, he tells his readers, has consequently been lost, never to be recovered (*PSO*, III, 199). In Du Camp's mind, ostensibly at least, there can be no question that the fires which destroyed, among other buildings, the Palais de Justice, the Hôtel de Ville, the Préfecture de Police, the Ministère des Finances and the cour des Comptes, were wilfully raised by the Communards in order to destroy not just the nation's history but also their own criminal records. Writing at the end of the nineteenth century, however, Armand Dayot suggests that the conflagrations were also the work of the Versaillais and, significantly, the Bonapartists, who seized the opportunity to destroy all the compromising archives they could find in the wake of Napoleon III's abdication.[20] Most modern historians tend to agree. Thousands of documents were lost in the process and contemporary observers noted that charred fragments, some of which were still legible, were blown about by the wind throughout the city and beyond.[21] After 1871, therefore, Du Camp's reference to the destruction of the archives in the Palais de Justice and the Préfecture de Police resonates with an irony that could not have escaped his contemporary readers, including Zola. The Palais de Justice, for example, is significantly the place where Lisa Quenu in *Le Ventre de Paris* is shown the file containing all the anonymous letters denouncing the would-be revolutionary Florent. Similarly, in *Son Excellence Eugène Rougon*, contemporary readers would have had no difficulty in associating Zola's portrayal of the fictional disgraced politician Eugène Rougon carefully burning any incriminating evidence of his five years in office before staging a come-back as a liberal progressive (*RM*, II, 38) with that of the Bonapartists first burning their archives in 1871 and then reinventing themselves in time to enjoy electoral success in 1874 and 1875. Finally, in *La Débâcle*, Zola describes the fragments of documents blowing in the wind over the city (*RM*, V, 902).

In his 1876 footnotes to the earlier volumes, Du Camp also records how the Parisian landscape has been irrevocably altered. In the introduction to the first volume, for example, he describes some of the city's most important buildings including the Palais de Justice, the Conciergerie, the Préfecture de Police, the Hôtel de Ville with its newly restored bell tower, and the linked Louvre and Tuileries palaces, which together comprise the modern city's central, strategic fortress (*PSO*, I, 6). His footnote then reminds the reader that the Commune has altered this 'tableau', as all of these buildings have now either been destroyed or still bear the wounds inflicted on them by the conflagrations. Meanwhile, his 1867 clichéd description of Paris as the 'beast of the Apocalypse', Babylon, Nineveh and Sodom, and his statement that, despite its decadence, the city will still be saved on the Day of Judgement because it contains sufficient numbers of 'the Just' for it to be spared complete destruction, can, following 1871, be read as an eerie prognostication. There are also passages that echo much of the Cornelian-style rhetoric that characterized Monselet's piece in *Le Monde illustré* in 1871, and which are therefore imbued with retrospective dramatic irony (*PSO*, I, 15). Attila, the archetypal 'barbarian of the north', may well have spared 'Civilized' Paris, but the Prussians certainly did not spare the city in 1871 and the predicted 'chaos' certainly ensued.

As discussed earlier in respect of Walker's Parisian 'promenades' in *Le Monde illustré*, the image of the storm came to be read as a metaphor for the Commune, but for Du Camp in 1867 it was to be applied to revolutions in general. In an 1876 footnote he adds the *coup d'état* of 4 September 1870 to his list of revolutionary dates, though interestingly he doesn't add 18 March 1871, the birth of the Commune. The storm that broke out on 4 September 1870, he tells us, was gentle and propitious for the German armies, whose task it made that much easier (*PSO*, I, 15, n. 1). In common with many of his contemporaries, Du Camp argues that if the republicans had bided their time in September 1870 and allowed Napoleon III to take full responsibility for the nation's humiliating surrender to the Prussians before forcing him to abdicate, the Prussian siege of the capital would have been avoided, the people of Paris would not have been provoked into making a stand against the new regime by declaring the Commune, and *la Semaine sanglante* would never have occurred. Du Camp even said as much at the time in a letter to Flaubert.[22] According to Du Camp, therefore, the revolution of 4 September 1870, deftly orchestrated by a number of comrades riding high on the emotions of a stunned nation, and against which no effective resistance was mounted, gave birth to the Commune, that 'monster of 18 March', which, after two months of alcohol-fuelled dementia, was destroyed by the conflagrations which consumed the city (*PSO*, VI, 362).

Exercising what Du Camp sees as the historian's prerogative, endorsed by Barante et al., to moralize, judge and condemn events and people as he sees fit, he accuses the Prussian siege and the Commune of having had a disastrous effect on the Parisian working class. During the siege 'the people' wanted to fight the (Prussian) enemy, he tells his readers, but were only given alcohol, while during the Commune they were given alcohol in order to make them fight the forces of law and order (*PSO*, IV, 339). He backs up his claim by stating that in the space of nine months Paris apparently drank the equivalent of five times its average annual consumption of alcohol, which led 'inevitably' to bouts of *delirium tremens* and what he calls 'pétrolomanie alcoolique' among the Parisian population, resulting in the destruction of the city (*PSO*, IV, 440). He goes on to say that more than one of the 'brutes' who ordered the burning of 'our' city had spent time in mental institutions and would no doubt do so again, just like those unfortunates who obeyed them and who find themselves there already. This is doubtless an oblique reference to Vallès, who had been mentally certified in 1851; however, along with alcoholism and disease, mental instability is of course just another stock attribute of the revolutionary in the anti-Communard imagination and a recurring theme not just in Du Camp (compare with *LC*, II, 244) but generally in the literature of the period.[23]

Given Du Camp's later stance in *Les Convulsions*, it is interesting to note also in volume VI of *Paris: ses organes* that the cause of the city's abuse of alcohol is to be traced back firmly to the hardships endured by the people of Paris during the Prussian siege, a situation which was exacerbated by the mismanagement of the population by the government of the new Republic (*PSO*, VI, 97). Du Camp's use of the first person singular pronouns *il* (he) and *on* (one) serves again to distance him and his intended readers from the government of the Third

Republic and their actions, and at the same time implies a collective responsibility on the part of the dominant social order. The accusation, made within the context of a discussion of the events of 1870, can also be read within the context of the period 1874–75 as a none too subtle accusation of the failure of MacMahon's regime to deal with the continuing problems faced by working-class Parisians and as a warning that, unless harnessed in a productive way, 'the passion of the people' may once more find its outlet in a recurrence of 'evil deeds'.

Later, in Volume VI, Du Camp returns to his analogy between Paris and the cities of antiquity. Now, however, the fall of Second Empire Paris is to be rationalized in accordance with the period's obsessive preoccupation with decadence; all the great cities, he opines, have met with a violent end. It is as if these plethoric and hydrocephalous bodies are destined to disappear in a cataclysm. They can be reborn, but in such a changed fashion that they are no longer themselves; 'dans la Constantinople des Padischahs, qui reconnaîtra la Byzance des empereurs d'Orient, et dans la Rome de la papauté, qui reconnaîtra la Rome des Césars?' (who would be able to recognize the Byzantium of the oriental emperors in the Constantinople of the Padishahs, and who would be able to recognize the Rome of the Caesars in the Rome of the Papacy?) (*PSO*, VI, 391).

With the excavations for the construction of the Sacré-Cœur basilica currently under way and the law of 12 July 1875 set to reinforce the power of the Catholic Church, Paris did indeed appear to have been reclaimed by the hard-line representatives of the Papacy who, as Du Camp was completing volume VI of *Paris: ses organes*, were busy effacing all traces not so much of Communard Paris but of 'Caesar' (Napoleon III) himself. Ironically, however, Du Camp's post-1871 readers would also have recalled that Napoleon III had similarly actively courted and supported the Pope before finally abandoning him over Italian unification: perhaps wisely, in Du Camp's estimation, given his own youthful support for Garibaldi. An additional twist is also provided by the knowledge that if Napoleon III himself had been disgraced, the Bonapartists, as a political faction, were similarly at this point trying to forge an alliance with the Catholic Church in a bid to defeat the republicans. Du Camp thus uses the apparently innocuous vehicle of a socio-historical-geographical and administrative account of the functioning of Paris in order to make a point about the political climate of 1874–75. Despite his moral stance, Du Camp reveals himself as no supporter of the interference of the Church in matters of state. He castigates the Commune for its persecution of the clergy but is also mindful of the Catholic Church's past misdemeanours in order to advance its own political ambitions, such as, for example, its involvement in the Holy League, the Fronde, and the Revolution of 1789 (*PSO*, VI, 275, 281). As for the deaths of Archbishop Darboy and his fellow clerics during the Commune, these exemplify, according to Du Camp, 'notre misérable état social' (our [that is to say *collective*] pitiful social state) (*PSO*, VI, 276). Later, in *Les Convulsions*, he would perform a characteristic volte-face. In that work, Du Camp's aim is to mobilize support against the granting of amnesty to ex-Communards and his emphasis accordingly shifts to the Commune's barbaric treatment of the clergy. Nevertheless, even in *Les Convulsions*, he does mention the fact that Thiers could easily have saved Darboy, if only he had agreed to exchange him for the imprisoned revolutionary Auguste Blanqui. Du Camp, no supporter of Thiers the man, is quick to note that Blanqui did not constitute a new danger to the state (*LC*, I, 232). Darboy, as Bernard Noël has since pointed out, was considered a liberal and consequently unpopular with the monarchists, and Thiers was in need of a suitable martyr.[24]

In *Paris: ses organes*, Du Camp goes on to accuse 'the people' of having killed the hostages in 1871 just as they had carried out the Saint Bartholomew's Day massacre of Huguenots in 1572 (*PSO*, VI, 276). However, as he and his contemporary readers would have known, the massacre had been instigated, not by 'the people', but by the duc de Guise, Catherine de' Medici, and the Catholic Church who, between them, manipulated Catherine's ten-year-old son, Charles IX, into giving the order for the attack. Since 1789, the massacre had become a clichéd metaphor for all revolutionary uprisings, and never more so than after the Commune.[25] Monselet, for example, was quick to see the analogy, describing the Commune as 'cette autre Saint-Barthélemy' (that other Saint Bartholomew's Day massacre) (*Le Monde illustré*, 27 May 1871), and Zola, as we shall see in the next chapter, provided his own ironic and original re-working of the cliché in the Louvre scene in *L'Assommoir* (*RM*, II, 445).

In 1882 Ernest Renan provided further evidence of the special place reserved for 'la Saint-Barthélemy' in French cultural memory. According to Renan, a nation consists of a group of people who have much in common with one another but who have also collectively (and knowingly) forgotten many things.[26] One of the things French citizens are required to have 'forgotten' is 'la Saint-Barthélemy'. Benedict Anderson posits that it was too soon in 1882, when Renan made this statement, to include the Commune as one of the fratricidal conflicts that French citizens are required to 'have already forgotten', because the memory of May 1871 was still too recent and too painful;[27] but in fact, as the above examples prove, Renan's reference to 'la Saint-Barthélemy' was quite indicative in itself of the Commune.

The Du Camp of *Paris: ses organes*, following in the deist tradition of the eighteenth-century *philosophes* Montesquieu and Voltaire, is also quick to remind his readers, not without some irony, of the Parisian clergy's reputation for hypocrisy and debauchery. Furthermore, at a time when the Catholic Church was actively campaigning for donations for the construction of the Sacré-Cœur, Du Camp's irony carries further contemporary resonance when he tells his readers that the French public does not take too kindly to requests for donations to churches or convents and, in this regard at least, he claims, the lessons of the past appear not to have been wasted (*PSO*, VI, 276).

At a time when MacMahon and the monarchists were firmly aligned with the Church, and willing to offer military support to the Pope in order to help him regain the territories he had lost when Italy was unified, Du Camp issues a further warning to his readers: if, under normal circumstances, it may not much matter if the Church is allowed a free rein to interfere in the affairs of the French state, when, as has happened in the past, matters abroad become complicated, such interference can become highly embarrassing for national governments, and foreign powers have been known to waste little time in proffering a military response to any objurgatory edicts issued by Rome. As Du Camp obliquely suggests, and as MacMahon's government soon realized, any military intervention in Italy by France would have proved very ill-advised indeed, for not only did the Italian government enjoy Bismarck's support, but also, closer to home, such an action would have further alienated the majority of the typically anti-clerical bourgeoisie and urban working classes. In the event, nothing was done to help the Pope.

Du Camp suggests that the Church will not achieve its ambitions, however hard it may try, and he looks forward instead to a new era when Paris will follow the example set by New York where, he says, all sects have the right to practise their beliefs in public. He looks forward too to a time when the ties that have traditionally bound 'us' (the French) to the Church and its leader in Rome will eventually loosen and give way to a spirit of free examination and rationalism and that, finally, a true spirit of impartiality and tolerance will reign. In this way, both Church and state would recover their individual freedom. In echoing

Voltaire's advocacy of religious tolerance ('Cinquième lettre: sur la religion anglicane', *Lettres philosophiques*), and in reprising his own youthful
admiration of America as the model for modern civilization,[28] Du Camp's
rhetoric also invokes Napoleon I's speech of October 1804, in which the
new Emperor similarly suggested that no matter what their creed or
sect, the souls of all men were welcomed equally into Heaven. The implication is that without exercising such tolerance, France will be doomed
(*PSO*, VI, 285). One of the reasons why *Paris: ses organes* was so well
received by its bourgeois readers can no doubt be attributed to the fact
that Du Camp voices, in the politically and religiously repressive years
1875 and 1876, the sort of anti-clerical opinions that appealed to the
majority of moderate bourgeois republicans, just as later, with *Les Convulsions*, he was to see the personal advantages of championing the cause
of the reactionary right in a bid to endear himself to the Académie.

   In *Paris: ses organes* Du Camp even goes so far as to single out Roman
Catholicism as the direct cause of all of France's ills. If decadence is, as
it is often claimed, simply a question of race, why is it, he asks, that all
Catholic nations appear to be so prone to it, regardless of whether they
are of Latin extraction or not? How is it, he asks, that Protestant nations
manage to prosper, found colonies, and become first-class states while
Catholic nations are all, without exception, languishing in the doldrums?
The answer is that Protestantism liberates people by making them responsible for their own consciences while Catholicism with its insistence
on divine intervention into people's lives in order to force them into
passive submission, invariably fosters revolt (*PSO*, VI, 360). Thus for
Du Camp, 1789 was a failure because it overturned the political and
social order without also effecting a religious revolution. This is a most
interesting reversal and a good example perhaps of Du Camp's oppor-
tunistic alignment with whichever cause suits him at the time as well
as an example of one of the ambiguities inherent in the text, for
anti-Communard rhetoric typically associated the Communards with
the heresy of Protestantism.[29] France has recovered in the past from the
mutilations she has seen fit to inflict upon herself, and will no doubt do
so again, but this transformation is unlikely, according to Du Camp, to
be brought about by an alliance between God and the monarchy; it
never has in the past and never will in the future. In typically misogynistic
fashion he declares that one might as well ask an old woman to grow
young again (*PSO*, VI, 359). Du Camp's ultimate message is, therefore,
to dispense with religious and political sectarianism and to concentrate
instead on the really important issue: the reforming and strengthening

of the nation's internal mechanisms in the same way that Napoleon I had been obliged to do after 1789. This would enable France to regain her credibility and standing in a world that has come to regard her as inherently politically unstable and thus vulnerable to attack on all fronts.

Du Camp is well aware that, throughout Europe, Paris is regarded as the world's *cloaca maxima*, and that many people consider the disasters of 1871 to have been deservedly meted out as a punishment to this 'modern Babylon', and yet, he claims, those who have cast the most virulent aspersions on the city have been those who have most availed themselves of the benefits afforded by 'our' way of life (*PSO*, VI, 288–9). While not disputing the fact that Paris is indeed 'démoralisé' (in the sense of corrupt or lacking in morals), this state of affairs is invariably, for Du Camp, and for the majority of anti-Communards, not the fault of 'true' Parisians but of outsiders (provincials in Du Camp's case). Furthermore, Parisians, from Du Camp's perspective, cannot be blamed for making a living out of pandering to the tastes of foreign visitors to their city and for enjoying themselves into the bargain. They have, after all, the apparent support of the authorities who, just days after the capitulation of the city, authorized the construction of four new theatres in the Place du Château-d'Eau (*PSO*, VI, 291). The choice of location for these new theatres, no less than Du Camp's reference to it, is particularly resonant, for the Place du Château-d'Eau (today's Place de la République) and its barricade played a major role during the events of May 1871, and it was on this spot that Charles Delescluze met his death and that his fellow Communard leader, Auguste Vermorel, was fatally wounded.[30] Another Communard *lieu de mémoire* was thus effectively effaced. The resurgence of the city's places of leisure and entertainment can be seen, therefore, not just as a means of generating revenue for Paris, though undoubtedly this was a major consideration, but also as a way of purging the Parisian body and psyche of the trauma suffered.

As an erstwhile Saint-Simonian as well as a supporter of the 'liberal' Second Empire, Du Camp fully supports the destruction of the old city to make way for the new, prosperous, healthy and law-abiding metropolis.[31] In the chapter entitled 'La Voie publique' (Public Highways), he states that Haussmann was right when he claimed that the more Paris was opened up, made light and airy, the more it would attract foreign visitors who would spend their money in the city and thereby enrich the whole population. Some buildings, which might at first have seemed to be expensive, frivolous follies, in fact generate wealth equivalent to four times the amount it cost to erect them (*PSO*, VI,

252). Du Camp also reminds his readers that Paris had become practically uninhabitable after 1848; everything was in dire need of a complete overhaul, from the city's lack of hygiene and inadequate policing and surveillance to its tortuous means of communication and antiquated infrastructure. It was crucial, on all fronts, to rebuild and regenerate the city, an enormous undertaking that had unfortunately ground to a halt owing to recent events (*PSO*, VI, 253). Therefore, just as Charles V, Henry IV, Louis XIV, Napoleon I and Napoleon III all effaced the past by rebuilding the city in order to consolidate their respective regimes, it was now obviously equally important for the Third Republic to do the same by completing Haussmann's projects. Du Camp's emphasis, however, is on banishing the physical, social and moral decay festering in the city's ancient streets. If Du Camp attempts to preserve the disappearing old city by meticulously documenting its history, as Walter Benjamin suggests, he equally champions the completion of Haussmann's projects as the means by which to preserve the legacy of the Second Empire. The sooner the new boulevard Saint-Germain is completed by demolishing the old alleyways on the Left Bank, the better, in his estimation (*PSO*, VI, 259–60). The same is true of the scheme to connect the avenue de l'Opéra with the Tuileries gardens by flattening the ancient, filthy slum area around the Butte des Moulins.[32] For Du Camp, the demolition of such 'cloaques' ('middens' and, figuratively, 'dens of iniquity') and their replacement with healthy homes is not before time (*PSO*, VI, 322–3). These schemes, together with the improvements in street lighting, he claims are doing more for the city's security than any moralist's sermon ever could.

Meanwhile, the planned (but ultimately uncompleted) road across the Tuileries gardens to align the Solférino bridge with the rue de Castiglione would, he believes, facilitate the flow of traffic between the two banks of the Seine. The linking of the boulevard Haussmann (conveniently razed to the ground by the conflagrations of 1871), to the avenue de l'Opéra, is also, according to Du Camp, not before time. In Paris, as if his contemporary readers needed any reminding after the repeated construction of revolutionary barricades, there could never be enough wide thoroughfares facilitating rapid movement across the city. The symbolic link between 1789 and 1871 is later made explicit in the comparison between the snow-covered Paris of December 1871 and that of the first French revolution. The city, Du Camp tells us, had not seen such an abundance of snow since 1789 and Parisians might well ponder on this historical 'rapprochement' at their leisure as they skate along as best they can through the blocked streets (*PSO*, VI, 263, 323). In Zola's *Une page d'amour*, this same image of a snow-covered Paris acts as a metaphor for the purification of the city.

In the last paragraph of the chapter on 'La Voie publique', Du Camp reiterates his support for Haussmann, and by extension Napoleon III. He suggests obliquely that much good had in fact been achieved under the previous regime, from a social perspective at least. Indeed, modern commentators agree that the urban poor did generally fare marginally better during the Second Empire than under the Third Republic.[33] Du Camp's aim is thus to reconstitute not just the textual but also the topographical archive of the Second Empire. *Paris: ses organes* itself as a *textual* and *commercial* product of the Second Empire ensured that after 1871 the Paris of the Caesars would indeed remain a part of French cultural memory, just as the physical Second Empire city, despite its threatened reappropriation by 'la papauté', remained tangible and recognizable.

The Commune as prostitute in *Les Convulsions de Paris*

Like *Paris: ses organes*, the four volumes which make up *Les Convulsions de Paris* were originally conceived by Du Camp as a series of articles, the first of which appeared in *La Revue de deux mondes* on 1 May 1877. However, unlike *Paris: ses organes*, which is a highly ordered text, *Les Convulsions* comes closer, in its fragmentary structure, to the oral form of reminiscence. In this respect, and surprising as it might seem given their opposing ideological positions and literary styles, Du Camp's *Les Convulsions* bears comparison with Vallès's *L'Insurgé*, the form of which Walter Redfern has similarly described both as being close to that of oral storytelling and as evidence that 'the frantic life of the Commune is irreducible to any classical kind of artistic representation'.[34] Neverthe-less, despite this uneven, collagist and fragmentary style which is a characteristic of all memory texts,[35] in both *Les Convulsions* and *L'Insurgé* there is still an internal structure of beginning, middle and end to each of the individual fragments, as there is in all storytelling; though *L'Insurgé*, as Redfern admits, is 'too disjointed to be easy listening for a public'.[36] In terms of the forging of group memories and myths, pro-Communard in the case of Vallès and anti-Communard in the case of Du Camp, the two texts are also very similar. Such 'life narratives' and storytelling, as Connerton (echoing Durkheim and Halbwachs) suggests, do not stand alone but form part of an 'interconnecting set of narratives' which is 'embedded in the story of those groups from which individuals derive their identity'.[37]

Du Camp's timing in publishing *Les Convulsions* was crucial because the Commune was once again high on the political agenda. Since the end of 1876, the call for amnesty for ex-Communards had been gaining ground, with more and more people appearing to be ready to forgive the Commune, or at least revise their original condemnation of it.[38] It is not coincidental, therefore, that the first article of *Les Convulsions de Paris* appeared in 1877 and the first volume in February 1878. Volumes II, III and IV followed respectively in February, April and November 1879 in an attempt by Du Camp to counter Marx's elevation of the Commune to mythological status and to refute pro-Communard accounts of *la Semaine sanglante*, most notably that by Prosper-Olivier Lissagaray.[39] *Les Convulsions* exemplifies the desire on behalf of the reactionaries of *l'Ordre moral* to keep remembering the Commune 'out of anger at harm done' to society (to borrow Nietzsche's words).[40] Those in any way involved in the Commune, and thus *de facto* criminals, still owed a debt to society, and by reminding the nation of this Du Camp hoped to mitigate calls for amnesty.

In his introduction to the first volume of the first edition of *Les Convulsions*, Du Camp declares that it is all very well making up myths and stories and disseminating these in prose and verse; that it is all very well talking about the great battle of Père-Lachaise, the supposed 40,000 summary executions, the heroism of the Communards, and the 'ferocity of our soldiers'; but that all of this counts for nothing if one studies the actual 'facts'.[41] The authors and propagators of such deliberate inaccuracies, he believes, will be suitably rewarded for their flights of the imagination when these fables eventually disappear into oblivion, but for the time being the bad influence such stories are exerting on the public needs to be pointed out. These stories, he says, would have one believe that the insurgents of 1871 were the 'knights and apostles' of a maligned cause, whereas in reality they were the 'knights of debauchery' and the 'apostles of absinthe'. For Du Camp, therefore, the granting of amnesty to such people constituted an affront to public morality, a denial of history since it would consign the Commune to oblivion, and was effectively the fast route to another popular uprising. In order to prove that they were not assassins themselves, some were now threatening instead to 'assassinate the historians' while others were pushing the bounds of buffoonery to the limit by calling for the executions ('réparation par les armes') of those who had made their crimes public knowledge. What they were all forgetting or pretending to forget, how-ever, is that an unbridgeable river of blood and paraffin separates them from honest, law-abiding people. In a perfect example of the exercise of the author's moral authority,[42] Du Camp declares that the granting of amnesty to ex-Communards may well excise the judicial and political consequences of the crime committed but it would never be able to erase the moral consequences of what they had done.[43]

Later, in the final melodramatic paragraphs of the last volume of *Les Convulsions*, in a stock Shakespearean allusion, this time to *Macbeth*, Du Camp rails not just against the amnesty but also against the granting of universal (male) suffrage on the basis that it might enable ex-Communards to take up public office again: 'ils ont aux mains la tache de sang que toute l'eau de la mer n'effacerait pas, et l'odeur de pétrole dont ils sont imprégnés ne s'évaporera jamais' ('all the water in the world could never wash away the blood stains on their hands and the smell of the paraffin that saturates them will never evaporate') (*LC*, IV, 330–1). Du Camp was to be disappointed in his wish, however, as several ex-Communards did in fact go on to take up public office, with several even being elected as deputies and senators.[44]

The four volumes of which *Les Convulsions* is comprised do not constitute a historical text in the manner of, say, Taine's *Les Origines de la France contemporaine*, but they do nevertheless exploit the generally accepted standards of late nineteenth-century historical discourse which took both literary fiction and scientific discourse as its model. There-fore, just as Taine claims to study his subject scientifically and objectively 'dégagée de tout parti pris' ('free from all bias'), in order to unravel and interpret the passions, ideas and collective will of each discrete group of people, so Du Camp claims to do likewise.[45] He allows his strong emotional involvement, moral judgement and creative imagination full rein while claiming simultaneously to be a completely impartial commentator who only reports truthfully what he has either directly witnessed himself or extrapolated from the exhaustive amount of factual and statistical evidence he has researched. By purporting to offer an eyewitness account of events he lends further weight to his claim of truthfulness:

Du 18 mars au 28 mai, je suis resté à Paris, attentif aux faits dont j'étais le témoin, me mêlant aux hommes, regardant les choses et prenant des notes; un goût inné pour la recherche des documents originaux m'a poussé à réunir de nombreuses pièces authentiques [. . .] Appuyé sur de tels éléments, j'ai pu écrire quelques fragments d'une histoire de la Commune et leur donner – je le crois du moins – un degré d'exactitude qui mérite d'inspirer confiance aux lecteurs. (*LC*, I, xiv–xv)

[From 18 March to 28 May, I remained in Paris, paying careful attention to the events I was witnessing, mixing with the men, observing things and taking notes; an innate love of research based on original documents led me to pull together numerous authentic pieces [. . .] Using these as evidence, I was able to write down a few fragments of a history of the Commune, the level of accuracy of which, I believe, should inspire confidence in my readers.]

The declared reliance on, and actual reproduction of, archival documents was just as much *de rigueur* for Du Camp as it was for Taine, who claimed that once readers were provided with such evidence they would be able to interpret it for themselves and form their own opinion. Taine's influence on Du Camp also manifests itself in his choice of medical and scientific metaphor. For example, Taine describes France as having undergone a metamorphosis after 1789 when her traditional state organization was destroyed and she proceeded to tear her own precious flesh apart as she fell prey to seemingly fatal convulsions.[46] Similarly, in *Les Convulsions* (the title of the work alone acknowledging a debt to Taine), Du Camp declares that his aim is to describe Paris in a state of convulsion, when the wind of folly and revolution was in the air and the cogs of this vast machine were paralysed or warped by revolt.[47]

Any errors that may have slipped into his own account of events, meanwhile, as he states in the preface to the first edition, are purely accidental ('involontaires'). Furthermore, as for any charge of political bias on his part, he affirms his impartiality and political non-alignment; he cares not what government is in power, provided that it is a regime that protects each and every taxpayer's safety. He has only researched the truth, he says; he has done everything possible to discover the truth and to make it publicly known (p. xv). These are all examples of the stock rhetoric common to all the Versaillais 'histories' and 'eye-witness' accounts of the Commune. Catulle Mendès, for example, also addresses his reader directly, claiming to offer a day-by-day account of 'our misfortunes', supplemented occasionally with the author's own 'sincere and open-minded' views.[48] And Mendès, like Du Camp, not only includes accounts of conversations he himself has actually witnessed but also interchanges which he has obviously 'reconstructed' (or invented/ imagined) such as those between the Communard leader Rigault and Archbishop Darboy (p. 95).

Curiously, there are also some apparently self-imposed and one might add highly convenient limits on Du Camp's representation of the 'truth'. In the preface to the first volume of the 1878 edition he manages deftly, through the use of a clever rhetorical device, to allude to the atrocities of *la Semaine sanglante* while implying that the blame for these lay firmly with the Communards:

> Je n'ai dit que la vérité, mais je n'ai pas dit toute la vérité. Celle-ci est parfois si particulièrement monstrueuse, elle révèle des actes de férocité, de débauche, de perversion tellement effroyable, que dans bien des cas j'ai dû garder le silence par respect pour le lecteur et par respect pour moi-même.

> [I have only told the truth but I have not told the whole truth. The whole truth is sometimes so monstrous, revealing acts of such ferocity, debauchery and horrific perversion, that in many cases I have had to keep silent out of respect for the reader and for myself.][49]

Similarly, in his revised preface of 1881 he states that there are some acts of debauchery and brutishness which should not be mentioned at all and that he has tried, as far as possible, only to discuss those incidents which have been reviewed by the justice system and which, as a consequence, have already been brought to light and discussed (*LC*, I, xv). In claiming to deal only with those incidents which were 'legally sanctioned', he thus gives himself permission to exclude all mention of the many indiscriminate and unlawful atrocities perpetuated by the Versaillais. Furthermore, to justify his own actions and protect himself from any accusations of having acted illegally, he admits to having purposely failed to denounce men he knew to be guilty because the authorities had not called them to account at the time (*LC*, II, 294–6). Du Camp is no doubt referring here to Vallès, whose life he had saved by not identifying and denouncing him to the Versaillais, who instead shot another man in his place. Vallès himself was to provide his own account of the incident in the newspaper *Gil Blas* (28 March 1882) and in *L'Insurgé*.[50] For all his faults, Du Camp clearly had enough compassion and integrity when presented directly with the opportunity to save the life of a fellow human being, even if that human being was a Communard. For his part, Vallès described *Les Convulsions* as the work of a 'carrion-eating hyena' but nevertheless declared that he respected Du Camp for being open and honest about his anti-Communard views and his bourgeois *parti pris*.

In print, however, Du Camp's claim to impartiality and truth telling is often contradicted in practice, but this fact is never the cause for any soul-searching. Like Taine, Du Camp has no qualms about exercising his imagination when concrete evidence is in short supply, missing altogether or when it runs counter to his argument. For Taine, a historian's power of 'divination' (imaginative conjecture) is an asset that has transformed the writing of history.[51] Du Camp, following his master, thus begins by claiming that it was impossible for him to produce a serious account of the events of the Commune without following modern historical practice and without passing judgement on several of the characters involved who, throughout this lamentable period, finally acted out the roles they had dreamed of playing for some time.[52] But he reassures his readers that this was all done with the firm conviction of a man for whom acts of hatred inspire nothing but the utmost horror. Echoing Taine, Du Camp likens the writing of his factual account of recent events that are still very much present in everyone's memory to that of performing a vivisection. He has tried his best, he says, to be scrupulously honest and has not put forward anything that cannot be supported by authentic documents. Not only has he been accurate in his reports of events but in spite of the personal indignation he has often felt he has remained impartial throughout, having written this volume without any ulterior motive '*ad narrandum, non ad probandum*' (pp. ii–vi). In quoting from Quintilian, Du Camp is also paying homage to Barante, who used the same quotation for the epigraph to the preface of his *L'Histoire des ducs de Bourgogne*.

Notwithstanding all these claims to his impartiality, Du Camp later freely admits to reconstructing the events that led up to the death of Delescluze according to his own conjecture, and at the same time accuses his detractors of lying in support of their revisionist agenda (*LC*, I, 294). This 'truth', Du Camp declares, he will now try to reconstruct, but the reader should be warned that (paradoxically) his account is based only on conjecture; such conjecture, supported by witness accounts, is so probable, however, that for all intents and purposes it may be taken as comparable to the truth ('la certitude'). He uses much the same rhetorical ploy, with echoes again of Taine, in the dedication to his semi-autobiographical novel *Les Forces perdues* (1867).

The fact that Du Camp only consulted official government sources and the private accounts of various members of the ruling class and *de facto* Versaillais sympathizers, and that he discredits or disregards any accounts that might conflict with his own interpretation of events, does not appear to trouble his conscience either (*LC*, I, xiv–xv). On the contrary, this supposed lack of 'reliable' factual documentation is used to justify having produced such a fragmentary and episodic piece of work rather than a comprehensive history of the Commune. Had he relied on newspaper accounts of the period or on those books which some had rushed to publish after the triumph of law and order ('victoire de la légalité'), Du Camp would, he claims, have been prey to reproducing much erroneous information (*LC*, I, i). The reference to the 'victoire de la légalité' exemplifies White's proposition that historiography is used by the dominant social order as a way to create law-abiding citizens.[53] Du Camp is thus implying that any account of events by the Commune's supporters is by definition not only mendacious but also likely to corrupt its readers, turning them also into criminals and revolutionaries.

Senneville's claim that Du Camp only took account of carefully veri-fied facts and that he discovered new evidence with regard to the corrupt practices of senior members of the Commune[54] needs to be offset by the knowledge that, firstly, Du Camp relied on official police sources and data made available to him by those same powerful contacts who had already facilitated his research for *Paris: ses organes* in the days of the Empire; and, secondly, that he often blatantly resorts to his own creative (and tendentious) imagination, as in the passage describing how Delescluze met his death. According to Du Camp, for example, the total number of *fédérés* killed between 20 and 30 May was only 6,500, and the total number of those arrested and tried only 36,309, of which only 10,131 received sentences (*LC*, II, 302–5). This conflicts with other his-torical accounts which put the total number killed, not just *fédérés*, at between 20,000 and 40,000 during *la Semaine sanglante* alone, and the figure of those subsequently arrested, tried and executed or deported at between 50,000 and 120,000. Modern historians have put the totals at about 20,000 killed and 43,522 arrested during *la Semaine sanglante*.[55] Within the context of the accepted blurring of historical and fictional genres in the nineteenth century, of course, Du Camp's method is nothing unusual. In the unlikely event that Du Camp required any justification for his method of interpretation, Taine (echoing Barante and before him, Aristotle), had already provided him with it when he declared that 'history is an art'.[56] Du Camp's method of re-presenting the 'facts' can also be usefully compared to that of the photographer Eugène Appert, whose series of composite images entitled *Les Crimes de la Commune* similarly reconstructs only those incidents that portrayed the Communards in the worst light such as their execution of Thomas and Lecomte, Archbishop Darboy, the Dominicans of Arceuil, and the hostages in the rue Haxo.[57] There is certainly no denying that Appert's images are overtly and virulently anti-Communard and that they were sold at the time as if they were actual photographic representations of the events they depict. Nevertheless, as Christine Lapostolle argues, composite photographs were generally perceived during this period as a useful method of recording those events which at this time could not be captured directly by the camera, and as a way of rendering the photographic image 'more real'.[58] Writing in the 16 October 1871 edition of *Le Moniteur de la photographie: revue internationale des progrès du nouvel art*, the influential journal he had founded and edited since 1855, Ernest Lacan, for example, states that historians (of the Commune) would be able to use photographic documents as irrefutable evidence of recent events and that, moreover, such documents would be a very useful aid for future generations in the teaching of moral lessons. Sentiments shared by, amongst others, Armand Dayot who, some twenty years later, similarly extols photography's historical uses through its ability to capture people, places and events with such precision.[59] Viewed within the context of traditional nineteenth-century historical practice, Du Camp's text, like Appert's constructed images, would have been considered to be perfectly acceptable to many people.

As in *Paris: ses organes*, Du Camp relieves the potential tedium of dry facts and statistics by entertaining his readers with a number anecdotes, personal reflections, flashbacks and Balzacian pen-portraits of the 'characters' involved, to whom he even ascribes dialogue. The most striking of these anecdotes, and the most telling in terms of how Du Camp interprets the Commune, is the entire chapter he devotes to the spectacle of the toppling of the Vendôme Column and to Gustave Courbet's involvement in the whole affair (*LC*, II, 180–212). Unsurprisingly, Courbet is ironically patronized throughout the story as a mentally deficient 'pauvre homme' (poor chap) whose extreme realism in art is the result of his own vanity and lack of imagination. As further 'proof' of Courbet's degeneracy, Du Camp cites the artist's infamous painting *L'Origine du monde* in which a naked woman is depicted 'émue et convulsée . . . donnant le dernier mot du réalisme' (impassioned and convulsed . . . representing the last word in realism). The fact that Courbet is capable of degrading his craft to such depths of abjection would suggest, according to Du Camp, that he is capable of anything. As Neil Hertz suggests, Du Camp, seemingly oblivious to his own voyeurism and sexual paranoia, goes on to link by something akin to Freudian free association what he considers to be the artist's own moral degeneracy and the erotic exposure of the woman's naked body in the painting to the political 'convulsions', 'fetishism' and 'disease' of the Commune as exemplified by the destruction of the Vendôme Column.[60] Also from a Freudian psychoanalytic perspective, Elaine Showalter suggests that Du Camp's shocked description of Courbet's painting is an example of the male fear of the *vagina dentata*.[61]

At one level there are clearly some Freudian comparisons to be made between the destruction by the Commune of the Vendôme Column – an obvious phallic symbol – and the emasculation of Paris itself (and by extension the French nation). The perfect 'masculine' body of the Vendôme Column is replaced by the 'imperfect' (in the Freudian sense) female body exposed in Courbet's painting. Furthermore, since Paris was routinely portrayed as a woman (if not a prostitute) in nineteenth-century literature and art, the 'convulsed', 'mutilated' or fragmented woman's body in the painting can be read as a striking metaphor for the city in its own convulsed, violated and destroyed state in the aftermath of the Commune. The automatic association between venereal infection (typically syphilis) and revolution was also commonplace during the period, and Du Camp's personification of the Commune as a woman is therefore certainly not new in anti-Communard discourse (see also Monselet's piece for *Le Monde illustré* in 1871).[62]

In his preface to the first edition of *Les Convulsions*, Du Camp also alludes indirectly to Courbet's *L'Origine du monde* when he personifies the Commune as a diseased prostitute:

> Comme une prostituée sans vergogne, [la Commune] a tout fait voir, et l'on a été surpris de la quantité d'ulcères qui la rongeaient. . . . elle est le produit du vice humain par excellence, de l'envie. Elle date de loin et remonte jusqu'à nos origines; son grand ancêtre est le fils aîné du premier homme et s'est appelé Caïn.[63]

> [Just like a shameless prostitute, [the Commune] put everything on display, and one was surprised at the number of ulcers that ravaged her . . . she is the supreme product of human vice and envy. She goes back a long way, to our very origins; her great ancestor was the elder son of the first man and was called Cain.]

This Commune/prostitute shamelessly displaying her genitalia unsurprisingly turns out to be none other than Eve, the first woman – *the first fallen woman* – whose son Cain was of course the world's first fratricide. Again, this is quite in line with anti-Communard discourse which routinely depicted Communard women as temptresses, prostitutes, amazons, harpies, and witches (Eve is not the only model, therefore, but also Lilith, Hecate, Brunhilde, et al.), and Communard men as drunken, lazy, greedy, cowardly (and by extension, effeminate), dishonest, envious, murderous Cains (a myth that is subtly subverted by Zola in *Le Ventre de Paris*, as I shall go on to show in the next chapter). For Du Camp, envy, or 'le Caïnisme', lies at the heart of all revolutions including the Commune (*LC*, IV, 326).

Du Camp's diseased prostitute also brings to mind Zola's portrayal of the pustule-covered Nana on her deathbed who, as Leslie Ann Minot has persuasively argued, bears comparison with the Communard *pétroleuse* in terms of her perverse sexuality and her ability, literally and figuratively, to send things ups in flames.[64] Zola began writing *Nana*, his great novel about prostitution in all its forms as an allegory of the decadent and corrupt Second Empire in August 1878 but did not complete it until January 1880. Given that the publication of the first volumes of *Les Convulsions* was in February 1878 it is conceivable that Zola's description of the diseased Nana owes just as much to Du Camp as it does to all the medical treatises the author is known to have consulted (*RM*, II, 1683–92, 1737). The automatic association in Du Camp's mind (and arguably also Zola's) between the Commune and the prostitute or the fallen Eve should also, however, be read as part of a wider discourse in which wars in general are perceived in gendered terms. Klaus Theweleit (drawing on Susan Jeffords) posits that after losing a war men become 'a sort of woman' for whom there is 'no resurrection, re-erection, re-election'.[65] In order to become men again and to feel like natural winners they must fight another war that they can win: 'winning a war against the people you live with is one of the real ways of re-winning lost wars.' With the Commune, therefore, Thiers and the humiliated French army were presented with the perfect opportunity to 'replay' the Prussian war they had just lost, only this time they would emerge as the victors. Thus the people of Paris – men, women and children – had to die *en masse* for the benefit of the nation as a whole but also to enable the French army to regain its self-esteem. Furthermore, the Commune itself had to be made feminine in order for the nation to regain its masculinity.

There are some interesting parallels to be drawn between America after Vietnam and France after the Franco-Prussian War. In both cases those accused of having lost the war were similarly brought into some humiliating connection with femininity.[66] The 'women wimps', 'not so good Americans', 'hippies, dems and fems' who were blamed for America's defeat find their counterparts in those Du Camp describes as 'traîtres à la patrie blessée' ('traitors to the wounded nation') who destroyed the Vendôme Column while the Prussians stood at the gates of Paris; those utopian socialists who preached against war and imperialism, those feminists who demanded equality, and those 'cowards' who preferred to strut around in their ribbons and medals amid barrels of wine and cognac rather than fight the enemy (*LC*, IV, 339, 331; I, 284–5). After Vietnam, fighting femininity and winning the Cold War against the communist bloc was seen as a way to reclaim Vietnam as a 'won war' and for American men to free themselves from 'that Asian communist prostitute'.[67] After their defeat by Prussia, Frenchmen similarly had to rid themselves of that shameless Commune-prostitute so that they and the French nation could similarly be reborn and 're-erected'. If, as Theweleit suggests, men are 'reborn through killing' and 'give birth to themselves living in New World Orders', then nowhere is this 'male logic' more effectively expressed than in the conclusion to Zola's *La Débâcle*. In that novel Jean, the strong, manly Versaillais soldier of solid, honest peasant stock, kills his young, weak, feminine 'brother', the Communard Maurice (representative of the diseased part of the nation made rotten by the decadent Second Empire) and then walks away into the proverbial sunset to take on the hard, manly task of building the new France. It comes as no surprise either to hear Zola declare on 30 May 1871 that the bloodbath Paris had just experienced was perhaps a horrible necessity, for it had succeeded in calming the city's fever and would enable it to grow wise and splendid.[68] The same sentiment finds its way into the final pages of *La Débâcle* twenty years later. Nor is it any surprise that soon after the defeat of the Commune the Vendôme Column was re-erected complete with its statue of Napoleon Bonaparte, and that the cost of the reconstruction was charged to none other than Gustave Courbet.

Du Camp's *Les Convulsions* was clearly in tune with its time but it did nevertheless have its serious critics, Flaubert for one. As with *Paris: ses organes*, Flaubert's objections were mainly aesthetic and stylistic and in accordance with his own view of what constituted good narrative and historical discourse. He approved of Du Camp's extensive use of supporting documentation and certainly did not deny his interpretation of the Commune, but he ironically pointed out to his friend in a letter dated 16 April 1879, that *Les Convulsions*'s condemnation of the Communards was excessively vicious and polemical.[69] He felt that this would only serve to weaken Du Camp's case and give his detractors the opportunity to question the integrity of the work as a whole. In an earlier letter dated 19 September 1878 to his niece Caroline, however,

Flaubert revealed himself to be quite disturbed by the furore and repercussions caused by *Les Convulsions*.[70] Referring to a hostile but in his view quite justified article which had just appeared in the newspaper *L'Evénement* accusing Du Camp of having been personally responsible for the sentencing of a man to penal servitude, Flaubert tells Caroline that he is glad not to have such a weight on his conscience. Flaubert suggests that through his continual meddling Du Camp has run the risk of committing a crime himself.

The incident to which Flaubert refers concerns one Ludovic Matillon, an ex-Communard who had held the post of Accountant-in-Chief at the Ministère de la Marine. On 15 March 1878 Du Camp published an article stating that he had uncovered evidence to suggest that Matillon had been one of those responsible for the setting alight of the rue Royale and the pillaging of the ministry building. The letters between the two men were published in *La Revue des deux mondes* between 1 December 1878 and 2 January 1879.[71] The unfortunate Matillon was found guilty and sentenced but was subsequently acquitted and granted amnesty on 5 June 1879. Senneville claims that Du Camp's articles could have had little influence on the decisions taken by the War Councils as, according to some accounts, the final sentence was issued in October 1872. The Du Camp–Matillon affair would suggest otherwise.

Du Camp republished his correspondence with Matillon together with the latter's trial report as an appendix to volume III of *Les Convulsions*. Volume III also includes the offending article itself and is another example of Du Camp's novelistic technique in what is supposed to be straightforward reportage:

> Il était un peu plus de minuit lorsque l'officier revint; il descendit de cheval sous la grande porte, rencontra Matillon et lui parla à l'oreille. Matillon dit à M. Le Sage: 'Emmenez votre femme, votre enfant, et filez sans vous retourner: on va faire sauter le ministère.' ... Dans une lettre écrite de Bruxelles, le 21 janvier 1872, Matillon affirme qu'il n'avait ménagé aucun effort pour faire révoquer l'ordre de destruction; cela est possible; mais en tout cas sa tentative a échoué et si le ministère a été préservé, ce n'est pas à lui qu'on le doit. (*LC*, III, 91)

> [The officer returned just after midnight; he dismounted his horse under the great doorway, went over to Matillon and whispered something in his ear. 'Take your wife and child, flee the building and don't look back', said Matillon to Mr Le Sage, 'the Ministry is going to be blown up.' ... In a letter dated 21 January 1872, written from Brussels, Matillon asserts that he spared no effort in trying to revoke the order for the destruction of the

building. That may well be possible but in any case his attempt failed and
if the Ministry was saved it is no thanks to him.]

Volume II of *Les Convulsions* was also subject to a hostile review in
the 11 March 1879 edition of the low-circulation but highly influential
republican newspaper *Le Siècle*. The paper's anonymous reviewer calls
Les Convulsions 'a detestable work', and accuses Du Camp of being a
self-styled upholder of the law. No one apparently would have known
anything at all about the Commune had it not been for Monsieur Du
Camp; he alone saw everything, knew everything, heard everything
and not only is he is vulgar, but also boring. Whatever his subject,
claims the reviewer, Du Camp's form is invariably shrill and unpleasant.
The reviewer concludes by stating that Du Camp's articles, which had
already been published over the course of the last seven or eight years in
various periodicals (namely, *La Revue des deux mondes and Le Moniteur
universel*) and which were now being republished in volume form, had
led to their author being recognized as one of the Duc de Broglie's most
useful allies during the 16 May 1877 electoral campaign but that unfortunately for 'le pauvre homme' ('the poor chap'), a partial amnesty had
nevertheless still been granted to all ex-Communards.

Undeterred by Flaubert's stylistic objections, the hostility of the
republicans, who recognized the electoral advantages of supporting
calls for amnesty and who accused him of trying to wreck their chances
of political success, or by any of the insults levelled against him by outraged ex-Communards who branded him a 'fusillard' and punningly nick-
named him 'Du Camp de Satory' (the military camp where Communards
were detained and executed), Du Camp forged ahead, completing all
four volumes of *Les Convulsions* and continuing to denounce what he
called the grotesqueness and total stupidity of the Commune.

Like *Paris: ses organes*, *Les Convulsions* sold well right up to the 1900s
(see Table 3 for estimates of the total number of print runs) with volume I, considered by Du Camp himself to be the most important, even
being published in an English translation in 1940.[72] As a product of its
time, *Les Convulsions* clearly fulfilled a need in the hearts and minds
of the reactionary and monarchist elite, but it also gained favour with
some conservative republicans, as evidenced by the hundred or so
letters Du Camp received from members of the public congratulating
him on his election to the Académie.[73] In one such letter, a self-
confessed committed republican named Frédéric Diéry tells Du Camp
that while he is disappointed to see a reactionary elected to the *Institut*

Table 3 *Les Convulsions de Paris*: number of editions and/or reprints

Year of publication or reprint	No. of entries[a]	Vol.	Estimated no. of copies based on average print run of 1,000 copies[b]
1878	2	I	2,000 of vol. I
1879	5	I, II, III and IV	1,000 or 5,000 of each vol. in the set[c]
1880	2	II and IV	1,000 or 2,000 each of vols II and IV
1881	1	I, II, III and IV	1,000 of each vol. in the set
1883	1	I and II and	1,000 of each vol. in the set
	1	II and IV	
1889	4	I, II, III and IV	1,000 or 4,000 of each vol. in the set
1897	1	I	1,000 of vol. I
1898	2	II, III and IV	1,000 or 2,000 each of vols II, III and IV
1905	2	II, III and IV	1,000 or 2,000 each of vols II, III and IV

Vol.	Estimated total no. of copies 1878 to 1905, depending on interpretation of entries
I	7,000 or 14,000
II	11,000 or 17,000
III	8,000 or 17,000
IV	13,000 or 17,000

Source: *Bibliographie de la France*

[a] NB: Figures in the 'No. of Entries' Column represent either the total number of print runs for all the volumes listed collectively or for each of the individual volumes listed.

[b] The estimate of 1,000 copies per edition (or reprint) is based on Zola's general statement regarding the average print run in *Œuvres complètes*, XI, 221.

[c] The entry appears to refer to all four volumes but does not indicate whether the five entries correspond to five re-printings of the total set, or one printing of each individual volume plus an extra reprinting of just one of the volumes.

de France, he nevertheless agrees wholeheartedly with him with regard to the Commune. Diéry even goes so far as to ask Du Camp for an autographed photograph of himself and to praise him as an excellent writer. Such responses to Du Camp's work demonstrate that for all his virulent, exaggerated rhetoric and tendentiousness, by the standards of the day, *Les Convulsions* displayed, for some at least, all the scholarly credentials and gravitas demanded of a historical account and that the text served to consolidate the constructed anti-Communard memory of Paris and the Commune. Dumouchel's exasperated wish in Flaubert's *Bouvard et Péchuchet* that, in order to put an end to the continual round of historical discoveries and re-writings, the *Institut* should establish a sort of canon of texts prescribing what should be believed as historically true appears to have been granted, at least where the history of the Commune was concerned, when the Duc de Broglie, Alexandre Dumas *fils*, and others, assured the election of the author of *Les Convulsions* to the Académie française in December 1880.[74] The extent to which Du Camp, the humanitarian Saint-Simonian turned arch-reactionary, was motivated to write his history of Paris and the Commune in the way he did in order to endear himself to the Académie is a matter for debate and conjecture. This was certainly the view of Antoine Albalat, one of Flaubert's early biographers.[75]

On 6 March 1880, *Le Monde illustré* published Du Camp's portrait on its back page together with an anonymous hagiography inside the journal describing the writer as 'one of our most distinguished writers' but, tellingly, omitting to mention any of his novels or poetry and instead placing the emphasis on the success of his works on Paris, especially his account of the bloody days of the Commune in *Les Convulsions*, sections of which had also appeared in the journal's sister paper, *Le Moniteur universel*. Later that year, on 23 December, on the occasion of Du Camp's formal election to the Académie, the philosopher Elme-Marie Caro made it abundantly clear in his welcoming speech that it was certainly not for his talents as a novelist or poet that Du Camp had earned his place in that august institution but, again, on account of his work on the history of Paris.[76] Caro goes on to praise Du Camp's exacting use of documentary evidence and brushes aside all the accusations levelled against the writer by his opponents; how could it be possible, he asks rhetorically, for it to be more dangerous to recount the history of certain crimes than actually to have committed those same crimes? In an oblique rebuttal of Gambetta's 1880 exhortation for everyone 'to place the tombstone of oblivion' over the Commune Caro states that while humanity may forgive and politics may forget the past, it is history's task to remember and to act as the conscience of the nation and the human race in general.

Following Du Camp's death on 8 February 1894, Paul Bourget, on the occasion of his own election to the Académie on 13 June 1895, also saw fit to praise all of his predecessor's historical works on Paris. Through the use of the same biological and medical metaphors beloved of Du Camp himself, Bourget declared his admiration for the latter's examination of that 'great organism' (Paris) while it stood in the grip of an attack of fever.[77] Finally, in terms that neatly sum up Du Camp's enduring contribution to the anti-Communard memory of Paris, Bourget reminded his audience that Du Camp's texts on the city would remain an indispensable resource for anyone wishing to understand contemporary French life. Nobody, Bourget opined, had condemned that criminal insurrection staged before a victorious (Prussian) enemy more than Maxime Du Camp, and nobody more than he had so detested that frenzy of savage vandalism that was suddenly unleashed against so many precious monuments.

Notes

1 Senneville, *Maxime Du Camp*, p. 292.
2 Zola, *Œuvres complètes*, X, 814–15.
3 Finot, *Maxime Du Camp* (Paris: Les Amis de Flaubert, 1949), p. 65.
4 See B. Bart, 'Is Maxime Du Camp a Reliable Witness?', *Modern Languages Review*, 47 (1953), pp. 17–25; W. Loftus, 'The Veracity of Maxime Du Camp's Reminiscences of Gustave Flaubert, 1849–51', *Les Bonnes Feuilles* (1974), pp. 61–72; and Rosa M. Di Stefano, 'Maxime Du Camp d'après sa correspondance avec Flaubert', *Les Amis de Flaubert*, 54 (1979), pp. 7–18.
5 See Jacques Thierry, *Histoire de la conquête de l'Angleterre par les Normands: Dix ans d'études historiques* (1830), in *Œuvres* (Brussels: Human, 1839), p. 10; the introductions to the first volumes of Hippolyte Taine's *Histoire de la littérature anglaise*, 5 vols, 2nd edn (Paris: Hachette, 1899) and *Les Origines de la France contemporaine* (Paris: Hachette, 1876); and Prosper de Barante, *Histoire des ducs de Bourgogne de la maison de Valois 1364–1477*, 13 vols, 3rd edn (Paris: Ladvocat, 1825–26), pp. 25–6. For a critical assessment of the major French historians, see the introduction to Camille Jullian's *Extraits des historiens français du XIXe siècle* (Paris: Hachette, 1897).
6 Hayden White, *The Content of the Form: Narrative Discourse and Historical Representation* (Baltimore: Johns Hopkins University Press, 1987), pp. 37–42.
7 See Roland Barthes, 'Le Discours de l'histoire' and 'L'Effet du réel', in *Essais critiques IV: Le Brunissement de la langue* (Paris: Seuil, 1984), pp. 153–74.
8 White, *The Content of the Form*, pp. 21–2, 24.
9 Casey, part 2, ch. VI, pp. 90, 93, 98–9, 329, n. 16.
10 Cf. Jacques Derrida, *De la grammatologie* (Paris: Les éditions de minuit, 1967), ch. 2, pp. 42–108.
11 Cf. Halbwachs, *Les Cadres*, p. 63.
12 Casey, pp. 186–7.

13 Henri Lefebvre, *La Vie quotidienne dans le monde moderne* (Paris: Gallimard, 1968), p. 325.

14 Benjamin, *The Arcades Project*, pp. 23, 469.

15 Du Camp, *Souvenirs littéraires*, 2 vols (Paris: Hachette, 1882–83), I, p. 417.

16 See Senneville, pp. 283–4.

17 See Pilbeam, ch. 10.

18 See Preface to Adolphe Joanne's *Paris illustré en 1870: Guide de l'étranger et du Parisien* (Paris: Hachette, 1871), p. xi.

19 The Municipal Council of Paris had bought the Hôtel Carnavalet in 1866 with the intention of converting it into a museum of the city. In 1880 the Carnavalet was finally opened to the public as a museum, but by 1889 the constant expansion of the library holdings and the museum's other collections was such that the library was moved to the adjacent Hôtel Le Peletier. Eventually, in 1968, the library collection was moved to the nearby Hôtel Lamoignon, to become, as it remains today, the Bibliothèque Historique de la Ville de Paris.

20 Armand Dayot, *L'Invasion, le siège, la Commune, 1870–1871* (Paris: Flammarion, 1895(?)), p. 318.

21 Morisot, p. 58.

22 Gustave Flaubert, *Correspondances, Flaubert-Alfred Le Poittevin, Flaubert-Maxime Du Camp*, ed. by Yvan Leclerc (Paris: Flammarion, 2000), p. 403.

23 Vallès was forced by his father to spend time in a mental institution in Nantes from 31 December 1851 to 2 March 1852, following his involvement in the resistance against Napoleon's *coup d'état*. Noted in Jules Vallès, *L'Insurgé*, ed. by Marie-Claire Bancquart (Paris: Gallimard, 1975), p. 338. See also Lidsky, Glazer, and Roger Ripoll's article, 'Zola et les Communards', *Europe*, 468–9 (April–May 1968), pp. 17–26.

24 Noël, *Dictionnaire de la Commune*, I, pp. 188–9.

25 See Philippe Joutard et al., *La Saint-Barthélemy ou les résonances d'un massacre* (Neuchâtel: Delachaux et Niestlé, 1976), and Roberts, pp. 187–205.

26 Renan, *Qu'est-ce qu'une nation?*, ed. by Joël Roman (Paris: Presses Pocket, 1992), p. 42.

27 Benedict Anderson, *Imagined Communities: Reflections on the Origin and Spread of Nationalism* (London and New York: Verso, 1999), p. 201.

28 See Du Camp, *Les Chants modernes*, p. 13.

29 See Roberts.

30 Noël, *Dictionnaire de la Commune*, II, p. 279.

31 Saint-Simonians are the followers of Henri de Saint-Simon (1760–1825), the founder of an early form of socialism that called for the reorganization of society under the leadership of an elite of philosophers, engineers and scientists so as to effect a peaceful process of industrialization based on Christian-Humanism. He influenced, among others, Auguste Comte, John Stuart Mill, Karl Marx and Napoleon III.

32 The Buttes des Moulins covered the triangular area nowadays bordered by the avenue de l'Opéra to the east, the rue St Roch to the west and the rue St Honoré to the south. The demolition of the old streets in this area was covered in *Le Monde illustré* (18 November 1876) and Zola paid his own tribute in *La Débâcle* by placing some of the action in the rue des Orties, which had long gone by the time the novel was published in 1892.

33 David Baguley, *Zola: 'L'Assommoir'* (Cambridge: Cambridge University Press, 1992), pp. 17–18.

34 Redfern, p. 196. See also Bancquart in the preface to Vallès, *L'Insurgé*, p. 32.

35 See Annette Kuhn, *Family Secrets: Acts of Memory and Imagination* (London and New York: Verso, 2002), p. 163.

36 Redfern, p. 196.

37 Connerton, p. 21.

38 See Georges Tersen, 'L'Opinion publique et la Commune de Paris (1871–79)', *Bulletin de la société d'études historiques, géographiques et scientifiques de la région parisienne*, 107–8 (April–September 1960), p. 30, and 114–15 (January–June 1962), pp. 25–7.

39 Prosper-Olivier Lissagaray, *Les Huit Journées de mai derrière les barricades* (Brussels: n.pub., 1871) and *Histoire de la Commune de 1871* (Paris: Maspero, 1970). Karl Marx, *The Civil War in France* (1871), ed. by Frederick Engels, 2nd edn (Moscow: Progress Publishers, 1977).

40 Nietzsche, *On the Genealogy of Morals*, pp. 45, 52–3.

41 Du Camp, *Les Convulsions de Paris*, 1st edn, 4 vols (Paris: Hachette, 1878–80), I (1878), p. vii.

42 White, *The Content of the Form*, pp. 21–2, 24.

43 Du Camp, *Les Convulsions*, 1st edn, I, p. viii.

44 Tombs, *The Paris Commune*, p. 189.

45 Taine, *Les Origines de la France contemporaine*, II, p. 111.

46 Ibid., I, iv.

47 Du Camp, *Les Convulsions*, 1st edn, I, p. i.

48 Mendès, pp. 1–2.

49 Du Camp, *Les Convulsions*, 1st edn, I, p. iii.

50 Vallès, *L'Insurgé*, pp. 330, 406–7 n. 5. See also Langford, p. 53.

51 Taine, *Histoire de la littérature anglaise*, I, xii.

52 Du Camp, *Les Convulsions*, 1st edn, I, p. ii.

53 White, *The Content of the Form*, p. 87.

54 Senneville, pp. 347–8.

55 Rougerie, *La Commune de 1871*, p. 118.

56 Taine, *Essais de critique et d'histoire* (1855), 3rd edn (Paris: Hachette, 1874), p. 111. See also Jullian, pp. xcv–xcvi.

57 For an analysis of examples of Appert's images, see English, pp. 33–48, and Quentin Bajac, ed., *La Commune photographiée* (Paris: Editions de la Réunion des musées nationaux, 2000), pp. 40–8, 96–105.

58 Lapostolle, 'Plus vrai que le vrai'.

59 Dayot, pp. 1–4. What is disturbing, however, is the fact that Appert's composites were still being reproduced in French school history books in the 1970s as if they provided evidence of actual events. See Gautrand, p. 53, who quotes André Zeller's *Les Hommes de la Commune* (1969) as a case in point.

60 Neil Hertz, 'Medusa's Head: Male Hysteria under Political Pressure', in *The End of the Line: Essays on Psychoanalysis and the Sublime*, ed. by Neil Hertz (New York: Columbia University Press, 1985), pp. 169–73.

61 Elaine Showalter, *Sexual Anarchy* (London: Bloomsbury, 1991), p. 148.

62 See Bertrand Taithe, *Defeated Flesh: Welfare, Warfare and the Making of Modern France* (Manchester: Manchester University Press, 1999), ch. 9 (p. 232), and also Kidd.

63 Du Camp, *Les Convulsions*, 1st edn, I, pp. iii–iv.

64 Leslie Ann Minot, 'Women and the Commune: Zola's revisions', *Excavatio*, 10 (1997), pp. 57–65 (p. 58), reprinted in *Writing the Feminine in Zola and Naturalist Fiction*, ed. by Anna Gural-Migdal (Bern: Peter Lang, 2003). See also, Taithe, *Defeated Flesh*, pp. 217–18.

65 Klaus Theweleit, 'The Bomb's Womb and the Genders of War (War Goes on Preventing Women from Becoming the Mothers of Invention)', in *Gendering War Talk*, ed. by Miriam Cooke and Angela Woollacot (Princeton: Princeton University Press, 1993), pp. 284–5.

66 Theweleit, p. 285. See also Susan Jeffords, *The Remasculinization of America: Gender and the Vietnam War* (Bloomington: Indiana University Press, 1995) and Sara Ruddick, *Maternal Thinking: Toward a Politics of Peace* (Boston MA: Beacon Press, 1989).

67 Theweleit, pp. 284–5.

68 *Le Sémaphore de Marseille*, cited in Ripoll, p. 17. See also Zola's preparatory notes, *RM*, V, pp. 1378–9.

69 Gustave Flaubert, *Correspondance supplément: juillet 1877–mai 1880*, ed. by René Dumesnil et al. (Paris: Editions Conrad, 1951), pp. 204–5. On Flaubert's views on the Commune see Lidsky, pp. 68–77.

70 Gustave Flaubert, *Œuvres complètes de Gustave Flaubert: Correspondance (1877–1880)* (Paris: Louis Conrad, 1930), pp. 147–8.

71 See Du Camp's letter of 7 February 1879 in Flaubert, *Correspondances, Flaubert-Alfred Le Poittevin, Flaubert-Maxime Du Camp*, p. 420.

72 Maxime Du Camp, *Paris After the Prussians* trans. by Philip A. Wilkins (London and Melbourne: Hutchinson, 1940).

73 See Fonds Maxime Du Camp, ref. 3723, Portefeuille des *Convulsions de Paris*, held by the library of the Institut de France.

74 See letter number 162, Fonds Maxime Du Camp, ref. 3723, for evidence of the duc de Broglie's involvement in Du Camp's election.

75 Antoine Albalat, *Gustave Flaubert et ses amis* (Paris: Plon, 1927), p. 40.

76 Elme-Marie Caro's speech reproduced in *Discours prononcés dans la séance publique tenue par l'Académie française pour la réception de Maxime Du Camp, le 23 décembre 1880* (Paris: Firmin-Didot, 1880), pp. 52–3.

77 Paul Bourget's speech reproduced in *Discours prononcés dans la séance publique tenue par l'Académie française pour la réception de Paul Bourget, le 13 juin 1895* (Paris: Firmin-Didot, 1895), pp. 22, 24. Republished in Paul Gautier, *Anthologie de l'Académie française: Un siècle de discours académiques 1820–1920* (Paris: Delagrave, 1921), pp. 186–96.

~4~

Zola's 'art of memory'

Zola was a very different man from Du Camp in terms of his temperament and social background. Du Camp was a supporter of the 'liberal' Empire while Zola was one of the severest critics of Napoleon III, but the two writers nevertheless shared a very similar moral and conservative world-view. Both were Versaillais supporters, though critical of the way Thiers had abandoned Paris and mishandled the Commune. Both shared a horror of bloodshed and were appalled by *la Semaine sanglante* and yet remained, as Lidsky and many other commentators have shown, unsympathetic to the aims of the Commune and particularly hostile to its leaders. Nevertheless, ambiguities abound in the writings of both. Du Camp, as we have seen, had no hesitation in helping Vallès escape the Versaillais, and we should certainly guard against seeing Zola as wholly against all those who supported the Commune.[1] Both men were sceptical of MacMahon and *l'Ordre moral*, particularly where censorship of the press was concerned, though Du Camp conceded that while this was not a regime that suited everyone, it did at least offer some guarantees for future stability.[2] Zola's impatience with the endless squabbles between the different factions within the government found its expression in his press articles and novels, most notably the overtly political *Son Excellence Eugène Rougon* (1876), a novel which is arguably as much a depiction of the political machinations of the early Third Republic as it is of those of the Second Empire. Neither Du Camp nor Zola was conventionally religious and yet both men shared the same biblical values. Both men were born in Paris and shared a passionate love for the city. Both were also, in their own way, highly complex, ambitious individuals who managed in their literary and journalistic output, as in life generally, to combine a strong passion for the modern, based on a Positivist belief in moral and social progress through science and technology, with a deeply regressive, pessimistic anxiety about the future.

For Walter Benjamin, Du Camp's presentation of the city from the administrative point of view in *Paris: ses organes* can be seen as deriving from the same inspiration that produced Baudelaire's idea of modernism.[3] Hugo, Baudelaire and the artist Charles Meryon were all acutely aware of how quickly Paris was changing after 1848 and Du Camp's *Paris: ses organes* is seen by Benjamin as yet another attempt, in a different register, to fix in memory the image of the old city before it disappeared forever. Paul de Man, meanwhile, has argued that the essence of Baudelaire's notion of modernity has much in common with that of Nietzsche, for whom 'life' is not conceived purely in biological terms but also in 'temporal terms as the ability to forget whatever precedes a present situation'.[4] For Paul de Man, Nietzsche's opposition between history and life and his advocacy of ruthless forgetting captures the authentic spirit of modernity. But for Nietzsche – as for Baudelaire and, by extension, Du Camp and Zola – this 'history-transcending life-process is counterbalanced by a deeply pessimistic wisdom that remains rooted in a sense of historical causality [that] reverses the movement of history from one of development to one of regression' (pp. 388–9).

It is surprising, therefore, that Benjamin does not also extend his analysis of Baudelaire and Du Camp to Zola, whose Parisian novels, it could equally be argued, are another manifestation of this same Romantic, nostalgic and memorialist urge. In his novels Zola, no less than Hugo in 'A l'Arc de Triomphe', Baudelaire in 'Tableaux parisiens' or Du Camp in *Paris: ses organes*, depicts the city as a topographical palimpsest or archive of the past; a past which he appears to know intimately but which is in fact filtered through collective myths and memories and subject to his own imaginative sensibility.

Despite Zola's use of the literary device of free indirect speech to create the illusion of distance between the author–narrator and his characters, and his technique of allowing his characters to express 'their own' thoughts and world-view as the means by which he pursues 'objectivity' and 'truth', he still attempts no less than Balzac, Hugo and Flaubert to include everything within his totalizing vision of the world. Zola also sacrifices that desired objectivity by positioning himself as an 'author/scientist' conducting a so-called 'experiment' with characters and situations he himself has created and by continuously resorting to the use of myth, allegory, parody and his own artistic imagination as the means by which to moralize consciously or not on the behaviour of his characters and society at large. In this he is no different from Du Camp, Barante, Thierry or Taine as discussed in the previous chapter.[5] Any claim to historical objectivity on Zola's behalf is compromised right from the outset given his own declared intention to manipulate the historical framework to his novels as he sees fit and his reliance on tendentious accounts by Taxile Delord of the Second Empire and by Théodore Duret of the Commune. It is significant too that Zola, while not quite to the same extent as Du Camp, deliberately marginalizes or ignores descriptions and interpretations of events that do not fit his own ideological agenda.[6]

Much has been written already about the complexities and contradictions inherent in Zola's political views and his response to the Commune.[7] Roger Ripoll and Aimé Guedj, for example, have explored how Zola's anti-Communard opinions expressed in his journalistic articles also manifest themselves in *Le Ventre de Paris* and several other of his novels. Marie Scarpa's detailed analysis of *Le Ventre de Paris* (which builds on the work of Ripoll, Lidsky, and R.A. Jouanny), is perhaps the most searching analysis of the influence of the Commune on the novel to date, but still does not go far enough, as I will highlight, in its analysis of the character of Florent as a proto Communard.[8] David Baguley and Robert Lethbridge have both studied some of the covert political references in *L'Assommoir*.[9] However, whilst these and several other scholars have analysed the embedded narratives and intertextual references in these novels, none has, to date, studied the relationship between the text, the city's topography, and the Commune as a function of the collective memory in either of these novels or in *Une page d'amour*.[10]

A great deal of critical attention has instead focused on Zola's multifaceted descriptions of Paris, often on evidence of his literary impressionism or on his place within the long-established tradition of the city and the urban panorama as literary topoi.[11] Meanwhile, Brian Nelson has studied *Une page d'amour* as another example, along with *La Curée* and *Pot-Bouille*, of Zola's condemnation of the decadence and hypocrisy of the bourgeoisie under the Second Empire, and Susan Harrow has taken a psychoanalytical approach to the novel and focused on the gender issues it raises.[12] For F.W.J. Hemmings, Henri Mitterand and Frederick Brown it is the autobiographical intertext of *Une page d'amour* that is of particular interest.[13]

What this chapter aims to contribute to all this existing scholarship is proof that the memory of Paris and the Commune lies at the very heart of Zola's carefully crafted descriptions of the city's topography in *Le Ventre de Paris*, *L'Assommoir* and *Une page d'amour*, giving a new meaning to the naturalist determinants 'le milieu et le moment'. The locations, monuments, streets and landmarks contained in Zola's descriptions of Paris are not innocent but *lieux de mémoire* forever inscribed on the contemporary national psyche so that they form an 'art of memory' evoking a unique time and place, in much the same way as Walker's *promenades* do in *Le Monde illustré*. We should also not forget the third naturalist determinant, 'la race', or inherited, biological characteristics, since this too – when applied to the perceived inherited characteristics of 'mentally disturbed' revolutionaries like Florent, the main protagonist of *Le Ventre de Paris*, or working-class alcoholics like Gervaise and Coupeau in *L'Assommoir* – finds its corollary in contemporary descriptions of the Commune's leaders. For Zola, like Du Camp (*PSO*, IV, 440), these men are 'fous furieux' (raging madmen) and their inebriated followers suffer from *delirium tremens*, a condition that afflicts Coupeau at the end of the novel.[14] Finally, in *Une page d'amour*, beneath the deceptively simple, moralistic tale of a woman's sexual awakening, transgression and subsequent punishment, there lies not only another covert allegory of the Commune and *Semaine sanglante* but also an allegory of the whole saga of the Franco-Prussian War, the fall of the Second Republic, and a city's attempt to bury and forget its past.

Le Ventre de Paris

Written in 1872 and published in 1873, *Le Ventre de Paris*, the third novel in the Rougon-Macquart cycle, contains several allusions to the Commune; of the three novels under consideration, it is the only one clearly to do so.[15] However, if critics have already highlighted the most obvious of these allusions, from a memorialist point of view, there are, I believe, several others which need exploring: for example, Florent's journey into the city by way of Courbevoie and Neuilly (two important Commune *lieux de mémoires*); the many images of fire embedded throughout the novel; and, most strikingly, the similarities between Zola's protagonist and the assassinated Communard leader Gustave Flourens, whose name alone echoes that of Zola's revolutionary.[16] All of these examples allude to the city's recent past but they serve also to structure the novel in such a way as to reinforce its essential underlying conservative ideology.[17]

For Christopher Prendergast, the long opening sequence which characterizes *Le Ventre de Paris* is no more than just another example of the typical nineteenth-century device which sees the arrival of the hero into the capital.[18] And yet, on closer inspection, this carefully constructed, selective and detailed street-level description of Florent's journey into Paris is very revealing. Florent could have reached Paris by any number of routes and, for the modern reader, Zola's decision to have his protagonist approach the city via Courbevoie and Neuilly might well appear to have been quite arbitrary or, if we believe Maurice Dreyfous's account, the author may have been influenced by his own experience when he and Dreyfous observed convoys of market gardeners making their way into the city centre over the Pont de Neuilly one autumn night in 1872.[19] For any Parisian, however, reading *Le Ventre de Paris* when it first appeared in its self-censored form as a *roman-feuilleton* in *l'Etat* between January and March 1873 or, subsequently, in its definitive 1873 Charpentier edition, the names Neuilly and Courbevoie would have been poignantly evocative. In 1872–73, these once beautiful, smart outlying suburbs where Parisians used to spend their Sunday afternoons still lay in ruins after enduring bombardment, first by the invading Prussians, and then again during the initial military engagements of the civil war in April 1871. Zola records having visited Neuilly in April 1871 during the Commune, and according to both Zola and Du Camp the crowds gathered on the hilltop in Montmartre to watch as the Versaillais fought the Communards and the small town was destroyed in the process (*RM*, V, 1366; *LC*, II, 224–5). Courbevoie, Neuilly, and the Porte Maillot, the next staging post on Florent's journey, formed the subject of innumerable prints and photographs that were still on sale in the city as the novel was going to press.

As contemporary readers would also have remembered, Neuilly had been in the news even before the start of the civil conflict when, on 12 January 1870, Gustave Flourens made an early attempt to launch the Commune there and then by trying to incite the vast crowd that had gathered in the town for the funeral of the journalist Victor Noir (shot by Prince Pierre Bonaparte, cousin to Napoleon III) to march on Paris, only to be held back by Henri Rochefort and Delescluze.[20] This was not the first time Flourens, a veteran of the Cretan and Polish uprisings of the 1860s, had actively participated in revolutionary action, and he went on to lead some 8,000–10,000 men from Belleville in bloodless insurrections on 5, 8 and 31 October 1870 in a bid to take control of the Hôtel de Ville. Lacking any coherent plan, all these attempts ended in confusion and failure and served merely to highlight the weaknesses and contradictions among the revolutionary leaders that were later to undermine the Commune itself and precipitate its demise.[21]

In *Paris livré*, a third-person account of his own revolutionary struggle, Flourens describes how the five Belleville battalions, each with its own leader, peaceably take possession of the Hôtel de Ville from a government considered treacherous, thereby carrying out the will of the people.[22] All government resistance subsequently subsides and the people thus reclaim their own sovereignty. *Paris livré* was published on 3 April 1871, the same day that Flourens was captured and killed by the Versaillais, and ran to five reprints (an estimated 5,000 copies) during that month alone. Flourens's plan, dependent on volunteer batallions consisting of 'excellent republicans' all devoted to their chosen leader, recalls the one placed by Zola into the head of his own utopian revolutionary. In a passage which strongly echoes Flourens's description, the naïve but heroically confident Florent dreams of dividing Paris up into twenty sectors, each with its own leader, and of taking possession of the city and marching straight to the Hôtel de Ville without as far as possible engaging in any armed struggle with the rank and file soldiers, guardsmen and firemen, but instead inviting them all to 'faire *cause commune* avec le peuple' (my emphasis) (make common cause with the people) (*RM*, I, 813).

After appropriating the Hôtel de Ville on 18 March 1871, the Commune's leaders proceeded to abolish conscription, an action that left the new administration grossly unprepared for the Versaillais attacks at Courbevoie and Neuilly. The Commune's counterattack consisted of only three columns of *fédérés* accompanied in a festive spirit by a number of women and children. This of course was no match for the Versaillais. Those Communards not killed outright at Neuilly were mercilessly hunted down and imprisoned, and, during the three-week siege that followed, the inhabitants of Neuilly were left to starve and the atrocities committed in the town proved far worse than those perpetrated during the Prussian siege. Zola was later to offer his own account of the Neuilly siege in *La Débâcle* (*RM*, V, 874–5). The anti-militaristic culture of the Commune was to be another cause of its downfall in that it gave the Versaillais the opportunity to deny the fact that the *fédérés* had any military status and to substantiate their claim that Paris was in a state of chaos that threatened to engulf the whole country, thus facilitating and justifying their slaughter of defenceless Communards.[23]

Zola's harsh judgement of the Commune's leadership, like that of many of his fellow writers and intellectuals, is well known: all are considered to be naïve, effeminate, hypersensitive fanatics, 'fous furieux' (raving madmen), and idealistic revolutionaries spouting dubious moral doctrines who think of themselves as martyrs but are in fact no more than criminals.[24] For his part, Du Camp describes Flourens as an 'aliéné' (lunatic) who, along with his accomplices, sought to represent 'la République universelle' at the heart of the Commune (*PSO*, VI, 339). Even Charles Prolès, Flourens's sympathetic biographer, draws attention to the man's apparent inherent naivety.[25] The image persisted. In 1914, for example, Lucien Nass in his 'medicalized history' of the Commune calls Flourens a Romantic utopian revolutionary, a hothead who, as a child, suffered hallucinations.[26] In 1927, Henri d'Alméras considered Flourens's blind sectarianism and fanaticism to be truly frightening.[27] Florent, no less than Zola's other revolutionaries, Silvère Mouret (*La Fortune des Rougon*), Etienne Lantier (*Germinal*), and Maurice Levasseur (*La Débâcle*), shares many of the same perceived physical and mental characteristics attributed to Gustave Flourens.

Given the success of Flourens's *Paris livré* and its author's notoriety as a republican journalist and Communard, there can be little doubt that Zola was all too well aware of this revolutionary hero whose reputation reached almost mythical proportions after his brutal assassination by one Desmarets, a captain in the Gendarmerie. Desmarets apparently received a tip-off from an informant suspected of being the inn-keeper with whom Flourens took refuge en route to Chatou during the Communard sortie to Courbevoie, and in *Le Ventre de Paris* Florent is similarly betrayed to the authorities by the café owner Lebigre.[28] Zola was also personally affected by the Communard backlash following the assassinations of Flourens and other prominent Communards when, in accordance with the Decree of 6 April 1871, he was himself detained and almost taken hostage on 10 May 1871 for alleged collaboration with the Versailles government. Zola was at this time commuting as a reporter between Paris and Versailles and, ironically, he was also stopped during a round-up of suspected rebels in Versailles.[29] Furthermore, Flourens appears to have been the inspiration for *César Panafieu*, a short story by Paul Alexis, which eventually formed part of a collection entitled *L'Education amoureuse* (1890). In an exchange of letters with Zola between February and June 1871, Alexis tells his mentor that he has created a character named Barbin, an embittered, drunken coward and thief based on Pierre Vésinier (a real-life, disgraced Communard) who is to play Sancho Panza to the other main protagonist, a tall, slim forty-year-old Don Quixote modelled on none other than Gustave Flourens.[30]

The *Avertissement* dated November 1874 that prefaces *César Panafieu* informs the reader that the text that follows is drawn from the fragments of a diary belonging to some half-demented, half-lucid fool which were found in the tunic pocket of a tall, thin, bony-featured, Quixote-like *fédéré* killed alongside Gustave Flourens. This description chimes, eerily, with the account given by Amilcare Cipriani of Flourens's own arrest and assassination. On being searched, Flourens was apparently identified when a letter addressed to 'General Flourens' was found in one of his pockets.[31] Alexis was not the only one to spot the apparent resemblance between Flourens and the famous Spanish knight-errant. Some thirty-five years later, Nass described him as 'a Don Quixote of social causes', a bragger who enjoyed parading around in his costume and whose boots were particularly striking.[32] If Florent does not quite share Flourens's coquettish passion for fine clothes and especially fine *boots*, then Zola's other revolutionary, Etienne Lantier in *Germinal*, most certainly does. No sooner does Lantier acquire such a pair than he finds himself transformed into an unelected leader with the whole mining village rallying to him (*RM*, III, 1281).

Alexis also confided to Zola that he was planning a much more ambitious project, an epic novel covering the Prussian siege and the Commune with a gigantic conflagration as the final tableau.[33] In the event Alexis abandoned this project but Zola went on to realize it on his behalf, to a certain extent, with *La Débâcle* and, in the meantime, created his own Don Quixote (Florent) and Sancho Panza (Gavard) in *Le Ventre de Paris*, lending them some of the traits and characteristics attributed to Flourens and Vésinier.

Zola, no less than Alexis or Du Camp, remained convinced that France had to rid herself of the Commune in order to achieve political stability and moral order. For Zola, therefore, there is no place in Paris for the thin, rake-like Florent ('un maigre'), and the city is described as being angry at his return from the penal colony of Cayenne where he was banished after unwittingly becoming involved in a round-up of insurgents following Napoleon III's *coup d'état* in December 1851 (*RM*, I, 606). Florent's anticipated failure is clearly announced at the very start of the novel when, his legs almost broken with exhaustion, he leans over the bridge at Neuilly under the watchful gaze of a red beacon likened to a bleeding eye floating in the Seine. This startling image finds its echo in the incriminating blood found on Florent's hands in December 1851, which led to his deportation.[34] It looks ahead also to the scene in which Quenu makes black pudding out of pig's blood while Florent recounts the gruesome story of his escape from Cayenne in a parody of *la Semaine sanglante* (*RM*, I, 683–93). It presages also the 'red' activities to be plotted later in the café Lebigre where even the bar bench and curtains are red and the marble surfaces red and white, and where the hot wine, grog, punch and rough cognac inflame the blood and spirits of Florent and his free-thinking companions (*RM*, I, 705), alcohol forming the vital link in the contemporary bourgeois imagination between revolution, low morals, fire and blood. However, in a novel written between 1872 and 1873, the red beacon/bleeding eye functions, above all, as an adumbrative reminder of the thousands of mutilated corpses that were cast into the river during the Versaillais repression, turning the Seine red. The returned convict's plan to conquer the city peaceably is destined to fail, like that of Gustave Flourens. Condemned like Sisyphus to an eternity of futile hard labour, Florent will never reach the city's glittering heights. In a parody of his whole tragic existence, his wanderings around Les Halles keep sending him back to the church of Saint-Eustache and finally back to Cayenne. At least Zola spares Florent the bloody fate that befell his alter ego, Gustave Flourens.

For Zola's contemporary readers, Florent's mode of transport into the city would also have evoked memories of the Commune. Firstly, and as a counterpoint to Maurice Dreyfous's anecdote, Armand Lanoux claims that Zola himself had entered the city from Versailles in a market gardener's cart during the Commune.[35] While Baroli dismisses this story as uncorroborated, it is interesting to note that, according to Du Camp (*LC*, II, 220), such a practice was in fact commonplace during both the Prussian and Versaillais sieges.[36] Secondly, the description of a semi-conscious Florent being transported in this way finds its sinister echo in the removal of Flourens's corpse from Chatou to Versailles in a dung-filled tipcart.[37]

Dreyfous also claims that the first chapter of the novel is a reworking of his own childhood memories of Paris during the outbreak of street violence which accompanied news of Louis Napoleon's *coup d'état* in December 1851, and which he recounted to Zola as the two men visited

Saint-Eustache in 1872, while the writer carried out his research for the novel. Dreyfous describes how, when he arrived at Saint-Eustache with Zola, the sight of the illuminated church clock caused him to experience what we might describe as a 'madeleine moment', an instance of involuntary Proustian–Halbwachian revelation, when he was suddenly transported back to the horrors he had witnessed as a child.[38] In the novel, Zola has his protagonist undergo a similar experience. On his return to Paris after seven years in Cayenne, Florent initially finds the city unrecognizable after its transformation by Haussmann, but the sight of Saint-Eustache with its distinctive clock and the adjacent entrance to the rue Montorgueil, one of the medieval streets left unchanged by the redevelopment of Les Halles (an anachronism in the novel),[39] causes him to recall a whole series of events (*RM*, I, 609). The juxtaposition between the modern Halles and the ancient streets and alleyways with their bustling, banal, present-day normality throws Florent's personal memories into sharp relief, reminding him of the slaughter of five insurgents manning a barricade in the rue Grenéta and that he himself narrowly missed being lined up and executed against the walls of Saint-Eustache (*RM*, I, 610–11). Human corpses on the streets are now replaced by something as mundane as cases of radishes, however, and instead of revolutionary barricades Florent now only sees carts loaded up with pumpkins. The carnage he witnessed is still there though, transmogrified into the carcasses and offal on a butcher's stall (*RM*, I, 627–31). The vocabulary and imagery in this passage bear comparison with Zola's account of Père-Lachaise in the days after the Versaillais executions of the Communards at the end of May 1871, where he saw mutilated bodies pinned to railings like sides of beef.[40]

The mass executions against the wall at Père-Lachaise, meanwhile, are transposed in the novel to the wall of Saint-Eustache and the indiscriminate shootings of civilians in the Boulevards Bonne-Nouvelle and Montmartre recall the wholesale slaughter on the streets of Paris by the Versaillais. The description of the young woman killed beside Florent, her white blouse dripping with blood, similarly resonates with the memory of the time when any innocent working-class woman caught out on the streets was likely to be accused of being a *pétroleuse* and summarily executed or deported.[41] The sensitive Florent is left traumatized by the sight of this dead woman; a shy thirty-year-old, afraid of looking at any woman directly, he is left with the permanent haunting memory of this one woman whom he feels he has somehow lost (*RM*, I, 610, 837), just as Zola himself, also aged thirty, was traumatized by the sight of a seventeen-year-old boy he saw lying dead at Père-Lachaise in 1871.[42] The dead woman in *Le Ventre de Paris* is reminiscent also of Miette, the victim of the *coup d'état* in *La Fortune des Rougon*, while Florent's reaction mirrors that of her young revolutionary lover, Silvère (*RM*, I, 220–1). Later, in *La Débâcle*, written after the myth of the *pétroleuse* had been discredited, Zola would depict another innocent woman, being mercilessly executed in front of a crowd of baying bourgeois spectators (*RM*, I, V, 904–5).

If the shooting of civilians by government troops was a regular feature of all Parisian insurrections, the conflagrations that overwhelmed and destroyed so much of the city were unique to May 1871. Thus in a novel which purports to deal with the 1851 *coup d'état*, it is important to note the recurrent image of fire and death. Right at the beginning of the novel, the city is discerned in all its 'flames' as it materializes on the horizon through a luminous, vaporous mist. The stereotypical image of Pairs as the 'City of Light' is disconcertingly juxtaposed, however, with the image of the city as a deathly desert, lit up by short yellow gas jet flames (*RM*, I, 605–7). Throughout the novel the fear of revolution and destruction is also closely allied with the image of fire. Gavard, for example, tells Lisa in a heated discussion, which serves to confirm her own worst fears, that it would only take two determined men, like Florent and himself, to set fire to her shop and later, as the women gossip, we are told that Florent clearly had evil intentions and that those of his ilk had only one thought in mind, to set everything on fire. Madame Lecœur also imagines Les Halles being set alight as Florent and his accomplices lie hidden in a cellar, biding their time before launching an assault on Paris (*RM*, I, 786, 829–30). Du Camp bears witness to a similar obsession among *petit bourgeois* shop-keepers in 1871 who, as in 1848, imagined their homes and businesses being set on fire by the insurgents and suspected every lighted lamp or candle of being used to transmit some mysterious message (*LC*, II, 287). In 1878 Zola accused Taine of depicting the 1789 Revolution from the point of view of someone who had lived through 1848 and 1871. The same criticism might well be levelled at Zola himself in *Le Ventre de Paris* for, as these examples demonstrate, the novel depicts the relatively minor insurrection and political unrest of 1851 from the traumatized perspective of 1871. Whether by design or not on Zola's part, the image of the city in flames recurs throughout his Parisian novels; at street-level again in *L'Assommoir*, and then becoming progressively more abstract and distant in the panoramas of *Une page d'amour*, *L'Œuvre* and, finally, *La Débâcle*, by which time the material effects of the conflagrations of 1871 had become less of a tangible reality and more like Chifflart's sublime image, 'Histoire de Paris: les nuits de mai' (Figure 5).

Despite their fears, the triumph of Zola's voracious 'dames de la Halle' in *Le Ventre de Paris* is as inevitable as the defeat of their quarry. As a vexed Lisa declares, with the same insistence on the fatal hereditary predisposition attributed to the revolutionary throughout antiCommunard discourse, 'Ah! le malheureux! . . . Il [Florent] était venu ici comme un coq en pâte, il pouvait redevenir honnête, il n'avait que de bons exemples. Non, c'est dans le sang; il se cassera le cou, avec sa politique' (Ah! the poor wretch! ! . . . He [Florent] came here for an easy life, to be fattened up and taken care of like a rooster; he could have become an honest man again, he had nothing but good examples all around him. No, it's in the blood; he'll break his neck, with his politics) (*RM*, I, 786). Apart from the obvious allusion to Florent's perceived state, and in keeping with the conceit of the 'bataille des Gras et des Maigres' ('battle between the Fat and the Thin') which underpins the whole novel, the description of Florent as 'un coq en pâte', an expression which also translates as someone who is 'in clover', 'living the life of Riley', or well-off and overly happy with himself, is particularly telling. In *L'Assommoir*, Lantier, another of Zola's 'Communards manqués', is also referred to as 'un coq' and, as a character, even more than Florent, conforms to the anti-Communard dual interpretation of the term to designate both a political revolutionary and a moral and sexual deviant (*RM*, I, 635). Furthermore, there is a direct link between the 'coq' and the conflagrations of 1871 for, as Philippe Régnier points out, in the slang of the period, 'le lancer du coq rouge' (literally, 'to throw the red cockerel') actually meant 'to commit arson'.[43] According to the Napoleonic Code, incendiaries and arsonists were classified as murderers and faced the death penalty. Arsonists were therefore criminals in civil as well as political terms, which is no doubt why any ex-Communard found guilty of murder or arson was specifically denied amnesty in 1880.[44]

Just like Nietzsche's criminal-debtor, Florent fails to appreciate all the material comforts and moral examples offered to him and to 'repay his debt' both to Lisa and to the good burghers of Les Halles.[45] He even goes so far as to try to launch a revolutionary attack on his 'creditors'. From then on, he is not only deprived of all the benefits of living in society but must also submit himself to the vengeful violence of all 'injured' parties. The *petits bourgeois* of Les Halles thus consider themselves justified in their decision to persecute him and eventually him cast out with impunity, for they consider him to be not only ungrateful but also a dangerous threat to their own comfortable lives and to the social order in general.

In much the same way that he disapproved of the inhumane measures used by Thiers to bring the Communards to heel, Zola feels contempt for Lisa and disapproves of her methods. The final line of the novel, uttered by the artist Claude, makes this clear: 'quels gredins que les honnêtes gens!' ('what scoundrels these so-called honest folk are!') (*RM*, I, 895). Though the language in which Zola chose to issue his condemnation of the Versaillais repression at the time is telling in itself – 'on soigne les fous, on ne les assomme pas' ('the insane should be healed, not killed')[46] – in the novel it is still Lisa, the 'honest' bourgeoise, who represents the triumph of social and moral order over unlawful, revolutionary chaos, of the all-devouring Cain over the starving Abel, in what constitutes an interesting reversal by Zola of the standard anti-Communard interpretation of the biblical story as rehearsed by Du Camp (*LC*, IV, 326).

For Zola, Cain is not the envious, lazy revolutionary of anti-Communard rhetoric, but neither is he the Romantic rebel opposed to the stolid conformist Abel we find in Byron's *Cain: A Mystery* or Baudelaire's 'Abel et Caïn' in *Les Fleurs du mal*. While still holding on to the biblical depiction of Cain as a dishonest glutton, Zola recasts him in the dual role of the overfed bourgeois capitalist and reactionary Versaillais, while turning Abel into the starving, idealistic, worker-revolutionary-Communard destined to be consumed and digested by some great machine (Paris) in some great holocaust (*RM*, I, 626, 805). 'La bataille des Gras et des Maigres', first conceived by Zola in 1868, thus acquires a new political and memorialist dimension after the Commune.

If Zola the bourgeois condemns the Cains of this world, he nevertheless still understands their point of view, even sharing some of their fears and obsessions and, in this respect, as well as in his cynical, mocking portrayal of the novel's revolutionaries, *Le Ventre de Paris* fully reflects the conservative and reactionary *Zeitgeist* of the immediate aftermath of the Commune. Zola the humanist, however, has no truck with either the Cains or the Abels of this world, whichever way one may wish to define them. In the final analysis, it is Madame François, who significantly belongs in neither camp and is the only character in the novel of whom Zola really approves, who perhaps best exemplifies his own ambivalent position (*RM*, I, 806).

L'Assommoir

Just as Zola's portrayal of Florent in *Le Ventre de Paris* owes much to real-life revolutionaries such as Gustave Flourens, so the character of Gervaise in *L'Assommoir* shares many of the traits attributed to the working-class women who participated in the Commune, not least the fact that she is a laundress. Since before the eighteenth century, laundresses had been saddled with a reputation as promiscuous, vulgar, hard-drinking women who often picked fights and enjoyed wrestling physically with other women.[47] To Zola's contemporary readers, therefore, the laundress was already a well-known stock character in bawdy vaudevilles and operettas. However, not only were laundresses considered especially erotic by the bourgeoisie during this period because of their loose, revealing clothes and because they handled men's underwear, they were also among those chiefly identified as *pétroleuses*.[48] With this thought in mind, it is worthwhile looking again at Edgar Degas's many studies of laundresses at work. *Les Repasseuses* (c.1884), for example, manages to combine the perceived erotic animality of the two women depicted with that classic emblem of the *pétroleuse*, the bottle. This painting, like Zola's novel before it, would therefore have appeared particularly shocking to a contemporary audience on several levels.

Relatively tame by today's standards, *L'Assommoir* caused a furore on publication owing to its language, subject matter and deliberate violation of the period's accepted literary conventions,[49] but arguably also because by setting the working classes centre stage the novel no doubt revived memories of the recent past that some of Zola's contemporaries would have wished to erase.[50] In 1875, while Zola was writing the novel, 'la question communarde' was very much back on the nation's agenda after a temporary hiatus from 1873 to 1874. Demands for amnesty for ex-Communards were now growing in number amid the strengthening of the republican position, and police registers for the period recorded that the Commune was again a topic of conversation in the city's bars and workshops.[51] For many this was all deeply troubling, for in the bourgeois public's imagination, and in Zola's own, the Commune was still inextricably bound up with a vision of the uncontrolled violence and passion of the mob, and the collapse of moral and social order; a perception that the state-commissioned inquiry into the causes of the Commune endorsed on the basis of a presumed causal link between working-class alcoholism and insurrection.[52]

Two cases involving laundresses are particularly worth noting in relation to the genesis of Zola's protagonist Gervaise, both of which would certainly have been well known to the author in his capacity as a reporter during the Communard trials in Versailles: that of Eugénie (*aka* Léontine or Léonie) Suétens, and that of Marie-Jeanne Moussu (reported in the *Gazette des Tribunaux* on 23 September 1871). Suétens was sentenced to death along with five other women for apparently having set fire to the Palais de la Légion d'Honneur and houses in the rue de Lille. The women were reported to have been heard screaming out 'Il faut que Paris saute' (Paris must be blown up).[53] However, while all the women admitted to having supported the Commune, they claimed to have gone to the barricades just to be with their menfolk and denied any involvement in the actual raising of the fires. Their pleas were ignored on the basis that the women had prior convictions for petty crimes and that their sexual histories contravened the bourgeois moral standards of the period, all of which constituted further 'proof' of their guilt. At the time of her arrest Suétens was twenty-five and had been living with a man who was not her husband for six years, and it is worth noting that Gervaise, when we first meet her, is aged twenty-two, unmarried and living with Lantier. The case was reported in both France and England and the severity of the sentences meted out to the women caused even *Le Figaro* and the writer Jules Claretie, both sympathetic to Versailles, to declare that the treatment of the women had been overly harsh given that only two of the seventeen male Communard leaders put on trial received the death penalty. The women's sentences were subsequently reduced to deportation and life-long hard labour.

Moussu, the other laundress of note, confessed that she had tried to set fire to her lover's house in June 1871. She too was duly sentenced to death in spite of the fact that her actions were clearly not politically motivated.[54] Her unhappy story finds its distorted echo in that of Gervaise, who, similarly fast approaching the end of her tether with Coupeau, feels that she would like to '[ficher] en personne le feu au bazar' (*RM*, II, 629) (set fire to the whole shebang). It is worth noting, too, that this insight into Gervaise's thoughts immediately precedes her ill-advised acceptance of her past lover Lantier's invitation to accompany him to a seedy café-concert in (revolutionary) Montmartre, where a flesh-baring Mademoiselle Amanda is to be heard singing obscenely suggestive and state-censored songs.[55] What starts out as an innocent respite from her daily drudgery soon turns into an alcohol-fuelled, sexually charged night out that leads directly to Gervaise's moral degradation.

While normally a gentle, loving and rather naïve woman, Gervaise proves herself capable of displaying uninhibited violence as demonstrated spectacularly in her washhouse fight with Virginie and again against her own daughter Nana, to whom she provides no moral guidance whatsoever. Gervaise is guilty of sexual transgression, religion plays no real part in her life apart from the perfunctory rituals of marriage, baptisms and funerals and, as the novel progresses, she becomes a dirty, foul-mouthed, lazy alcoholic attempting to sell herself on the streets. It could be argued that Zola's laundress lacks what might be taken to be the most obvious attribute of the Communard woman – an interest in politics – but, as the above cases demonstrate, many of the working-class women involved in the insurrection were not particularly politically motivated either. If there were indeed some women who like Louise Michel were activists and who did fight on the barricades out of political conviction, or who at least became politicized during the conflict itself, many others joined the Commune as *cantinières* and *ambulancières* in order to help their men by providing food and tending to the wounded.[56] Thus it is not her politics (or lack of them) that would have made Gervaise seem so shocking to Zola's contemporary readers but rather the fact that she shares so many of the pejorative characteristics of the laundress/*pétroleuse* stereotype exemplified by women such as Moussu and Suétens.[57]

As the novel progresses, Gervaise's husband Coupeau displays certain characteristics attributed to the lazy, working-class alcholic buffoon of anti-Communard discourse. Polichinelle and Guignol, as discussed earlier in the texts by Monselet and Du Camp, were terms regularly applied to the Communards, and it therefore comes as no surprise to find Coupeau described as such, significantly in the same passage where Gervaise dreams of committing arson (*RM*, II, 629). The reference to Coupeau as Polichinelle then is not only in keeping with the carnivalesque aspect of the novel, which in itself recalls the Commune, but it also looks ahead to the end of the novel when Coupeau, now suffering from *delirium tremens* as a result of his alcoholism, is once again likened to Polichinelle as he dances round his padded cell tormented by visions of fiery skies and of being executed by some 'machine' set up against a wall (*RM*, I, V, 787–8, 793). Where do such hallucinations come from? There is nothing in Coupeau's previous life that would provoke these particular thoughts in him, rather they come from Zola's own overheated imagination influenced by representations of the *Semaine sanglante* and Versaillais summary executions by machine-gun, in images such as those by Chifflart and Pichio, and written accounts by Monselet, Du Camp and others of Communards who supposedly suffered from *delirium tremens* and were locked up in mental institutions.

If Zola does not directly acknowledge the influence of contemporary depictions of Communards on the creation of his characters, and if he claims that *L'Assommoir* is primarily a novel about the everyday lives of the working-class and that any engagement with politics is to remain quietly in the background, it is important to note that in his more detailed plan for the novel he nevertheless specifically states that the wedding episode is to have a political dimension: 'le mariage de Coupeau et Gervaise. La politique' (*RM*, II, 1546, 1550). As with Florent's journey from Neuilly to Les Halles, the apparently arbitrary route followed by Gervaise and her wedding party from the heights of Montmartre (the birthplace of the Commune) to the city centre soon reveals itself to be an allegory of the Commune's struggle and ultimate failure to re-appropriate urban space on behalf of the Parisian working class and, in addition, much like volume VI of Du Camp's *Paris: ses organes*, as an ironic commentary on some of the debates and preoccupations of the early Third Republic.

Like Gervaise's saint's-day feast later on in the novel, the wedding-party's descent into Paris is a key moment in the novel when the lower classes are seen to assert their fundamental right to free speech in a display of what Bakhtin refers to as the 'culture of the marketplace and of folk laughter' that, while it has always existed, has never merged with the official cultural and aesthetic values of the bourgeoisie.[58] Just like the Roman Saturnalias that preceded them, carnivals and folk festivals exist, according to Bakhtin, as 'second worlds': they are subject only to their own laws, and express a universal spirit of freedom and renewal, and a (temporary) return to a golden age. As Charles Rearick also reminds us, with particular relevance to *L'Assommoir*, *fêtes* are 'revivers of communal spirit or safety valves releasing tensions built up from workaday cares and discontents'.[59] They were also long known to governments and the Church as potential *trouble-fêtes* where the celebrations often turned to protest and violence.[60] Unlike Lefebvre – who sees the *fête* as a positive phenomenon, as a spontaneous, euphoric 'moment' which has the potential to effect change and even revolution[61] – other commentators have argued that carnivals are by their very nature a mere interruption of normal behaviour not a transformation of it.[62] The Commune lasted just seventy-two days, too short a time to implement any lasting social reforms, though one could argue that the separation of Church and State and the educational reforms of the Third Republic in the 1880s had originally been on the Commune's stated agenda, and certainly there is no denying the Commune's inspirational power for working-class and socialist movements throughout the world. Nevertheless, at the time that Zola was writing *L'Assommoir*, the Communards, at least those who survived the slaughter of May 1871 and who had not been imprisoned or deported, were back in their *faubourgs* seemingly no better off than they had been before 18 March 1871. Similarly, the wedding-party's spontaneous descent into Paris is no more than a fleeting diversion from everyday life. It is all over in a flash during the course of a summer storm, an image that as already noted had come to be synonymous with the Commune. As with Florent's inevitable return to Cayenne in *Le Ventre de Paris*, Zola takes Gervaise and Coupeau back full circle to Montmartre where they belong, to eke out their miserable existence.

Let us turn now specifically to the details of the wedding party's descent into the city centre. The first stop en route to the Louvre via the rue Saint-Denis, the rue de Cléry and the rue du Mail is the place des Victoires where, at the foot of the statue of Louis XIV, Gervaise pauses to retie her shoelace. The reference to the statue is by no means a casual one. As Zola's contemporary Parisian readers would no doubt have known from all the press coverage and cartoons devoted to the subject – such as that by Cham in *Le Monde illustré* on 5 May 1877 (Figure 17, third row on the left) and the satirical daily *Le Charivari* on 26 October 1876 and 15 April 1877 – the monarchists had been actively campaigning amid predictable republican opposition to have the statue cleaned and restored. The restoration of the statue – if not of the monarchy itself – finally took place in 1877. In the novel, meanwhile, Gervaise's pause at the foot of the statue provides an excuse for much predictable bawdy banter at her expense; but the carnivalesque juxtaposition of the Sun King in all his pious majesty and the laundress irreverently lifting her skirt is symbolic of the working-class Parisian's and the Communard's contempt for monarchy and authority in general. It is also symbolic, to a qualified extent, of Zola's own contempt. However, this is not the only important link between the place des Victoires and the Commune. A contemporary engraving that appeared in one of the souvenir collections of illustrations of the two Paris sieges published in 1872 shows the people of Paris and the National Guard driving the cannon they appropriated on the butte Montmartre on 18 March 1871 down into the city centre via the place des Victoires.[63] Zola's contemporary Parisian readers would certainly have also remembered the part played during the

Figure 17 'REVUE COMIQUE, PAR CHAM'. *Le Monde illustré*, 5 May 1877.
(© British Library Board. All Rights Reserved. Shelfmark F23)

Commune by the church of Notre-Dame des Victoires, which is located just around the corner from the place des Victoires and adjacent to the rue de Mail. On 17 May 1871, the day after demolishing the Vendôme Column, the Commune carried out a raid on Notre-Dame des Victoires taking possession of some of its precious objects and relics and displaying a number of skeletons recovered from the crypt outside the church itself. These, they claimed, were the remains of people murdered by Catholic priests. Such gruesome anti-clerical purges emulated those that had taken place in July 1848 when various nuns and priests were similarly accused of, among other things, 'hysterical behaviour', sexual perversity and paedophilia.[64] The Commune was, of course, renowned for its anti-clericalism, and not surprisingly during *la Semaine sanglante* the clergy was the only civilian group to be systematically targeted as hostages.[65]

Notre-Dame de Paris and the Panthéon – significantly, two of the monuments singled out by Monsieur Madinier from the top of the Vendôme Column, when Gervaise's wedding-party climbs it – were also the focus of Communard anti-clerical aggression. Notre-Dame only narrowly escaped complete destruction when chairs in the choir were set alight, and the arms of the cross on the Panthéon (which had been reinstated as a secular building) were sawn off and replaced by a red flag. However, the type of anti-clericalism which brought about the purge of Notre-Dame des Victoires had its roots in a much more fundamental and deep-seated peasant and working-class tradition of hatred and suspicion towards an authoritarian Catholic Church, which was increasingly perceived as being out of touch with the real needs of the people; as imposing its views, hypocritically according to some, on public morality; and as suppressing popular culture.

Consequently in *L'Assommoir*, as later in *La Terre* (1887), the Church is often ridiculed and its rituals looked on as incomprehensible or irrelevant (*RM*, II, 436, 668, 769; IV, 527). In a social milieu where even if workers had wished to attend church, they were prevented from doing so by having to work twelve-hour days, including Sundays, it is not surprising that the old French tradition of 'contes gaulois' (farces and obscenities directed at the clergy), and stories of occultism such as those to be found in *Le Juif errant* by Eugène Sue (significantly one of Lantier's favourite authors), were very popular, fuelling old fears of clerical perversity and Jesuit Inquisition-style activities. The apparently innocent episode in the place des Victoires, under the gaze of a king who was renowned for his strong Jesuit sympathies, exemplifies the Commune's 'victory' over the monarchy and the Catholic Church. Having 'conquered' the place des Victoires, the wedding-party proceeds to the Louvre via the rue Croix-des-Petits-Champs.

If we wipe away some of the layers of the city's topographical palimpsest we find that the rue Croix-des-Petits-Champs originally formed the outer western reaches of the ancient burial wasteland of Les Saints-Innocents, which stretched out as far as the rue Saint-Denis to the east and to the church and cemetery of Les Saints-Innocents, which today forms part of Les Halles. According to Du Camp, this vast area was notorious from the Middle Ages right up to the eighteenth century, when it was finally sanitized and paved over, as the cause of the many plagues that afflicted the city. Du Camp also states that while the rich enjoyed dignified burials, the bodies of the poor were just thrown into large communal ditches containing some 1,200 to 1,500 bodies. Once the ditches filled up, the oldest bones were disinterred and stacked up in the eves of the arches that surrounded the cemetery (*PSO*, VI, 124–6). As is usual in *Les Rougon-Macquart* all comic interludes are underpinned – literally, in this case – by a much darker pessimism. As they walk over old ghosts, Gervaise and Coupeau's happiness, such as it is, can only be short-lived.

In a novel set in the 1850s but written and published after 1871, any mention of the Louvre would inevitably have acted as a sobering reminder for Zola's contemporary readers of all the treasures that would most certainly have been lost had the museum not miraculously escaped the flames in May 1871. Furthermore, if for today's reader Madinier's inaccurate historical reference to the balcony from which Charles IX had supposedly once fired on the people of Paris is no more than another example in this whole set-piece of Zola's apparent collusion with his implied educated bourgeois reader or yet another distorted political echo in the novel,[66] for the contemporary reader it would immediately have triggered an association with the infamous Saint Bartholomew's Day massacre, which, as discussed earlier, was yet another coded reference to the Commune (*RM*, II, 445–7; *PSO*, VI, 276). The already droll image evoked by the phrase 'ça leur cassait le cou' (it was neckbreaking), the reference to the people being shot, and the final retreat from the Louvre by the members of the wedding-party who are so tired their legs are said to be 'broken' ('les jambes cassées') – an image which, incidentally, is also used to describe Florent in *Le Ventre de Paris* (*RM*, I, 606) – can no longer be read innocently following 1871. In the same way that Balzac in *Sur Catherine de Medicis* uses the Saint Bartholomew's Day massacre as the means by which to comment on recent events in France in his own time and extrapolates from his comparison a pattern underlying all popular uprisings, so Zola uses the reference to Charles IX in *L'Assommoir* to comment on the indiscriminate slaughter of the people of Paris by Thiers during *la Semaine sanglante* and also, like Du Camp in *Paris: ses organes*, as another warning against the dangers, in 1875, of allowing the Catholic Church to interfere yet again in matters of state.

Meanwhile, in yet another space and time, as we rejoin the wedding party outside the Louvre, we should pause to note that Gervaise's wedding takes place on 29 July 1850. This is consequently before the clearance of the notorious slums (immortalized by Balzac in *La Cousine Bette*), which, for centuries, had crowded the area between the Louvre and the courtyard of the Tuileries palace until the completion of the Louvre extensions in 1857 by Napoleon III. While the clearances had in fact started in 1849, in 1850 most of this area remained untouched, and both the large cour du Carrousel and the smaller cour Carrée still formed part of the city's public space. Napoleon III's scheme, which inspired Baudelaire's meditation on the death of the old city in 'Le Cygne', not only displaced the slum dwellers but also effectively closed off these areas to the people of Paris. It is perhaps not coincidental, therefore, that while people of Gervaise's class were encouraged to visit the Louvre for their edification during both the Second Republic and the Second Empire, the wedding-party only feels comfortable once it has left the museum and gained access to the Louvre courtyard where, finally, it can breathe easily again. The slum dwellers have thus, symbolically, reclaimed a part of the city centre, if only momentarily.

Having left the Louvre completely disorientated but suitably edified, the members of the wedding-party seek shelter from the pouring rain under the Pont-Royal where they appear, at last, to find a space in the city where they feel at home. After making an (unsuccessful) effort to be on their best behaviour in the Louvre, the women now relax by the river while the men amuse themselves throwing stones and listening to the echoes of their cries of 'cochon' (swine) under the arch of the bridge. Despite the apparent carnivalesque jollity, however, this scene is unsettling on several levels. The cries of 'cochon' look ahead to Coupeau's rendition of *Qué cochon d'enfant* during Gervaise's *fête*, but they also echo Gervaise's own anguished and disgusted 'Oh! le cochon! Le cochon! ... il a tout sali ...' (oh! the swine! the swine! ... he's made a mess everywhere ...) on discovering the inebriated Coupeau asleep on the marital bed in a pool of vomit, the turning point in the novel which forces Gervaise back into Lantier's bed (*RM*, II, 593, 631). Zola's use of 'cortège', rather than 'noce' to is also interesting, since it carries with it overtones of a funeral, as well as a wedding, procession while the references to the countryside seem distinctly at odds with the image of a black and filthy river, a dark vault-like bridge, and Mademoiselle Remanjou's tears for a lost lover (*RM*, II, 447–8). The image evoked here is, again, one of death and a descent into hell. The Seine could be the Styx or the Acheron, the dark vault of the bridge a tomb, and the men's disembodied voices, the voices of the dead. The description of the space under the bridge, 'comme du fond d'un trou' (like the bottom of a pit) looks ahead to Le Père Bru's 'Trou la, trou la, trou la la!' at the *fête*, and presages Gervaise's death in his vacated 'trou' under the stairway (*RM*, II, 588, 796).[67] In Zola's version of carnival, laughter and festive madness do not act as a regenerative force but instead leave the individual trapped and alienated in a terrifying vacuum with death as the only possible release.

Images of death and foreboding haunt the whole of the wedding episode from Gervaise's dress, which belonged to a dead woman, to the sphinxes and the *Radeau de la Méduse* in the Louvre, to Bazouge's final, unequivocal 'quand on est mort, c'est pour longtemps' (you're a long time dead) (*RM*, II, 463). The earlier suggestion of a visit to the tombs of Abélard and Héloïse in the cemetery at Père-Lachaise, as a way of passing the time before the wedding dinner, foreshadows Gervaise's visit to Coupeau at Lariboisière, where the white-sheeted beds in the hospital ward are likened to a row of headstones, 'un petit Père-Lachaise', and also Coupeau's and Gervaise's own deaths (*RM*, II, 440, 696). Père-Lachaise and the Pont Royal also bring us back, inevitably, to the Commune; to the massacres and burials at Père-Lachaise itself, but also to the mass burials in the rest of the city's cemeteries, all along the banks of the Seine and around the base of the Tour Saint-Jacques (another of the monuments picked out by M. Madinier from the Vendôme Column) in the aftermath of *la Semaine sanglante*. *Le Moniteur universel*, and Zola himself, were to describe how the city had been turned into a charnel house.[68] Later, however, Du Camp was to pour scorn on such reports, claiming that only sixty-two bodies had been exhumed from around the Tour Saint-Jacques, the square des Batignolles and the square du Temple (*LC*, II, 304).

From the Seine, one of the grisliest parts of the city connected with the Commune, the party moves on to two locations associated with its fleeting triumphs: the Tuileries and the Place Vendôme. Zola does not let the wedding-party linger in the Tuileries gardens and yet, in just one simple sentence he effectively evokes the special atmosphere of these most urban of gardens and recalls one of the key images depicted in many impressionist paintings, most notably Manet's *La Musique aux Tuileries* (1862). The suggestion that the 'bel ordre' (orderliness) of the wedding-party couples would be upset by the children playing in the Tuileries gardens is heavily ironic since it is far more likely that the rowdy wedding-party would have disrupted the genteel strollers and the games of the middle-class children than the other way round, and is reminiscent of Edouard Hubert's account in *Le Monde illustré* in 1871 of the invasion of the Tuileries by 'la canaille' (the rabble) (*RM*, II, 448). While Zola has Gervaise's wedding-party walk freely across the gardens, in 1850 this may well not have been possible as the gardens were not opened to the general public until after Napoleon III became emperor, and even then visitors would not have been allowed in unless suitably attired.

Where once bourgeois Second Empire audiences of the kind parodied by Manet listened to Offenbach and popular café-concert songs at the Tuileries, during the Commune audiences 15,000–strong sang along to *L'Internationale*, listened to edifying arias by Gounod, Verdi and Meyerbeer, laughed at satirical political sketches, and enjoyed recitals of Hugo's poems. It was on Sunday 21 May 1871, however, that, during one such fund-raising Commune concert, the Versaillais began their entry into the city virtually unhindered. The concert planned for the following Sunday, 28 May, did not take place and by then not only were some 25,000 people dead, but the Tuileries palace had been turned into a burnt-out ruin. Zola's reference to the Tuileries gardens, no less than the unspoken reference to the palace (still hauntingly present in the Paris of the time), would therefore have evoked several disturbing memories for ex-Communards, monarchists, Bonapartists, as well as bourgeois republicans.

The wedding-party, still with time to kill, finally makes its way to the Place Vendôme and at Monsieur Madinier's suggestion reluctantly agrees to climb the Column. The long dark climb up the Vendôme Column's narrow spiral staircase provides yet another opportunity for bawdy humour and behaviour barely disguised by a thin veneer of so-called 'honnêteté' (respectability) with the women, like mice, giggling as they are teased, tickled and pinched in the legs by the men. The reference to mice is one of many examples in the novel, as in most of the literature and visual arts of the nineteenth century, of the natural association in the bourgeois mind between the working classes, particularly working-class women, and animals. Gervaise, for example, is repeatedly eroticized as a cat or dog. The image evoked by Zola here, however, is also sugges-tive of vermin (the working-class) gnawing away at the very heart of the Column (imperialism) and shaking it to its very core (*RM*, II, 449). A further allusion to the Column's destruction is discovered later, during the contest of strength at the foundry, when we are told that Bec-Salé would have happily flattened the Vendôme like a pancake (*RM*, II, 532). But here, in the Place Vendôme itself, the scene is reminiscent of the many anti-Communard caricatures and photographs which circulated in Paris in 1871, and in particular of Jules Raudnitz's 'Saturnales de la place Vendôme', one of the images in his series of stereographic *diableries* entitled *Le Sabbat rouge*, where grotesque plaster-cast figures are used to represent the Communards.[69]

The laughter rings hollow once again and the suggestion of possible entrapment and suffocation in the dark and claustrophobic Column is deeply troubling. The physical constriction in this 'trou' or 'tuyau de cheminée' (hole, chimney flue) of these working-class characters in their seemingly never-ending struggle to ascend the Column, and the sense of dysphoria and disorientation they experience can be seen as symbolic of their political and social condition (*RM*, II, 449). When the party finally reaches the summit there is a distinct sense of emptiness and disem-bodiment which recalls the scene under the Pont Royal, except that now the laughter has stopped: 'quelle culbute, sacré Dieu! Les hommes, un peu pâles, regardaient la place. On se serait cru en l'air, séparé de tout' (Holy God, what a tumble! The men, rather pale, looked out on to the square. It felt like falling through the air, separated from everything). The 'culbute' (tumble, fall) is another reminder of the Column's fate. It also anticipates Coupeau's fateful fall while working as a roofer which precipitates his decline into a slothful alcoholic and, along with Monsieur Madinier's reference to Les Invalides, is also symbolic of Gervaise's own physical deformity. It announces too her later 'culbute dans la boisson' (descent into alcoholism) and in its sexual sense her promiscuity and moral 'fall' (*RM*, II, 705). And, finally, in the penultimate chapter of the novel we are told that her grotesque shadow 'faisait la culbute à chaque pas' (somersaulted at every step) and that she looked like something out of a Punch and Judy show, 'un vrai guignol!' (*RM*, II, 772). The coded contemporary shorthand for the Commune and Communards hardly needs stressing yet again. The whole Vendôme set-piece can therefore be interpreted as an extended metaphor for Gervaise's struggle to elevate herself socially while the 'culbute' represents a sober warning that her bid for independence and her success will come to nothing and that disillusionment and death will soon follow; a fate she shares with the doomed Communards who posed so triumphantly for Bruno Braquehais's lens at the foot of the Column before its demolition on 16 May 1871.[70]

Like Florent in *Le Ventre de Paris* the members of this errant wedding-party have little control over their own lives. The salvation and purification offered by the final panoramic view from the Column of a cleansed and reborn Paris is for society as a whole, not for the individual. Like the unfortunate Parisians who supported the Commune, Gervaise and Coupeau are condemned to play out their allotted roles in life. For Zola as for many of his contemporaries it would appear that individual suffering and death are the terrible price to be paid to ensure the survival of the city and, by extension, the nation.

If *Le Ventre de Paris* betrays Zola's hostility to the Commune's leaders, *L'Assommoir* can, broadly speaking, be read as an example of Zola's compassion for those innocent, working-class men and women who, while he was actually writing the novel, were still being executed and deported on the most tenuous of evidence. Zola's apologia dated 1 January 1877, after the scandal caused by the novel, makes this clear:

> Il ne faut pas conclure que le peuple tout entier est mauvais, car mes personnages ne sont pas mauvais, ils ne sont qu'ignorants et gâtés par le milieu de rude besogne et de misère où ils vivent. (*RM*, II, 374)

> [We should not conclude that all working-class people are bad because my characters are not bad, they are only uneducated and damaged by the rough and poverty-stricken environment in which they live.]

He expressed much the same sentiment in an article in *Le Sémaphore de Marseille* on 17 August 1871 with regard to the otherwise innocent individuals who, he believed, had been persuaded through a combination of ignorance, mental weakness and sheer desperation to support the Commune.[71] And yet, in the novel itself, the strong implication is that Gervaise herself is responsible for the wretched life she has led and for her slow agonizing death (*RM*, II, 796). Like Florent in *Le Ventre de Paris* and like the Communards, she fails to take advantage of the opportunity offered to her to become a respectable member of society and consequently deserves her punishment. If Zola was eventually to condemn the actions of the Versaillais, if the counter-republican *Ordre moral* was to replace Napoleon III as his *bête noire* and if he was to feel sympathy towards the innocent people who suffered the brutal consequences of the repression, he was never able where the Commune was concerned to shake off the prejudices and myths of his own social class.[72]

Une page d'amour

Une page d'amour is not normally regarded as a novel with a political subtext. In fact, like *L'Œuvre*, which followed *Germinal* and *Le Rêve* after *La Terre*, *Une page d'amour*, written straight after *L'Assommoir* and before *Nana*, is usually seen as an interlude providing Zola with an opportunity to put aside, temporarily, the great historical and political themes of *Les Rougon-Macquart* and to concentrate on a more intimate psychological drama.[73] And yet, as the following analysis will demonstrate, this novel no less than *Le Ventre de Paris* and *L'Assommoir* contains a number of coded political references that modern readers may overlook but which, for contemporary Parisian readers, would have evoked memories of the recent past. The children's fancy-dress ball given by Juliette Deberle is one such example. The episode can be read as a miniature version of the costumed ball in *La Curée*, and thus as another indictment of Second Empire decadence (*RM*, I, 537–80). Zola's targets in *Une page d'amour* are again: bourgeois superficiality and extravagance in the form of the shallow, gossipy socialite Madame Deberle; voraciousness exemplified by the greedy, spoilt children at the party; and moral depravity among the adults, children and servants. But it is in the apparently innocuous (to the modern reader) marionette-show – a common vehicle for politically subversive satire in nineteenth-century France particularly during the Second Empire, with Napoleon III as the main target – that we should look to discover Zola's coded political satire on recent events.

Napoleon III was often caricatured as the bellicose and immoral Polichinelle and this could well be the case in the marionette scene in *Une page d'amour* (*RM*, II, 894–5), with the 'Commissaire' (Superintendent) as Alexander II of Russia or, more likely, Franz-Joseph of Austria in his capacity as occupier of Italy, and the 'Gendarme' (Policeman) as a good candidate for Pope Pius IX, whose power and position many devout French Catholics believed Napoleon III had undermined over the issue of Italian Unification in 1860. The 'Devil', meanwhile, could be taken to represent William of Prussia and the ensuing 'greatest battle of all' the French defeat at Sedan. Against this rich historical and memorialist background the marionette show is anything but a banal piece of children's entertainment used by Zola merely to bring Hélène and Deberle together. Their inclusion in the scene as spectators serves to illustrate the moral depravity that for Zola typified the imperial regime. Hélène's respectable reserve breaks down during the show and we are told explicitly that she and Deberle fall prey to Polichinelle's bad example. Hélène becomes aware of Deberle's hot breath on the back of her neck as she sits back in her chair and presses against Deberle's hand just as the performance comes to an end, with the red stage curtain reminiscent both of the red flag of the Commune and the red blood of *la Semaine sanglante* that together concluded the 'theatrical performance' of the Second Empire itself.

As already discussed, however, the figure of Polichinelle also came to be readily associated with the Communard. Du Camp, for example, in recalling the Punch and Judy performances in the Champs-Elysées during the Commune to the accompaniment of artillery fire around the Arc de Triomphe, talks of 'Polichinelle et le commissaire' dealing each other blows until the Devil finally appeared and carried away the 'Communard Polichinelle' (*LC*, II, 218). In *Une page d'amour*, therefore, Polichinelle could equally stand for the Communard, with Thiers as the Commissaire and MacMahon, who led the actual assault on Paris, as the Devil: 'au dénouement du drame, lorsque le diable parut . . . il y eut une suprême bataille, un égorgement général' (*RM*, II, 894) (then at the end of the drama, when the Devil appeared, there was an almighty battle and everyone's throat was cut.).

As is often the case with Zola, in satirizing the Second Empire he is also commenting on more recent events, and in addition to these two interpretations of the characters in the marionette show in *Une page d'amour* we should also consider yet another possible connection with the politics of the Third Republic. Just a few years before Zola wrote *Une page d'amour*, yet another Polichinelle made the news. At a time when all caricatures of MacMahon were strictly illegal, Manet's lithograph *Le Polichinelle* (1874), which many believed to bear a striking resemblance to the Marshal, had caused the authorities such concern that the image had been confiscated.[74] The timely inclusion of the puppet Polichinelle in Zola's novel of 1878, when MacMahon's unpopularity was reaching its peak, can therefore also be read as a subversive reference to the man first manipulated by Napoleon III during the Franco-Prussian war and then by Thiers before finally, and ironically, being elected head of state in 1873 only to be manipulated by the monarchists.

Meanwhile Zéphyrin, the 'petit soldat' (little soldier) may at first also appear to be another superfluous addition to the novel. With his shako and red trousers he bears more of a resemblance to Manet's *Le Fifre* (1866) than to any real soldier, at least until the army corrupts him. And yet, within the historical and political context outlined above, Zéphyrin symbolizes the amateurish and inadequate French army that stood little chance against the superior might of the Prussian military machine. Rosalie's comment: 'tous les garçons qui tombaient soldats devenaient bêtes à crever' (*RM*, II, 865) (all the boys who succumbed to (literally, fell into) soldiering became stupid to the point of bursting/dying), is a play on words in the sense of 'beasts to the slaughter' and is doubtless also indicative of Zola's own opinion of soldiers and military conflict.[75] The exaggerated and slangy use in this passage of the words 'tombaient' (fell), 'bêtes' (stupid) and 'crever' (die) add to the humour of the scene but also neatly sum up the whole disastrous episode of the Franco-Prussian War and the Commune. As he acquires the brash manners and low morals of the working-class Parisian lad-about-town, Zéphyrin also begins to resemble the anti-Communard stereotype of the undisciplined *fédéré*. His jauntiness also brings to mind again, as in *L'Assommoir*, the young National Guardsmen who posed for the photographer Braquehais in front of the Vendôme Column prior to its demolition and who most certainly did not survive *la Semaine sanglante*. Even more disturbingly, in his ill-fitting uniform Zéphyrin also brings to mind the contorted image of the young man in Alfred Roll's *L'Exécution d'un trompette sous la Commune* (1871?).[76]

Earlier in the novel the reference to Walter Scott's novel *Ivanhoe* is also imbued with dark symbolism. At one level Hélène, like Flaubert's Emma Bovary, is dangerously influenced by Scott's Romanticism and her reading of the novel contributes to her moral downfall.[77] However, the reference to *Ivanhoe* in particular can also be read as another condemnation of the atrocities and absurdities of civil wars. Rebecca's nursing of the wounded Ivanhoe as the battle rages beneath her window presages Hélène's later nursing of the invalid Jeanne, but the scene also looks ahead to *La Débâcle*, when Henriette similarly tends to her brother the Communard Maurice who has been accidentally fatally wounded by his friend the Versaillais Jean Macquart, and all the while Paris burns below their attic window (*RM*, V, 907).

If the Punch and Judy scene is Zola's way of covertly allegorizing the political causes of the Commune in *Une page d'amour*, the panorama provides the means by which he allegorizes its social causes. Whereas *Le*

Ventre de Paris and *L'Assommoir*, as their titles suggest, engage with the visceral reality of life in the city at street level, *Une page d'amour* offers a quite different perspective on the city's topography. With only one notable exception, Hélène's visits to la Mère Fétu in the sordid tenement reached by way of the passage des Eaux, all the descriptions of Paris in this novel are panoramic cityscapes. Prendergast's suggestion that the distance afforded by the panoramic view provides 'a structuring device which – especially when placed at both the opening and close of the novel – serves to hold the teeming life the [novel records] in an ordered artistic representation' would certainly seem applicable to *Une page d'amour*, where each of the five parts of the novel concludes with a panorama of the city which mirrors the unfolding drama of Hélène's life.[78] However, taken together, the panoramas of *Une page d'amour* also comprise an allegory of the history of the other main protagonist in the novel, the city of Paris.

Zola's use of the panorama is also important for two further reasons: firstly, it enables Zola to suggest the totality of the dramatic effects of the Commune on the city, and secondly the panoramic view can be seen as emblematic of the nineteenth-century bourgeoisie's distanced relationship with the city. Prendergast suggests that 'the transcendent view can easily become the comfortable view'. In *Une page d'amour*, it is precisely this 'comfortable' high view from the elegant bourgeois apartments of an *hôtel particulier* in Passy that Zola wishes to portray. The closeted life of the women in the novel, therefore, is emblematic of the life led by the bourgeoisie in general, who did all they could to distance themselves from working-class Parisians. The Impressionist artist Berthe Morisot's *Vue de Paris des hauteurs du Trocadéro* (1872–73) exemplifies this same bourgeois distance from the great teeming mass of the city, which she depicts as a blurry haze on the distant horizon in the painting. Morisot's two bourgeois women turn their backs on Paris; they do not know the city and do not wish to know it. Only the little girl in the painting looks, out of curiosity, in the direction of the city, but still without crossing the divide. As for Hélène and Jeanne, we are told that they have only ever ventured out into the city three times since their arrival in Passy, and each time they have returned to their apartments, their heads in a spin, having been overwhelmed by the chaos of the city streets. The city is an entertaining spectacle for the bourgeoisie to enjoy, but only, it would seem, from a respectable distance (*RM*, II, 854).

Juliette Deberle's excursions into the city to attend the theatre or a dress-fitting at her high-class couturier, excursions which we only hear about, are really only an extension of her salon and garden-based social life, and even the male characters in the novel have little to do with life outside the strict confines of Passy and their own social class. If Zola has Deberle tend to la Mère Fétu, he does so for the purposes of the plot since, unlike the altruistic Docteur Pascal, the main protagonist of the final novel in the *Rougon-Macquart* series, Deberle does not appear to have any other working-class patients. Similarly, little is made of the fact that Rambaud, Hélène's future second husband, has a business in the rue Rambuteau in Les Halles. He never talks about it and certainly does not take Hélène there at the end of the novel when they return to Paris to close the business down. If Hélène and Rambaud do not belong to the upper bourgeoisie and are not even native Parisians, they neverthe-less share the same sense of class distance from the city as the Deberles and their circle. The panorama in *Une page d'amour*, therefore, serves to make manifest the gulf which exists between the bourgeoisie and working-class Parisians, particularly those living in the slums on the city's periphery such as Montmartre, which, importantly, is often re-ferred to in the descriptions of the city. And, from the social and political point of view, it was this physical and mental gulf between the bour-geoisie and the working classes that contributed to the social unrest experienced by the city during the latter part of the Second Empire and which was one of the factors that led to the Commune.

In social and geographical terms Passy is the complete antithesis of Montmartre, but when we consider the roles these districts played in relation to the Commune the difference between them becomes even more acute. Montmartre, of course, was where the Commune origi-nated while the upper-class residents of Passy, like Morisot's parents, for example, supported Versailles.[79] It is no coincidence, therefore, that after entering Paris at the Point-du-Jour on 21 May 1871, the Versaillais were able to advance swiftly through the friendly territory of Passy to take the heights of the Trocadéro by the early hours of 22 May. As in *Le Ventre de Paris* and *L'Assommoir*, Zola's choice of location is not innocent in *Une page d'amour* and nor are his panoramic descriptions.

In the panorama at the end of Part One of the novel, Paris is dis-cerned as soft and radiant on an early spring morning, like a beautiful woman gently rousing herself from her slumbers. Hélène, like bourgeois Paris on the eve of the Franco-Prussian War and the Commune, leads a quiet, respectable life, but already she begins to suffer from an indefin-able malaise that both troubles and excites her (*RM*, II, 846–7). If the city at first appears soft and feminine, its hard, disquieting, masculine side soon surfaces. Paris is, and will remain, distant, turbulent and unknowable. It could be argued, as in *Le Ventre de Paris*, that Zola's description of Paris is very much in keeping with stock Romantic representations of the city and that its 'devouring flames' are merely a clichéd reference to the sexual passion that will soon burn and devour Hélène, but after 1871 such imagery acquires further resonance. The active description 'incendié le soir' (set on fire in the evening) acts as a powerful adumbrative reminder of the conflagrations, the frenzied passion of the Parisian mob, and the bloodletting of the civil war (*RM*, II, 908–9). Eventually Paris becomes like an inferno or volcano emitting blood-red clouds of fire and brimstone (*RM*, II, 974). Zola's descriptions bear close comparison with contemporary accounts such as that by Théophile Gautier, who similarly talks of 'ce Vésuve ouvert au milieu de la ville' (this gaping Vesuvius in the middle of the city).[80] The image of the volcano reappears in Zola's description of the city at sunset in *L'Œuvre*, another Paris-set novel inspired by sublime and apocalyptic visions of Paris in May 1871 (*RM*, IV, 340),[81] while in the closing scenes of *La Débâcle* the author, drawing on imagery reminiscent of Chifflart's 'Histoire de Paris: Les nuits de mai' (Figure 5), finally grants his imagination free rein as he describes the city being devoured by flames during *la Semaine sanglante*.

Hélène, like the Communards, is swept up in a passionate frenzy and, try as she might, she cannot defeat the passion that threatens to destroy her, and in the end she knows that she must succumb to her strong desire for life and love (*RM*, II, 906–7). She makes her bid for independence and believes that she is strong enough to survive and consummate her happiness. But passion, like fire, is by its very nature ephemeral; it is exciting while it rages and burns, but ultimately, in Zola's universe at least, it must die out, leaving only spent ashes in its wake. Paris, that beautiful, decadent fairytale city of the Second Empire, has finally to be destroyed, like Babylon, Sodom and Gomorrah, or Rome (*RM*, II, 911–12).

For Hélène and for the bourgeoisie of the Second Empire, the warnings are there right from the start; Paris, we are told, often worried Hélène and Jeanne with its 'haleines chaudes et troublantes' (hot, disturbing vapours) (*RM*, II, 854). But the warnings remain unheeded. The 'haleines chaudes' look ahead to Deberle's hot breath on Hélène's shoulders and his declaration of love during the children's ball, but also to the end of Part Four of the novel, when Jeanne sits alone contemplating the turbulent city below her, inhaling its miasma of crime and filth and looking at Les Invalides, the Panthéon and the Tour Saint-Jacques on the horizon, while at the same time Hélène and Deberle have sex in Malignon's attic room above the dark, muddy waters of the Passage des Eaux (*RM*, II, 1030). Given what we know already about Les Invalides (here symbolic of Jeanne's infirmity), the Panthéon (a mausoleum), and the Tour Saint-Jacques (a makeshift burial site for Communards), this passage would appear to be more than just a Freudian allusion to Hélène's descent into moral depravity.[82] It is highly significant that these are the only monuments Jeanne recognizes and that they all represent death. The description of Paris as if it were a cesspool of filth, crime and wretchedness once again, as in *Le Ventre de Paris* and *L'Assommoir*, recalls Zola's own sense impressions in the wake of *la Semaine sanglante* when he walked the city streets, his hand over his nostrils so as to keep out the stench of putrefying bodies lying under the hot sun.[83]

Hélène's nightmarish walk under the arch of the Passage des Eaux on her way to seek out Malignon's attic rooms also recalls the disturbing scene under the arch of the Pont Royal and in the confined space of the Vendôme Column in *L'Assommoir* (*RM*, II, 995). Hélène experiences the same sense of dysphoria and disorientation, mixed with an element of illicit excitement, as Gervaise and her wedding-party. Zola's vocabulary and imagery in very similar in both novels – 'voûte' (vault), 'trou noir' (black hole), 'boyau' (bowel/gut) – and the overall sensation evoked is again one of fear, powerlessness and of a descent into the putrid rivers of hell.

As in most naturalist novels, water is a very important image in *Une page d'amour* and as the storm clouds gather in Part One, blotting out the horizon 'dans la débâcle d'un chaos' (in a chaotic struggle), Zola warns that soon the whole city will be engulfed (*RM*, II, 846–7). While the references to the 'débâcle' and the submerged city can again be read as Freudian allusions to Hélène's forthcoming moral struggle and subsequent submersion into the dark depths of sexual passion, the choice of metaphor is not without resonance in relation to the 'débâcle' of the Franco-Prussian War and the 'chaos' of the Commune. It is no coincidence, either, that soon afterwards Zola specifically singles out Montmartre on the horizon as if shrouded by glowing gold and crimson embers, reminding us once again of the conflagrations and bloodshed. Tellingly, the Ecole Militaire lies under an ominous dark cloud while distant crowds of people on the vast concourse in front of the building and on the pavements on both sides of the river Seine appear like ants soon to be destroyed and scattered along with the carriages, like grains

of sand in the approaching storm until all that remains of the city is a
giant carcass, empty and devoid of life (*RM*, II, 851). The panorama at
the end of Part Four, seen through Jeanne's tears and the pitiless rain,
foreshadows her own death, but in its depiction of a depopulated Paris
it also alludes to the aftermath of *la Semaine sanglante*.

The vocabulary used to describe Jeanne's rag-doll, whose fixed stare
the child often finds upsetting, again recalls the mutilated bodies Zola
saw at Père-Lachaise and stacked under the city's bridges. The doll's
head looks as if it has been flayed from chin to cheek and its arms look
as if they have been dislocated (*RM*, II, 1015). The Commune imagery is
reinforced as Jeanne remembers another doll she once had that she
secretly buried because its head has been broken, and how horrified she
was when she later exhumed it and found that it had turned black and
ugly. She remembers everyone she has ever loved and lost and those
who, like her mother, she believes have betrayed and abandoned her
(*RM*, II, 1026). This whole passage is a meditation on the injustice and
cruelty of existence and, as such, echoes Zola's own emotional response
to the events of April and May 1871 which saw thousands of children
traumatized by the deaths of their parents in summary executions
and left to starve on the city streets.[84] Despite the bleakness of Jeanne's
vision, however, the heavy rain begins the process of purifying the city.
If Jeanne is soon to die – there is no place for her in a Darwinian
universe, any more than there is for the deranged leaders of the Commune and their doomed followers – the sun breaks through the clouds
and the city slowly comes back to life.

Finally, at the end of the novel, as Hélène returns to visit Jeanne's
grave in the cemetery at Passy she, like the city, has regained her pride
and respectability (*RM*, II, 1084). For the city also, the 'débâcle' is over
and Montmartre re-emerges on the horizon beneath a pure, blue-white,
satin-like glow which brings to mind the purificatory white of the Sacré-
Cœur erected on that very spot (*RM*, II, 851). Paris as a whole emerges
bright and vast in the gleaming silvery light cast by its covering of snow,
beneath which the twin towers of Notre-Dame, the Panthéon, the Louvre and the Tuileries (symbolically at least) are restored to their former
glory (*RM*, II, 1091). This image of purification and regeneration is,
however, counterbalanced by the description of the city's sense of de-
solation. Despite the clear blue skies, Paris lies frozen, its streets and
houses ruined and spectral, while the waters of the Seine remain dark
and muddy with debris gathering under the bridges, again recalling
the corpses Zola saw floating there in May and June 1871 (*RM*, II, 1087,

1091). If Paris is destined to survive, the traces of its past are still difficult to erase completely, and the novel ends with the image of Jeanne, lying in her grave in the cemetery in Passy forever looking out across Paris, as a final reminder of those other victims whose memory lives on across the city in that other cemetery, Père-Lachaise (*RM*, II, 1092).

Zola wrote the greater part of *Une page d'amour* during the five months he spent away from Paris in 1877 at L'Estaque on the Normandy coast and, while he clearly drew on his own pre- and post-Commune memories of the city, including the articles he had written for *Le Sémaphore de Marseille*, his own physical distance from Paris during the composition of the novel may perhaps have had a bearing on its political and memorialist dimensions. Consciously or not, Zola may be seen in this novel to be attempting to distance himself from the events of the recent past in order to come to terms with the physical and psychological damage caused by the Commune; in effect, to rid himself, and the city, of the weight of the past. The restoration of the city to its former monumental glory in *Une page d'amour* mirrors the more optimistic mood of the city in the years 1877 and 1878 when Haussmann's schemes, revived by the new regime, were nearing completion and preparations were under way for the forthcoming *Exposition universelle*. But Zola's apparent desire to depict the rebirth of the city is counterbalanced by the overwhelming sadness of the novel's conclusion.

Unlike *La Débâcle*, which at least appears optimistic in its conclusion, with the hero Jean Macquart looking towards the future and the reconstruction of a new France, *Une page d'amour*, despite the clear blue skies and the birds singing among the gravestones, suggests an ambivalent and deeply depressing future for its female protagonist. Certainly Hélène, like the city, will survive, but at what cost? She has lost her daughter and her lover, and her second marriage looks set to be as solitary and as unfulfilling as her first. For if Zola appears to pity Hélène and to want her story to have a happy ending by marrying her off to Rambaud, the course of the novel itself suggests the complete opposite for, yet again, as in *Le Ventre de Paris* and so many others of Zola's classically structured novels, everything returns to the *status quo ante*: psychologically, emotionally and physically. Later, in *Le Docteur Pascal*, we learn that Hélène remains childless, and in his preparatory notes for that novel Zola makes it clear that this is to be 'her punishment' and that a 'shadow of sadness' clouds her otherwise happy existence (*RM*, V, 1648).

Ultimately, *Une page d'amour* shares the same deeply pessimistic, cynical and conservative moral world view that characterizes *Le Ventre de*

Paris and *L'Assommoir*, where the 'mad' revolutionary idealist and the 'fallen' woman invariably pay the highest price for not conforming to bourgeois society's moral codes, while the likes of 'honest' Lisa Quenu and the Deberles emerge triumphant. It takes Jeanne's death to make Hélène recognize her past passion for Henri Deberle for the aberration and act of blind folly it really was; like the temporary blindness induced by lightning during a storm (*RM*, II, 1089). The incomprehension and contempt that Hélène feels for her former self at the end of the novel, and the pity Zola would like his readers to feel for her, mirrors Zola's own incomprehension and contempt for the Commune's leaders inter-mixed with his pity for those who were their unwitting victims. The image of lightning and thunder, so strong in the novel, recalls the wedding-party's similarly short-lived diversion from everyday life dur-ing the course of that summer storm in *L'Assommoir* and, by association, the brevity of the Commune itself, which for Zola, like Du Camp, constituted a similar aberration from 'normal' life, an aberration that Paris was trying very hard to forget. As she leaves Paris to start her new life with Rambaud in Marseilles, Hélène, like Old Father Time and his sack in Edmond Morin's 1871 illustration 'L'an mil huit cent soixante et onze!' (Figure 7), remains saddled with her own 'grosse malle' (large trunk) which, while firmly shut, nevertheless contains all the weighty memories and psychological baggage of her recent past (*RM*, II, 1092). For Zola and his contemporaries, Paris was their 'grosse malle', their archive of the past and the symbol of their debt to Prussia; a debt that had to be repaid, and a past for which they had, like Hélène, to atone. However, while the city itself, and by extension the nation, may have managed to discharge itself of the debt in the literal sense, since repara-tion had been made to the Prussians and Paris was, ostensibly, 'herself again' (to borrow Sala's apposite description), the individual, that is Hélène (and before her Florent and Gervaise), no less than Zola himself (or Du Camp, or *Le Monde illustré*'s roving reporter Walker), is incapa-ble of breaking free from the chains of the past. To reinvoke Nietzsche: 'however far and fast he may run, this chain runs with him'.[85] Part of the contemporary appeal of the novel, which proved to be an unexpected bestseller (*RM*, II, 1622–5), must therefore be attributed to its strong moral message as well as its psychological insights. It is perhaps not insignificant in this respect that Zola's fellow writers Mallarmé and Flaubert were both very impressed with *Une page d'amour* and that it is the only one of his novels to be singled out by Emile Faguet, one of Zola's severest critics.[86]

The covert allegory of the Franco-Prussian War, the Commune and the *Semaine sanglante* which supports the thematic and narrative structure of *Une page d'amour* strongly suggests that this novel is anything but the parenthesis to *Les Rougon-Macquart* it is normally considered to be; a misconception that makes it today one of the least read novels of the whole cycle.[87] If its romantic title and Zola's own description of the novel as an intimate, even lightweight drama appear to set it apart from the trenchant and dark social, political and historical polemic of his previous novels (*RM*, II, 1622), a close examination of the text itself shows that in fact the very fabric of *Une page d'amour* is no less encoded with the collective memory of Paris and the Commune than either *Le Ventre de Paris* or *L'Assommoir,* and indeed the novel anticipates the expressionistic descriptions of the city in flames during the *Semaine sanglante* in *La Débâcle.*

The theme of purification and regeneration already evident in *Une page d'amour* is developed and brought to its conclusion in *La Débâcle.* By the time Zola came to write that novel, however, there was also an appreciation in France that the generation of 1870–71 was beginning to disappear. *La Débâcle,* therefore, differs from the novels of the 1870s in that by 1892 the Franco-Prussian War and the Commune had crystallized into distant historical events. The time had come with *La Débâcle* for Zola to record not just the memory but also the pedagogical history of the Franco-Prussian War and its bloody epilogue the Commune. *La Débâcle* presents history as both narrative and explicit discourse, which accounts for the novel's somewhat didactic and very retrospective tone. During his lifetime it remained the most widely read of all of Zola's novels and even in 1928 it was second only to *Nana* in popularity.[88] Today it is still regarded by many as the quintessential modern war novel, dealing as it does with the timeless issues of military conflict and the subjection of human beings to forces beyond their control. *La Débâcle,* however, is also concerned with all the wider political issues raised by the Franco-Prussian War and the Commune that still remained unresolved as France hurtled towards the First World War. If *Le Ventre de Paris, L'Assommoir* and *Une page d'amour* are a product of the 1870s, then *La Débâcle* is very much a product of the 1890s.

La Débâcle tackles the issues raised by the Franco-Prussian War and the Commune head on. On the basis of the evidence discussed in this chapter, however, it would perhaps be of more interest to re-read the rest of Zola's Parisian novels for further examples of the covert influence of the Commune. *La Curée* in particular might prove to be a particularly interesting text in this respect, since all but the first chapter of this novel was completed after May 1871, in other words at a time when Zola's experiences and sense impressions of the city during *la Semaine sanglante* would have been particularly acute.[89] All the main Commune *lieux de mémoire* are retraced in *La Curée* (1871) from the butte Montmartre to the Place Vendôme, the Hôtel de Ville, the Tuileries and the Bois de Boulogne. A close reading just of the scene where Saccard and Angèle look down on the city from a restaurant high up in Montmartre (*RM*, I, 388), for example, soon reveals much of the same symbolism to be found also in *Le Ventre de Paris*, *L'Assommoir* and *Une page d'amour*. The references to gold ingots, crucibles, alchemy and stills may be symbolic of Saccard's speculations and riches to come, but the 'nuage rouge' (red cloud) hanging over the city, the houses said to look like they are on fire, the Vendôme Column in the distance, and the ominous 'tout va brûler!'(everything will burn) are once more familiar covert references to the Commune.

In *Au Bonheur des dames* (1883) the eponymous department store is repeatedly described as if it has been set alight, and the shopgirl Denise's walk through the Tuileries gardens can again be seen in terms of the re-appropriation of city space by the working classes as in *L'Assommoir*. The panoramic views of the city in *L'Œuvre* also, as already briefly noted, bear close comparison to those in *Une page d'amour* and *La Débâcle*, as indeed do the descriptions of the night sky in *La Bête humaine* (1890) (*RM*, IV, 1024).

Allusions to *la Semaine sanglante* are also to be found in novels which do not overtly feature Paris such as *La Conquête de Plassans* and, more obliquely, *La Faute de l'Abbé Mouret* (1875) where the description of the ruined chateau and gardens of Le Paradou (*RM*, I, 1248–9) bears comparison with Soulier's photographs of the ruined Tuileries palace. No doubt many more such examples exist in these and several other novels in the *Rougon-Macquart* cycle, and probably where we would least expect to find them providing yet more evidence that Zola's response to the Commune lies at the heart not just of his descriptions of urban topography but also of his literary project as a whole. In this respect, it might prove fruitful to follow the lead set by Philippe Régnier in his study of Zaccone and Bion and his comparison of the themes and imagery to be found in their novels and Zola's *Germinal*, by identifying further instances of the cross-fertilization of ideas, themes and images relating to the memory of the Commune in their respective novels.[90]

Notes

1 Henri Mitterand, *Zola: 1. Sous le regard d'Olympia 1840–1871* (Paris: Fayard, 1999), p. 800.

2 Maxime Du Camp, *Les Ancêtres de la Commune: L'Attentat Fieschi* (Paris: Charpentier, 1877), p. 11.

3 Benjamin, *Charles Baudelaire: A Lyric Poet in the Era of High Capitalism*, trans. by Harry Zohn (London and New York: Verso, 1989), p. 87.

4 Paul de Man, 'Literary History and Literary Modernity', *Daedalus, Journal of the American Academy of Arts and Sciences*, 99 (1970), pp. 395–6.

5 Emile Zola, 'M.H. Taine: Artiste', in *Ecrits sur l'art*, ed. by Jean-Pierre Leduc-Adine (Paris: Gallimard, 1991), p. 81. On Zola's use, and abuse, of *style indirect libre* see: Roy Pascal, *The Dual Voice: Free Indirect Speech and its Functioning in the Nineteenth-century European Novel* (Manchester: Manchester University Press, 1977), pp. 112–22; Gilbert D. Chaitin, 'Listening Power: Flaubert, Zola, and the Politics of *style indirect libre*', *French Review*, 72: 6 (May 1999), pp. 1023–37; and Jacques Dubois, *'L'Assommoir' de Zola*, 2nd edn (Paris: Belin, 1993), ch. 5.

6 *RM*, V, pp. 1416–20.

7 For example: F.W.J. Hemmings, *Emile Zola*, 2nd edn (Oxford: Oxford University Press, 1970), pp. 69–86; Mitterand, *Zola: 1. Sous le regard d'Olympia*, ch. 5; and Frederick Brown, *Zola: A Life* (London: Macmillan, 1995), ch. 9.

8 See Ripoll; Aimé Guedj, 'Les Révolutionnaires de Zola', *Les Cahiers naturalistes*, 36 (1968), pp. 123–37; and Marie Scarpa, *Le Carnaval des Halles: une éthnocritique du 'Ventre de Paris' de Zola* (Paris: CNRS, 2000), pp. 246–56.

9 See David Baguley, *Zola: 'L'Assommoir'*, and three articles by Robert Lethbridge: 'Reading the Songs of *L'Assommoir*', *French Studies*, 45 (1991), pp. 435–47, 'Reflections in the Margin: Politics in Zola's *L'Assommoir*', *Australian Journal of French Studies*, 30: 2 (1993), pp. 222–32, and 'A Visit to the Louvre: *L'Assommoir* Revisited', *Modern Language Review*, 87 (1992), pp. 41–55.

10 See, for example, Pierluigi Pellini, ' "Si je triche un peu": Zola et le roman historique', *Les Cahiers naturalistes*, 75 (2001), pp. 7–28. See also James H. Reid's *Narration and Description in the French Realist Novel: The Temporality of Lying and Forgetting* (Cambridge: Cambridge University Press, 1993), on the memorialist and political aspects of *L'Œuvre*, and Peter Starr, *Commemorating Trauma: The Paris Commune and its Cultural Aftermath* (New York: Fordham University Press, 2006) on *La Débâcle*. Starr's book was published just as my own book went into production and I was therefore unfortunately unable to take account of his interpretation of the novel.

11 For example, Stefan Max, *Les Métamorphoses de la grande ville dans 'Les Rougon-Macquart'* (Paris: Nizet, 1966); Nathan Kranowski, *Paris dans les romans d'Emile Zola* (Paris: Presses universitaires de France, 1968); William

J. Berg, *The Visual Novel: Emile Zola and the Art of His Times* (University Park: Pennsylvania State University Press, 1992); Christopher Prendergast, *Paris and the Nineteenth Century* (Cambridge MA and Oxford: Blackwell, 1995); Jean-François Thibault, 'Zola et l'horizon parisien', *French Literature Series*, 24 (1997), pp. 33–49; Olivier Lumbroso, 'Le Passage des panoramas (poétique et fonctions des vues panoramiques dans *Les Rougon-Macquart*)', *Littérature*, 116 (December 1999), pp. 17–46; Claude Duchet, 'Pathologie de la ville zolienne', in *Du Visible à l'invisible: pour Max Milner*, ed. by Stéphane Michaud (n.p.: José Corti, 1988), pp. 83–96; Michael Wetherill, 'Visions conflictuelles: le Paris de Flaubert, Zola, Monet, Degas, Caillebotte', in *Le Champ littéraire 1860–1900: Etudes offertes à Micheal Pakenham*, ed. by Keith Cameron and James Kearns (Amsterdam: Rodopi, 1996), pp. 27–38; Marie-Claire Bancquart, *Paris 'fin-de-siècle': de Jules Vallès à Remy de Gourmont*, 2nd edn (Paris: Editions de la Différence, 2002), chs 1, 2; Priscilla Parkhurst Ferguson, *Paris as Revolution: Writing the 19th-Century City* (Berkeley, Los Angeles and London: University of California Press, 1994), chs 2, 4, 5.

12 Brian Nelson, *Zola and the Bourgeoisie: A Study of Themes and Techniques in 'Les Rougon-Macquart'* (London: Macmillan, 1983), pp. 96–128; Susan Harrow, 'The Matter with Jeanne: Narrative and the Nervous Body in Zola's *Une page d'amour*', *Excavatio*, 12 (1999), pp. 60–8 (reprinted in Gural-Migdal *Writing the Feminine*, pp. 237–50).

13 Hemmings, p. 129; Mitterand, *Zola: L'Histoire et la fiction* (Paris: Presses universitaires de France, 1990), pp. 137–55; Frederick Brown, pp. 220–394.

14 Ripoll, p. 19.

15 See Mitterand's commentary in *RM*, I, 1613; Marc Baroli in Zola, *Le Ventre de Paris* (Paris: Lettres Modernes Minard, 1969), pp. 93, n. *b*, 233, n. *a*, and 451, n. *b*; and Scarpa, pp. 246–56.

16 On Gustave Flourens, see Noël, *Dictionnaire de la Commune*, I, 288–90.

17 An earlier version of the following analysis of *Le Ventre de Paris* appeared as 'Florent/Flourens: du nouveau sur la dimension politique du *Ventre de Paris*', in *Les Cahiers naturalistes*, 79 (2005), pp. 77–87.

18 Prendergast, *Paris in the Nineteenth Century*, p. 67. See also Prendergast, 'Le Panorama, la peinture et la faim: le début du *Ventre de Paris*', *Les Cahiers naturalistes*, 67 (1993), pp. 65–71.

19 Maurice Dreyfous, *Ce qui me reste à dire*, 2 vols, 3rd edn (Paris: Paul Ollendorff, 1912), II, pp. 290–1.

20 See Serman, pp. 89, 100 and Noël, *Dictionnaire de la Commune*, I, pp. 288–90.

21 See Taithe, *Citizenship & Wars: France in Turmoil 1870–1871* (London and New York: Routledge, 2001), p. 2; and Serman, pp. 101–2, 122, 133, 138–9.

22 Gustave Flourens, *Paris livré* (1871), 6th edn (Paris: A Le Chevalier, 1873), pp. 137–8. See also Taithe, *Citizenship & Wars*, pp. 31–3.

23 Taithe, *Citizenship & Wars*, p. 137.

24 See Ripoll, p. 19.

25 Charles Prolès, *Gustave Flourens: insurrection crétoise 1867–1868. Siège de Paris 1870–1871* (Paris: Chamuel, 1898), p. 50.

26 Nass, pp. 328–9.

27 Henri d'Alméras, *La Vie parisienne pendant le Siège et sous la Commune* (Paris: Albin Michel, 1927), p. 116.

28 On Flourens's assassination see Prolès, p. 88; Amilcare Cipriani's first-hand account reproduced in Louise Michel, *La Commune: histoire et souvenirs*, 2 vols (1898) (Paris: Maspero, 1970), I, pp. 161–7; and Du Camp, *LC*, I, 37. Du Camp justifies Flourens's assassination by the Versaillais on the (disingenuous) pretext that the regular army were merely following the example set for them by the *fédérés* themselves.

29 See *Emile Zola: Correspondance*, ed. by B.H. Bakker, 10 vols (Montreal: Presses universitaires de Montréal, 1978–95), II, pp. 287 n. 2, 293, 295 n. 3.

30 Paul Alexis, *'Naturalisme pas mort': Lettres inédites de Paul Alexis à Emile Zola 1871–1900*, ed. by B.H. Bakker (Toronto: University of Toronto Press, 1971), letter dated 5 June 1871, p. 46. See also pp. 38, 39 n. 9–10, 47 n. 4–5, 48–51. On Vésinier, see Noël, *Dictionnaire de la Commune*, II, pp. 280–1.

31 Cipriani, quoted in Michel, p. 165.

32 Nass, p. 329.

33 Alexis, p. 46.

34 See also David Baguley, 'Image et symbole: la tache rouge dans l'œuvre de Zola', *Les Cahiers naturalistes*, 39 (1970), pp. 36–41.

35 Armand Lanoux, *Bonjour Monsieur Zola* (Paris: Le Livre Contemporain-Amiot-Dumont, 1954), p. 120.

36 See Baroli, in Zola, *Le Ventre de Paris*, p. 7.

37 See Cipriani quoted in Michel, I, p. 166.

38 Dreyfous, II, pp. 292–3.

39 See Geoff Woollen, 'Zola's Halles, a *Grande Surface* before their time', *Romance Studies*, 18 (June 2000), pp. 21–30.

40 See Zola's descriptions from *Le Sémaphore de Marseille* dated 2 June 1871 quoted in Mitterand, *Zola, I: Sous le regard d'Olympia*, p. 811.

41 See Du Camp, *PSO*, VI, p. 318; Gullickson; and Thomas.

42 See Mitterand, *Zola, I: Sous le regard d'Olympia*, p. 811.

43 See Philippe Régnier's analysis of Pierre Zaconne's novel *Le Coq rouge* (1872) in his 'Genèse d'un discours romanesque sur la Commune', in Bellet and Régnier, pp. 139–57 (p. 139).

44 Taithe, *Citizenship and Wars*, p. 114.

45 Nietzsche, *On the Genealogy of Morals*, pp. 45, 52–3.

46 Cited by Ripoll, p. 22.

47 See Eunice Lipton, *Looking into Degas: Uneasy Images of Women and Modern Life* (Berkeley, Los Angeles, London: University of California Press, 1986), ch. 3.

48 On working women and the Commune see Gullickson, chs 5, 6. On the nineteenth-century perception of laundresses see Mary Donaldson-Evans, 'The Morbidity of Milieu: *L'Assommoir* and the Discourse of Hygiene', in *Literary Generations*, ed. by Alain Toumayoan (Lexington: French Forum, 1992), pp. 150–62.

49 See Baguley, *Emile Zola: 'L'Assommoir'*, pp. 15–25.

50 An earlier version of this analysis of *L'Assommoir* appeared as 'City Space and the Politics of Carnival in Zola's *L'Assommoir*' in *French Studies*, 58: 3 (2004), pp. 343–56 and I am grateful to Oxford University Press for allowing me to reproduce this material.

51 Tersen, 'L'Opinion publique et la Commune de Paris (1871–79)', 107–8 (April–September 1960), pp. 35–6.

52 Susanna Barrows, 'After the Commune: Alcoholism, Temperance, and Literature in the Early Third Republic', in *Consciousness and Class Experience in Nineteenth-Century Europe*, ed. by John M. Merriman (New York and London: Holmes & Meier, 1979), pp. 205–18 (p. 208).

53 Thomas, pp. 195–9; Gullickson, pp. 207–9. According to Du Camp, for whom the women were obviously guilty as charged, they screamed out 'Il faut que Paris crève!' (*LPC*, II, p. 86).

54 See Thomas, pp. 193–4.

55 Lethbridge, 'Reading the Songs of L'Assommoir'.

56 See Tombs, *The Paris Commune*, pp. 132–43.

57 See the contemporary description of the *pétroleuse* in Gullickson, p. 171.

58 Mikhail Bakhtin, *Rabelais and his World*, ed. by Krystyna Pomorska and Michael Holquist, trans. by Helene Iswolsky (Bloomington: Indiana University Press, 1984), pp. 4–10, and *Problems of Dostoevesky's Poetics*, trans. by R.W. Rotsel (n.p.: Ardis, 1973), pp. 100–8, 134.

59 Charles Rearick, 'Festivals in Modern France: The Experience of the Third Republic', *Journal of Contemporary History*, 12 (1977), pp. 435–60. The whole subject of the *fête* was very topical at this time owing to the debates surrounding the staging of the *Exposition universelle* in 1878 as well as the celebrations to commemorate the centenaries of Voltaire, Rousseau and Joan of Arc. Following their electoral success of 1876, the republicans were also actively campaigning for a national celebration, eventually held as the *Fête du 30 juin* in 1878.

60 See Emmanuel Le Roy Ladurie, *Le Carnaval de Romans: de la Chandeleur au mercredi des Cendres, 1579–1580* (Paris: Gallimard, 1979), where the political context and the carnival in question can be fruitfully compared with the events of the Commune and the early Third Republic.

61 Lefebvre, *La Proclamation de la Commune*, p. 133. On Lefebvre's notion of 'le moment' see his *La Somme et le reste* (1959) (Paris: Méridiens, Klincksieck, 1989), part 3.

62 See Tombs, *The Paris Commune*, p. 106; and Peter Stallybrass and Allon White, *The Politics of Transgression* (London: Methuen, 1986), pp. 6–26.

63 Reproduced in Lorédan Larchey, *Mémorial des deux sièges de Paris, 1870–71* (Paris: 1872).

64 See Tombs, *The Paris Commune*, pp. 8–9; and Du Camp, *LC*, VI, pp. 239–40; *PSO*, VI, pp. 121–2.

65 Tombs, *The Paris Commune*, pp. 99, 124–6.

66 Lethbridge, 'A Visit to the Louvre', p. 45.

67 See also Valerie Minogue, *Zola: 'L'Assommoir'* (London: Grant & Cutler, 1991), pp. 45–6.

68 See Mitterand, *Zola I: Sous le regard d'Olympia*, pp. 810–81; and Noël, *Dictionnaire de la Commune*, II, pp. 153, 224.

69 See Denis Pellerin, 'Le Sabbat rouge', in Bajac, pp. 49–54, and the illustrations on pp. 104–5.

70 Image reproduced in Bajac, p. 65.

71 See Ripoll, p. 19.

72 'il faut bien admettre ... que les thèses de Zola sur la guerre civile ... n'ont rien qui puisse le distinguer de ses contemporains les plus conservateurs' [it has to be admitted ... that Zola's ideas on the civil war ... have nothing that can distinguish him from his most conservative contemporaries]. Mitterand in *RM*, V, p. 1378.

73 An earlier version of my analysis of *Une page d'amour* appeared as '*Une page d'amour*: un panorama politique', in *Les Cahiers naturalistes*, 76 (2002), pp. 177–91.

74 See Marilyn R. Brown, 'Manet, Nodier and *Polichinelle*', *Art Journal*, 45: 1 (1985), pp. 43–8.

75 For examples of Zola's long-standing anti-militarism see Lethbridge's introduction to Dorday's English translation of *La Débâcle*, pp. xiii–xvi.

76 Reproduced in Milner, p. 181.

77 See Pellini, pp. 7–28.

78 Prendergast, *Paris and the Nineteenth Century*, pp. 68–9.

79 Morisot, pp. 56–7.

80 Gautier, p. 325.

81 See Reid.

82 Nelson, pp. 119–21.

83 See Mitterand, *Zola I: Sous le regard d'Olympia*, p. 810.

84 Ripoll, p. 21.

85 Nietzsche, 'On the Uses and Disadvantages of History', p. 61.

86 Faguet, III, p. 247.

87 Nelson, p. 96.

88 See Lethbridge's introduction to *La Débâcle*, p. xiv.

89 See Lethbridge, 'La Préparation de *La Curée*: mise au point d'une chronologie', *Les Cahiers naturalistes*, 51 (1976), pp. 37–48.

90 Régnier, in Bellet and Régnier, *Ecrire la Commune*, pp. 139–57.

5

Paris and the Commune in the photographic imagination

Ever since its invention, much has been written about the nature of photography and whether it is an art, and therefore 'subjective', or a science, and therefore capable of offering an 'objective' glimpse of reality. Depending on the point of view adopted, such philosophical debates have led many critics to question the whole way in which we look at, and react to, what we see in photographs. Does the fact that a photograph is infinitely reproducible and lacks what Walter Benjamin calls the 'aura' of an original painting mean that a photograph cannot ever be a true work of art, that it is somehow only a rather cheap (in all the senses of the word), and therefore rather suspect, form of visual representation? [1] Are photographs a sinister product of the same rapid technological development which, in Benjamin's view, formed part of the 'phantasmagoria' of capitalism which would inevitably lead to the creation of Hell on earth (or Nazism)?[2] On the other hand, does the very fact that photography is essentially a mechanical process, ostensibly free of the artist's hand and replacing the artist's eye with an 'objective' lens, make photographs more 'truthful' in their representation of reality than other visual and textual forms? Indeed, as Roger Scruton argues, are photographs actually 'representational' at all in the sense of *re-presenting* an object, or are they effectively showing the object itself? For Scruton, the camera is 'used not to represent something but to point to it', and if a photograph holds our interest, it is 'because it acts as a surrogate for the represented thing'.[3] Or, as Susan Sontag maintains, since a photograph is the product of a chemical process whereby light is reflected off an actual object, are photographs not actual 'traces' of that object? For Sontag, photographs are 'miniatures of reality'; they have a unique, direct and causal relationship with the photographed object that any handmade visual or textual representation could never have.[4] For Barthes also, there can be no photograph unless there is something or someone to photograph in the first place.[5] A subject may be infinitely reproducible photographically but it can never be repeated or recreated in an existential sense (p. 15).

Notwithstanding their persuasive arguments in favour of photography's special relationship with 'reality', these critics are all ultimately obliged to acknowledge the unavoidably subjective nature of the photographic act. Even Scruton concedes that photographers are free to choose their subject and that they do exercise some control over point of view and lens angle. Any more interference than that, however, and, according to Scruton, the photographer becomes a painter.[6] Sontag admits that no object is identical in different photographs taken of it.[7] Barthes states that photography can be used to promote certain moral and political values and that if some photographs are not shocking *per se*, viewers may well perceive them as such.[8]

Sontag also considers that photographs function as 'a grammar' and, importantly, 'an ethics of seeing', but claims that they cannot create a moral position in the viewer, only reinforce an existing one or build a nascent one.[9] Stephanie Ross, on the other hand, contends that just as paintings like Géricault's *Le Radeau de la Méduse*, or Picasso's *Guérnica*, can have a moral import, so 'photographs have a comparable power to inform us about events in all their horror or all their glory and thereby teach moral lessons'.[10] While one would agree with Sontag that appearances can mislead, Ross's suggestion that judgements go beyond appearances and that different moral labels apply under different circumstances is perhaps more compelling, since it would reinforce the notion that photographs cannot be viewed in isolation from the society and culture that gave rise to them.

Any discussion regarding the interpretation of photographs and their relationship with history, memory and reality, however, must also take account of how photography was perceived in the nineteenth century. John Snyder and Neil Walsh Allen, for example, note that photographs at that time were perceived 'first and foremost [as] *pictures*, and that like other pictures they may serve to provide information (the "scientific dimension") or to provide aesthetic pleasure (the "art dimension")'.[11] The aim of the nineteenth-century photographer was no different from that of the artist in any other media, namely 'naturalistic' representation. As Sontag states, the history of photography can therefore be summarized as the struggle between artistic beautification and a moralized ideal of truth-telling, adapted from nineteenth-century literary models and from journalism; like the realist novelist or journalist, the photographer was required 'to unmask hypocrisy and combat ignorance'.[12] Consequently, there is a useful parallel to be drawn between nineteenth-century photographers, many of whom significantly started out as artists, and Zola the Naturalist author, or Du Camp the investigative journalist.

In the final analysis, however, the interpretation of any photograph requires the viewer, as Pierre Bourdieu suggests, not only to uncover its more obvious significance and the explicit intentions of the photographer who created it but also to decode the hidden meanings it betrays in terms of the social and aesthetic conventions of the period in which it was produced, and the expectations of the artistic group and/or audience for which it was intended.[13] All photography, amateur and professional, according to Bourdieu, is a regulated and conventional practice not just in terms of the traditional and cultural occasions that give rise to it, but also in its very composition of pictures where everything seems to conform to implicit 'canons' that dictate what is aesthetically acceptable or technically inept.

Thus, Soulier and Baldus specialized in panoramic cityscapes and monumental and architectural photography, including Romantic ruins, and Marville is best known as a street photographer. All three photographers can be seen to conform to the demands and expectations of the genres in which they worked as well as to the requirements of those who commissioned or purchased their photographs. In exploring the technical, commercial, aesthetic, cultural, political and memorialist context in which they produced their images in the period from 1871 to 1878, this chapter will identify some of the 'moral lessons' that contemporary viewers might have drawn from their photographic images.

In the immediate aftermath of the Versaillais repression, the proliferation of photographs of Paris and its environs in ruins (such as those depicted in Soulier's *Paris incendié, mai 1871*) and the thousands of *carte de visite* portraits of those deemed to be responsible for the destruction was initially seen as a deterrent to further insurrection. It soon became apparent to the government, however, that in some quarters, quite the reverse was true and that the Communards were fast acquiring a reputation as heroes and martyrs. Unsurprisingly, therefore, by 1873 the diffusion of Communard portraits was banned and even the most aesthetic views of ruins became subject to the strictest censorship.

It was only in 1881 with the passing of the Press Laws that the circulation of images of the Commune was again to be permitted.

A plethora of government restrictions had, of course, been plaguing photographers ever since the days of the Second Empire. From 1852 until 1891, when restrictions were finally lifted, all printed materials, including photographs, were subject to authorization by the Ministry of the Interior or the Departmental Prefect. Article 115 of the *Ordonnance du 25 juillet 1862 sur la Circulation* further stipulated that all photographers had to acquire authorization from the Préfecture de Police in order to take or sell photographs in the streets of Paris.[14] If photographers wished to photograph any of the city's open spaces such as the Bois de Boulogne or the Buttes-Chaumont, they also had to submit an application to the Director of Public Works in Paris. Some ten days later, the Municipal Council of Paris might grant the photographer a permit so long as it was collected in person and formal agreement given to supply the authorities with two copies of each photograph taken.[15] All photographers were required to obtain a separate permit from the Ministère des Beaux-Arts for each state-owned monument and museum they wished to photograph, and professional practitioners also had to conform to Article 22 of the *Ordonnance*, which required that all illustrations, medals and emblems be approved by the Ministre de Police or Departmental Prefect before they could be offered for sale. Anyone contravening these legal requirements risked anywhere between one and twelve months' imprisonment and a fine of between 100 and 1,000 francs.[16] Professionally produced photographs also constituted an extra-special case owing to their perceived realism, particularly in respect of pornographic images, and the law courts were kept busy each day serving sentences on photographers whose work was deemed to offend public morals.

Enforcement of all these and many other regulations was problematic, however, as Government resources were limited and could not keep pace with the huge number of photographers operating in the city and the thousands of images in circulation.[17] That said, it is not surprising that by 1873 Paris as a photographic theme had fallen distinctly out of favour with photographers who, if they wished to continue to earn a living, preferred to turn their attention instead to more readily accessible and less contentious subjects, such as family portraits, celebrity *cartes de visites*, and reproductions of paintings and maps. Thus while the 1869 and 1870 exhibitions mounted by the *Société française de photographie* (*SFP*) included a large number of photographs of Paris and its environs, the city featured in none of the exhibits on show in the 1874 exhibition. And, as further evidence of the decline of Paris as a photographic subject (or at least evidence of the reluctance of photographers to register their prints with the *Dépôt légal*), while the vast majority of photographs registered by the *Dépôt* for the period 1871 to 1873 are connected with Paris and the Commune, by 1874 only three items relating to Paris are listed, and these are none other than more reproductions of Appert's composites: 'Massacre de la rue Haxo', 'Exécution des otages à la Roquette', and 'Massacre des dominicains d'Arcueil, 25 mai 1871'.[18] After 1873, then, all new photographs of Paris consisted of officially commissioned images of the reconstruction of the city and the completion of new boulevards and other public schemes such as those produced by Marville.

After the republican electoral victory in 1876, there was a modest improvement in the fortunes of Paris as the object of the photographer's attention. The entries in the *SFP*'s exhibition for that year, for example, include photographs of the Tuileries palace, the new Opéra, and the Arc de Triomphe, but Alphonse Davanne, president of the *SFP*, clearly acknowledges the difficulties still being experienced by photographers in the city at this time.[19] Baldus, like Marville, also undertook public commissions such as recording the reconstruction of the Hôtel de Ville during this period, but like other photographers he appears to have stopped photographing the city on a private, commercial basis. Instead he remained in his studio in 1875 and re-created Paris from prints he had been officially commissioned to produce during the Second Empire in the 1850s and 1860s, and included them as part of the collection entitled *Les Principaux Monuments de France*.

State-sponsored photography occupied a major place at the *Exposition universelle* of 1878, where the special *Ville de Paris* pavilion housed a showpiece gallery devoted exclusively to this unique industry which was seen to cross the boundaries between art and science.[20] Virtually all areas of public life, not just in the city but across the country as a whole, were represented. The *Ecole des ponts et chaussées*, for example, submitted twenty-two albums comprising views of the nation's infrastructure including bridges, canals, railways, stations and lighthouses. Public and community works were also well represented and included photographs of churches, town halls, markets, abattoirs, fire stations, drains and sewers, hospitals and schools. The Fine Arts section included documentary photographs of the restoration of historic monuments and examples of teaching aids for painting and drawing. The Astrological section submitted works on scientific missions, observations of the sun, Venus and Mercury, and early versions of microscopic photographs, while the Civil Engineering and Public Works stand showcased the latest French inventions and technological achievements. Of the thousand photographs exhibited, some two-thirds were of architectural sites including two special displays focusing on Paris past and present.[21] These before and after shots of the city were produced by Marville and taken partly from his *Album du vieux Paris* (*Album of Bygone Paris*), containing some 425 images commissioned by Haussmann prior to the reconstruction of the city during the Second Empire, and two series of photographs *Travaux* (*Public Works*), numbering a hundred total, dating from 1876 and 1877, which he had produced as part of a special commission from the Municipal Council of Paris to document the new city in time for the *Exposition universelle* in 1878. Significantly, no photographs of Paris in ruins after the Commune were on display at the *Exposition*.

Politics, memory and aesthetics in Soulier's *Paris incendié, mai 1871*

Political readings of the photographs of a ruined Paris in the immediate aftermath of the Commune by Gautrand and Lapostolle, for example, have typically focused on thematic content and point of view, but it is arguable that these aspects alone provide conclusive evidence of a photographer's ideological stance.[22] As Alisa Luxenberg's analysis of Jules Andrieu's series *Désastres de la guerre* has highlighted, there are inherent ambiguities in that photographer's depiction of the destroyed city which suggest a shared irony with Goya's *Los desastres de la Guerra*.[23] Furthermore, as Donald English points out, it may well have been enough for some contemporary viewers to believe that the Commune had been responsible for the destruction of the city for all photographs of ruins to take on a political meaning, but without a caption pointing towards an anti-Communard interpretation viewers were free to read such images as they wished.[24] In this respect, Charles Soulier's shots of the Tuileries in ruins, as seen for example in Figures 18, 19 and 20, could be read by those sympathetic to the Commune, as well as those generally hostile to the Second Empire, as representing the inevitable, justifiable even, destruction of a decadent regime. The Tuileries was the only building that the Communards did not deny having wilfully set alight; an act that many conservative republicans certainly did not condone, but nevertheless understood.[25] The same photographs, however, could equally be

Figure 18 Charles Soulier. The ruined Tuileries Palace, interior view, the peristyle, south side, looking out towards the Arc de Triomphe du Carrousel, *Paris incendié, mai 1871.* Photograph. (V&A Images/Victoria and Albert Museum.)

Figure 19 Charles Soulier. The ruined Tuileries Palace, interior view, *Paris incendié, mai 1871*. Photograph. (V&A Images/Victoria and Albert Museum.)

Figure 20 Charles Soulier. Salle des Maréchaux, *Paris incendié, mai 1871.*
Photograph. (V&A Images/Victoria and Albert Museum.)

construed as the depiction of the results of a calculated attack on the monarchy or the nation by an immoral, inebriated, mentally disturbed horde of murderous barbarians, to recap all the anti-Communard stereotypes. And certainly such photographs, which were much copied and reproduced as engravings in the illustrated press of the period, served Thiers's government well as an effective means by which to propagate the reactionary myth of Paris and the Commune. The Commune, as both Barthes and Sontag remind us, saw the first use of the camera record to incriminate.[26] In looking for evidence of Charles Soulier's hostility to the Commune in *Paris incendié: mai 1871*, therefore, we should look to his choice of title for the series as a whole. For without such a *textual* frame, Soulier's images can be seen merely to conform to contemporary photographic and artistic conventions and, as such, would indeed remain open to interpretation depending on the viewer's own political bias.

While little is known of his private life, and even the precise dates of his birth and death are unclear, Soulier's successful career as one of Napoleon III's favourite photographers would suggest that he was very much a Second Empire establishment man.[27] In the 1850s he was one of the first to photograph the streets of Paris and was particularly celebrated, like Baldus, for his panoramic views of the city.[28] He exhibited his work at the *Exposition universelle* in 1855 and in 1859, along with fellow photographers Ferrier and Bérardy, accompanied Napoleon III and Victor Emmanuel II on their campaign in Italy against the Austrians, where he photographed the emperor and the departure of the French army for Magenta. In the 1860s he journeyed to Italy via the Alps, photographing Mont Blanc along the way. He exhibited his work widely in France, London, Amsterdam, Berlin and Boston, and by 1867 he had become a respected member of the *SFP*. That year he was also awarded a first-class medal in Paris as well as Napoleon III's special gold medal for photography, and was duly named an official photographer to the Emperor. Ernest Lacan praised his technical expertise and considered him the leading landscape photographer of the day.[29] In the immediate aftermath of *la Semaine sanglante*, Soulier joined the ranks of the photographers who flocked into the city to capture the spectacle of Paris in ruins. For many photographers, the destruction of the city provided a unique and irresistible commercial opportunity that helped to mitigate the hardships they had endured during the war and the two sieges. While conditions were far from ideal, photographers tenaciously and competitively fought their way through blockaded streets, piles of rubble, dead bodies, soot and dust, with the result that not one fire-damaged building or monument escaped being captured by the camera from all points of view, and in all possible forms and formats.[30]

Soulier's *Paris incendié, mai 1871* comprises eighty-three albumen prints probably made from wet collodion glass negatives, each measuring approximately 25 × 20 cm and mounted on larger cards. The odd number of prints would suggest that some might be missing, but research to date has not confirmed this, or indeed whether further collections by Soulier – identical in size and presentation to those under discussion here, and which form part of the Victoria and Albert Museum collection in London – are in existence. None of the prints bears the stamp of the *Dépôt légal*, but this, again, is not unusual, since not all photographers registered all of their prints, despite the legal requirement to do so.[31] The title of the collection is inscribed in large capitals on the mounts, with the subtitle in smaller capitals underneath. The inscription 'Photographiée par CH. SOULIER' appears directly beneath each print and, right at the bottom of each mount, the statement, 'Publié, 141 Boulevard Sébastopol, Paris', Soulier's last known address, to which he moved in 1867.[32] The subjects of the prints are not individually identified.[33] In common with many photographers of the period, Soulier presumably felt that images of such well-known sites and monuments did not require specific identification.

As with the majority of similar albums and collections, Soulier's series comprises a mixture of traditional, aesthetic, Romantic architectural ruins, as well as reportage-style shots of damaged blocks of flats and shop fronts, debris-strewn streets and public squares, and the toppled Vendôme Column.[34] In this respect his series closely resembles, among others, Andrieu's *Désastres de la guerre* and Liébert's bound album accompanied by an anti-Communard text, *Les Ruines de Paris et ses environs. 1870–1871. Siège et Commune.* By contrast, Braquehais, another photographer who has commanded a certain amount of scholarly attention and who is often perceived as being sympathetic to the Communard cause, does not appear to have produced any aesthetic shots; this leads Lapostolle to conclude that he was less concerned with conveying any historical perspective in his work than with the desire to record events as he saw them. Lapostolle contrasts Braquehais's approach with what she defines as the main characteristics of anti-Communard photography, namely: the production of distant, unsentimentalized, serial location shots, usually devoid of human subjects, Communard or Versaillais; and an emphasis on the romantic beauty of the architectural ruins, photographed for their own sake, and where the formal and aesthetic perfection of the photographs themselves appears to be at odds with the images of devastation they depict. Anti-Communard photography thus appears more 'scientific' in its execution and consequently would have been considered to be more 'truthful'.[35] The aim of such photographs, therefore, was the sublime fusion of beauty with 'truth', as the photographer understood it, at least. While she concedes that the depiction of the ruins cannot be considered as an anti-Communard act *per se*, Lapostolle maintains that the aesthetisization of the ruins was yet another attempt by those hostile to the Commune to deny the political and social causes underlying the uprising by depicting the events of May 1871 as apocalyptic and tragic.[36] These are certainly the sentiments expressed by the known anti-Communard Ernest Meissonier in his monumental painting *Les Tuileries (mai 1871)*, which he started in 1871 but did not complete until 1883.[37] The painting bears close comparison with photographs such as those by Soulier and Andrieu, but Meissonier claimed not to have been influenced by photographs of the same scene.

Lapostolle's classification of what constitutes anti-Communard photography notwithstanding, and whilst not denying that aesthetic photographs of the ruins can be seen as forming part of a broader anti-Communard discourse, it is nevertheless important to remember photography's artistic as well as informational and propagandist function. Like most photographers of the period, Soulier considered himself to be an 'artiste-photographe' and, as such, was bound by the same formal aesthetic and thematic conventions which had long governed the representation of the ruin in European art such as framing, perspective, chiaroscuro (enhanced by the use of the wet collodion process), and the use of the decadent classical temple, ghostly gothic castle or fairytale palace, all of which served to turn the ruin into a spectacle for the macabre delectation of the viewer. As Flaubert was later to note ironically in *Le Dictionnaire des idées reçues*, 'RUINES: font rêver et donnent de la poésie à un paysage' ('RUINS: make one dream and add poetry to a landscape').

At one level, therefore, Soulier's *Paris incendié, mai 1871*, like all the photographs of Paris in ruins, can be interpreted as yet another expression of the period's obsession with decadence and as part of the same industry which, even before 1871, had already produced a whole array of illustrations, guidebooks and nostalgic literary meditations on 'les ruines de Paris' and the disappearance of 'le vieux Paris', by the likes of, among many others, Meryon, Baudelaire, Hugo and the Goncourt brothers.

In his classic text 'A Small History of Photography', Walter Benjamin emphasizes the important early connection between photography and capitalism. Sontag develops this notion by suggesting that photography turned the discovery of the beauty of ruins into a genuinely popular taste.[38] Much like the poet Théophile Gautier, Soulier and Andrieu both share an appreciation of the sheer dramatic beauty of the ruins and anticipate, or wish to create, such a response in the potential purchasers of their large-format, high-quality photographs. Theirs was a discerning market that sought pictures which were informative, memorialist, historical but, above all, conventionally aesthetic. Such a market would have consisted primarily of affluent Parisians, tourists and overseas buyers. We do not know how much Soulier was charging for his series or for individual prints. However, we do know that a bound album containing twenty smaller photographs of a quality inferior to those by Soulier, entitled *Album historique des ruines de Paris* with an anti-Communard 'Historique' by Justin Lallier, sold for 16F (or the cost of forty loaves of bread). Only the relatively rich, therefore, would have been able to afford Lallier's album, and only the richer still, Soulier's *Paris incendié, mai 1871*. But again, the images of ruins were not just popular among the higher echelons of society. Less affluent souvenir collectors were also attracted to them and could choose from the hundreds of thousands of relatively cheap, mass-produced stereographic and postcard-size images widely on sale in the city. Soulier had produced a series of stereoscopic images of Paris back in the early 1860s with his then partners, Claude-Marie Ferrier and A. Ferrier, so it is highly likely that, like most of his contemporaries, he also produced images of the city after the Commune in this format, thus greatly broadening his market.

In contrast to Andrieu's similar collection, *Désastres de la guerre*, where, as Luxenberg points out, we are left wondering exactly 'whose disasters, whose war, whose ruins?' are being depicted,[39] Soulier's chosen title harbours no such ambiguity. *Paris incendié, mai 1871* as a generic title for such a series is certainly not original. Several other collections and albums refer either to the conflagrations or to the ruins in their titles or captions. In choosing *Paris incendié, mai 1871*, however, rather than, say, *Les Ruines de Paris*, Soulier is making a specific statement about the way he understands May 1871. *Les Ruines de Paris* would privilege the notion of decadence and the fall of the Empire. In addition, *ruine* has distinctly class-based connotations since the term has traditionally been applied only to palaces and other grand public buildings and monuments.[40] By referring instead to the burnt-out city and the specific year and *month* in his title, Soulier puts the emphasis firmly on Paris as a whole (monumental and bourgeois) and on the *civil war* it has just experienced, thereby rendering highly contentious his inclusion in the series of a number of shots of Neuilly, Courbevoie, and, most tellingly, Saint-Cloud, destroyed not by the Commune in May 1871, but during the Franco-Prussian War which ended in February 1871. Unlike Andrieu's *Désastres de la guerre* which is more open to interpretation, Soulier's *Paris incendié: mai 1871* predisposes his intended viewer to meditate primarily on the enormity of the physical damage done to Paris and, by extension, to the French nation, and to view all the destruction as the work of the Commune. The use of an active verb, *incendié* (which translates in English as: on fire, burning, burnt down, victim of a fire), implies an active subject and tells the viewer that what is being depicted was certainly no accident and consequently all the worse for that. The figurative definitions of *incendier*, to set fire to something, give some measure of the impact and ideological nuances of such a title: *enflammer, exciter, ravager, saccager, violence, combat, guerre* (to enflame, excite/arouse/incite, to wreak havoc, to sack/pillage/turn everything upside down, violence, combat/battle, war). In addition, fire carries with it connotations not just of destruction but also of uncontrolled sexual passion and political frenzy, more often than not fuelled by alcohol. And it is precisely in these terms that the Commune and its supporters were perceived in the minds of their detractors.

The symbolic associations evoked by fire, however, are more complex still. Fire is not just representative of animal passion but also of spiritual strength and thus represents both good and evil, or the dualism of the human predicament. At one level, there is the Heraclitean notion of fire as an 'agent of transmutation' which, like water, is central to life and symbolizes purification, transformation, generation, and the destruction of the forces of evil (Gaston Bachelard's 'Prometheus complex').[41] Thus for those who sought salvation in a return to the Catholic Church after May 1871, Soulier's light-filled archway in Figure 18 would no doubt have had a strong appeal. The archway, like the gates of heaven, rises high above the rubble of the palace and the Arc de Triomphe du Carrousel, both representative of the material world and of all the failed political regimes associated with them, culminating in the Commune. On another level, however, fire can consume and destroy life. It is representative of the Last Judgement, hell, and eternal damnation (Bachelard's 'Empedocles complex'). Fire, according to Bachelard, is more a *social* rather than a natural phenomenon. In the social context, fire is something to be both respected and feared and is thus subject to universal interdiction. It is this *social* sanctioning that Bachelard believes informs and conditions our knowledge and experience of fire (pp. 18, 23–5). Therefore, whilst the destruction of the earth by divine fire would be deemed acceptable, for humans to attempt to do the same would be considered as an illegal and sacrilegious act that is again precisely what conservatives and reactionaries believed the Communards to have perpetrated. Following their appropriation of the Tuileries, the torching of the palace by the Communards can be seen as the final violation of the body of the building and that of the nation itself. With the loss of the famous dome that once crowned the dominant central vertical section, the Pavillon de l'Horloge (or Pavillon du Trône), both building and nation have been 'decapitated'. The Communards have thus also severed the perceived natural link between God and ordinary mortals embodied in the monarchy and represented by the vertical structure of the palace itself, which traditionally symbolizes the union between heaven and earth.

Ruins are often seen to symbolize the mutilation of the body, and in Figures 18, 19 and 20, for example, we see the exposed 'bones', 'entrails' and 'sinews' of the Tuileries in the form of the calcinated shell of the building with its crumbling columns and masonry, broken pipes, bent metal tubing, exposed wires, and fragments of window frames and floorboards. The Tuileries, like a dissected corpse, exposes all its secrets to anyone who cares to look at its naked infrastructure.

Despite making use of a similar traditional classical 'mise-en-scène' in these photographs, Soulier eschews the starkness and precision that characterizes comparable shots by Andrieu, and emphasizes instead the soft powdery texture of the ruins. The viewer is thus almost able to smell the ash and the dust, to feel those calcinated walls and columns that would surely crumble at the slightest touch. By setting his camera angle low, Soulier is able to foreground and heighten the impact of the debris on display, leaving the viewer in no doubt that these are modern ruins. Part of the shock-value of the ruins of 1871, compared with those routinely encountered by contemporary travellers to Rome, Greece or Egypt, was the fact that they had been created so suddenly. For all their dreamy beauty, what these modern ruins lacked was the gently acquired patina of time.[42] A further ironic reminder of the recent nature of the destruction is to be found in another of Soulier's photographs of the palace from the Tuileries gardens, where one of the posters still attached to its walls beside the central entrance advertises the Commune's Sunday fund-raising concerts, the last of which took place on the evening of 21 May 1871 just as the Versaillais were entering the city heralding the start of *la Semaine sanglante.*

For his contemporaries, Soulier's photographs would no doubt have evoked all the sense impressions and emotions that they themselves had experienced during and after the Commune; such images would have been perceived as tangible, if fragmentary and selective, physical memory traces of the ruined monuments and buildings they depict. Victor Hugo, for example, is known to have bought similar photographs of the ruins and been inspired by them as much as by the sight of the actual burnt-out Tuileries and Hôtel de Ville.[43] According to Sontag, 'photography [is] one of the principal devices for experiencing something'.[44] That 'something', as the psychiatrist and psychoanalyst Serge Tisseron explains, is never experienced in a linear fashion, and nor it is purely visual, as it can just as well include sounds and smells; a photograph is thus capable of evoking the emotive and sensory experience of a memory.[45] For Casey, a viewer's memory of the taking of the photograph itself also has the effect of confirming and fixing in his or her own mind the moment of the experienced event, thus underlining the person's emotional response to that event. Casey suggests, therefore, that the photograph plays a very special and complex role in the actual experience of the event itself, not only providing documentary proof of the historical fact of the particular moment in question, but also very likely contributing to the survival of the viewer's own recollection.[46] Tisseron, drawing on Roland Barthes, goes even further and suggests that a photograph may even create a memory in the mind of a viewer for an event which s/he did not in fact experience but which nevertheless conforms to that person's chosen vision of the world.[47] Soulier's contemporaries and generations of Parisians to come, therefore, would have been able to remember or imaginatively (re)construct their 'experience' of the Commune by means of his images and others like them. In 1871 Soulier's photographs may have acted as material substitutes for souvenir shards of the ruined palace itself but, in 1883, when the ruins were finally removed it became possible to acquire those actual shards or, failing that, to buy souvenir paperweights made from them.

Bernard Noël suggests that the complete removal of the Tuileries provided the new Republic with a convenient pretext by which to accuse the Commune for all time of having destroyed one of the nation's greatest public monuments.[48] Kirk Varnedoe, however, suggests the opposite.

For him, those on the Left wished to demolish the Tuileries ruins in order to complete the work of the Commune 'by excising the vestiges of the monarchy from the spiritual heart of the nation'.[49] This may well have been the case among some sections of the radical Left. Vallès, for example, wanted the ruins removed and a new building in glass and steel erected in their place to celebrate the virtue of labour, and for this new 'Palace of Progress' to be open to all. I would suggest, however, that for Gambetta and many other moderate conservative republicans, who right from the outset had done everything they could to distance themselves from the revolutionary Commune, the desire to rid the city of this relic was motivated more by the need to efface not just the memory of the monarchy, Napoleon III and the Second Empire, but more specifically the memory of the Commune in an effort to reunite the nation and consolidate the new republic. In 1882 the republicans finally achieved their objective when the bill recommending that the Tuileries palace be demolished was finally passed. The ruins were duly removed the following year amid accusations of vandalism by the re-actionary Right.

Only the palace's foundations remained, accidentally rediscovered when the whole Louvre site was excavated and redeveloped between 1989 and 1990.[50] Above ground many Parisians and tourists alike would indeed be hard-pressed to tell exactly where the palace once stood. The Tuileries gardens remain deprived of the palace that gave them their identity and the Arc de Triomphe du Carrousel stands alone with no entrance to guard. Up until the time of writing, there is nothing to obstruct that world-famous perspective which runs from Pei's glass pyramid through the Arc du Carrousel to the Obelisk in the Place de la Concorde, along the Champs-Elysées to the Arc de Triomphe and then beyond to the Grande Arche at La Défense, the district named to com-memorate the defence of the city against the Prussians. The three arches stand in line as if that had been the plan all along, whilst the Tuileries palace remains out of sight, a locus, not of memory but of forgetfulness, 'un lieu d'oublie'.

There is, however, a further development to the story of the Tuileries palace. In December 2002 the *Académie du Second Empire* and *Demain le Louvre* (the association responsible for the Grand Prix de Rome and the Prix d'architecture de l'Académie des Beaux-Arts) launched a campaign to build an exact replica of the Tuileries palace. The joint sponsors stress the practical and economic advantages for the city that the reconstruction would provide, such as the creation of an extra 20,000 square metres (excluding basement levels) of much-needed additional exhibition space for the Louvre and the provision of a major new national and international conference centre. They stress also the patriotic, historic, aesthetic and above all moral benefits of returning the Tuileries palace to the nation. It is argued that the project is of considerable moral importance not only because it would serve to familiarize and reconcile young French men and women (perceived as being sorely ignorant of the nation's glorious past) with their own history, but also to remind them that 'modern, noble France' did not come into existence in 1789, much less in 1968.[51] The faithful reconstruction of the palace is described as a 'revolutionary act', as a way of contesting Paris's modern architecture which, it is claimed, is not only lacking in style and of mediocre construction to boot, but (significantly) is devoid of any French features whatsoever. A rebuilt Tuileries palace would, therefore, make Parisians and French people in general aware once more of what is beautiful, ancient, everlasting, solid and spiritually aspirational. Furthermore, it is suggested that the return of the palace would serve to reconcile all the 'tribus gauloises' with their 'History'. In a multicultural present-day France such a statement is somewhat contentious, for how can it still be possible to speak specifically of 'gallic tribes' and one overriding 'History'? If it goes ahead, the rebuilding the Tuileries palace will serve to resurrect the memory of Napoleon III's Paris as well as, paradoxically, to vindicate the reactionary *Ordre moral* and at the same time condemn the topographical memory of Paris and the Commune to oblivion for a second time. However, the apparent lack of engagement on the part of the Left in France with the proposed reconstruction would suggest that the site of the Tuileries is no longer a contested space.

Changing perspectives: Baldus's *Les Principaux Monuments de France*

Edouard-Denis Baldus, a naturalized Frenchman born in Westphalia, Prussia in around 1813 or 1815, moved to Paris in 1839, where he proceeded to set himself up as an artist before subsequently moving to New York. Throughout the 1840s he pursued a career as a portrait painter before returning to Paris and taking a serious interest in photography.[52] In 1851, along with the other 'greats' of early French photography, Bayard, Le Gray, Le Secq and Mestral, Baldus joined the *Mission héliographique*, undertaking a number of official commissions to photograph the great monuments of France.[53] Following the end of the *Mission*, Baldus gained government support for a vast new four-year project, beginning in 1853, and entitled *Villes de France photographiées*. Paris was chosen as the first city and it was at this time that Baldus perfected his method of architectural photography, which would soon come to be recognized as the model of the genre. His most famous project, however, proved to be his series of photographs commissioned, in 1857, by Archille Fould, the Minister of State and the Emperor's Household, documenting the controversial construction of the new Louvre and the extensions that were to link it to the Tuileries palace.

The publication of the Louvre series in 1869 proved timely, for no sooner had it appeared as a three-volume album collection than the Empire collapsed and the Tuileries lay in ruins. Following the demise of the Commune, Baldus does not appear to have joined many of his fellow photographers in their rush to photograph the fire- and bomb-damaged city. Whatever his reasons for not doing so – Malcolm Daniel suggests that Baldus may have felt uneasy photographing the horrors resulting from the aftermath of war between his country of adoption and that of his birth[54] – the success of his earlier volumes on the Louvre would appear to have encouraged him, in 1874, to publish a portfolio of a hundred heliogravures depicting the interior and exterior of Versailles and the Grand and Petit Trianon.[55] He was duly rewarded for his efforts with a medal at the *SFP*'s 1874 exhibition.[56] Baldus's work on Versailles certainly proved popular with illustrators and architects,[57] but it is also perhaps true to say that Versailles, at this point still the official seat of government, was the perfect choice of subject under *l'Ordre moral* and could not have failed to endear Baldus to the new regime and help to cushion the harsh blow dealt to him by the demise of his erstwhile patron, Napoleon III.

In 1875, Baldus followed the success of his series on Versailles with *Les Principaux Monuments de France*, which was published initially by the photographer himself and subsequently by A. Morel. According to Maia-Mari Sutnik, an expanded edition was published the following year and Daniel states that the collection was originally to consist of three volumes or *cahiers*, each containing twenty prints to be marketed at a cost of 80 francs per *cahier*.[58] It is not known how many *cahiers* Baldus actually produced, but as quite costly, high-quality objects they would necessarily have appealed only to wealthy bourgeois and aristocratic collectors, as well as to establisments teaching fine art and architecture. The album in the Victoria and Albert Museum collection, for example, from which the illustrations have been reproduced, consists of plates measuring, on average, 30 × 40 cm (excluding the border), and the album itself, rebound with a gold-embossed leather spine, measures 42 × 61 cm. Thus while these heliogravures cannot be considered as 'popular' in the sense of being extensively diffused, as for example the thousands of photographs of Paris and the Commune which flooded the city in 1871, they nevertheless do provide us with an important insight into the type of pictorial representation of the city which was deemed to be acceptable under *l'Ordre moral*.

Evidence of Baldus's undeniable success among the photograph-buying public is to be found in the *Guide Joanne* guides to Paris, which consistently recommended his landscape views and reproductions of monuments to both Parisians and visitors to the city from the 1850s to the 1870s.[59] It is believed, also, that many of the photographs in Napoleon III's collection, and destroyed in 1871, were the work of Baldus. If the cost of *Les Principaux Monuments de France* put the collection as a whole beyond the reach of most souvenir hunters, Baldus's reprints of photographs or heliogravures, and particularly his smaller format prints and stereographic images of Paris, would certainly have been well within the reach of the average middle-class buyer, as had been the case with Soulier and *Paris incendié, mai 1871*. Such reproductions sold in large numbers and represented a significant proportion of commercial sales during the period.[60] After completing a final project consisting of a hundred photo-engravings of the new Hôtel de Ville in 1882, however, Baldus's popularity went into rapid decline, his work being increasingly perceived as outmoded and technically regressive.[61] Despite still winning a prize in 1878, Baldus was eventually declared bankrupt in 1887 and by the time of his death, in 1889, he was virtually forgotten.[62]

Modern commentators, however, have been quick to observe the avant-garde nature of Baldus's œuvre, particularly his poetic urban panoramas and his depiction of the rapidly developing rail and road infrastructure in France under the Second Empire.[63] But in the case of *Les Principaux Monuments de France*, Baldus can be seen to have reverted voluntarily to the very traditional and classical conventions of architectural photography, which he himself had done so much to establish during his time with the *Mission héliographique*. In one sense the album can be considered, along with Marville's *Album du vieux Paris*, as the photographic equivalent of the memorialist and nostalgic aspects of Du Camp's *Paris: ses organes. Les Principaux Monuments de France* thus reconstructs the nation's glorious religious and secular architectural archive after the humiliation and destruction of national and civil war.

Taken as a whole, the monuments represented in the collection can be seen to celebrate the nation's great medieval, Renaissance and overwhelmingly Christian heritage. Out of a total of forty-five prints, it is significant that twenty are of churches, including four of Notre-Dame de Paris, three of the Sainte-Chapelle, and one each of Saint Germain l'Auxerrois and La Trinité in Paris. It could be argued, therefore, that, unlike Du Camp who, in volume VI of *Paris: ses organes*, actively warns against the interference of the Catholic Church in the nation's affairs, Baldus's collection actually constitutes an endorsement of *l'Ordre moral*. It is equally possible to argue that – by also including amongst his chosen principal national monuments the Palais de Justice, the Pavillon de Flore, the new Opéra and especially the Tuileries (all associated with Napoleon III) – Baldus was equally currying favour among affluent Bonapartists, whose star was now, once again, in the ascendant after their electoral victories in 1874 and 1875. However, the inclusion of the last two heliogravures in the collection, a panoramic view of the Tuileries palace and the Arc du Triomphe du Carrousel with the Tuileries palace in the background reduced to a ruin, not by the events of May 1871, but by Baldus's own artistic hand, would suggest that there is more to Baldus's engagement with the city of *l'Ordre moral* than might at first be apparent.

L'Ordre moral was becoming increasingly unpopular with the general population at this point and forced to fend off attacks from both the Bonapartists and Gambetta's republicans. The Commune was once again top of the agenda following a resurgence of demands for amnesty for ex-Communards and, furthermore, there was a debate raging between the republicans and monarchists over the fate of the Tuileries palace ruins themselves. Many republican deputies wished to remove the ruins altogether in preparation for the forthcoming universal exhibition in 1878, while the monarchists in the National Assembly were campaigning to reconstruct the palace for the eventual restoration of the monarchy.[64] The inclusion by Baldus of these particular images of the Tuileries palace and the Arc de Triomphe du Carousel in *Les Principaux Monuments de France*, therefore, can be interpreted as a desire on the photographer's part, much like Du Camp in the concluding volume of *Paris: ses organes* and Zola in *L'Assommoir*, not just to engage with the issues surrounding the fall of the Empire and the Commune but also to

Figure 21 Edouard-Denis Baldus. 'Palais des Tuileries. (Avant l'incendie de 1871)', *Les Principaux monuments de France*, 1875. Heliogravure. (V&A Images/Victoria and Albert Museum.)

reflect on the nature of MacMahon's regime. This runs contrary to the accepted view that Baldus avoided making any overt political statements through his photographs.[65]

Baldus's inclusion of a panoramic view of the Tuileries palace in *Les Principaux Monuments de France* (Figure 21) entitled 'Palais des Tuilieries (Avant l'incendie de 1871)' ('The Tuileries Palace (Before the fire of 1871')) stands out in marked contrast to the majority of the other important national monuments and buildings depicted in the collection, which tend to be closely focused architectural shots. In this image Baldus has attempted to include as much of the wide palace façade as possible and, by choosing his angle carefully, has prevented the Arc du Carrousel from masking the central domed Pavillon de l'Horloge, with the result that the Pavillon, the focal vertical point of the building, can be seen almost in its entirety to the left of the triumphal arch. This has the effect of drawing the viewer's gaze to the giant domed roof of the Pavillon de l'Horloge, the most dominant object on the skyline. As an example of photographic technique, there is nothing particularly unusual in Baldus's choice of perspective. The majority of contemporary photographs of the eastern aspect of the Tuileries, whether taken from the left- or right-hand side of the main entrance, follow much the same strategy in order to privilege both the palace and the Arc du Carrousel.

Baldus's panoramic view, on the other hand, inevitably privileges the Pavillon de l'Horloge, with the Arc being almost lost against the background of the palace itself. Given the strong association between Napoleon III and the Tuilieries, Baldus's representation might be seen to celebrate the emperor's power over the city and the nation, were it not for the fact that the initial impact of the Pavillon de l'Horloge on the horizon is soon diminished as the eye becomes distracted by the unevenness of the rest of the palace façade and the various levels of rooftops and chimney pots. Furthermore, the panoramic perspective results in the privileging of the vast expanse of courtyard and gardens in the foreground rather than the Tuileries palace itself. The eye is therefore also distracted by the rows of rather ghostly, oddly-placed streetlights, and by what appear to be an old cart, bins, pieces of scaffolding, and piles of sand or cement to the left of the picture.

One is tempted to ask why Baldus should have chosen to include this particular shot of the Tuileries, which appears to have been taken very shortly after the completion of the new Louvre extensions when the trees in the foreground had only just recently been planted. While the angle of the shot succeeds in including most of the palace façade within the picture frame, with the notable exception of the Pavillon de Flore, controversially demolished and reconstructed by Napoleon III, which lies hidden behind part of the southern wing of the new Louvre exten-sion on the left of the picture, it necessarily reduces the power and impact of what had once been indisputably one of France's finest Renaissance buildings. Why also, since the next image in the collection focuses specifically on the Arc du Carrousel, did Baldus choose to repre-sent the palace from its eastern perspective rather than from its more noble western side from the vantage point of the Tuileries gardens? His choice may have been made out of convention but, taken from the garden side, the Tuileries would have benefited from the inclusion of the lake and fountains in the foreground. The western perspective would have offered the eye an unimpeded and far more aesthetically pleasing view of the palace. Baldus has also eschewed the other two familiar photographic vantage points, the oblique perspective from above the rue de Rivoli and that from the Quai des Tuileries alongside the Seine. The prosaic answer to these questions may quite simply be that Baldus did not have any other suitable negative of the Tuileries to hand in 1875.

Figure 22 Edouard-Denis Baldus. 'L'Arc de Triomphe du Carrousel', 1875, *Les Principaux monuments de France*. Heliogravure. (V&A Images/Victoria and Albert Museum.)

However, more attractive versions of the Tuileries from this perspective by him are known to exist, though, of course, we cannot be sure he still had access to these.[66] By including this panoramic view of the Tuileries taken before the fire of 1871 in his collection of 1875 Baldus certainly guaranteed the palace a place in the nation's archive, but by purposefully or unwittingly choosing to include a view of the Tuileries which physically relegates the palace to the margins Baldus can also be perceived to be undermining not just the building itself but also, by implication, the regime which had been most closely associated with it.

In the final image in the collection, 'L'Arc de Triomphe du Carrousel' (Figure 22), Baldus returns to his monumental architectural style of photography. Taken at face value, this imposing image of the Arc du Carrousel can be seen as a reaffirmation of the survival of the city and the nation itself, much as we already saw in Soulier's interior view of the palace looking out towards the Arc (Figure 18). The archway, as an archetype, is said to represent a triumph over the banalities of the material world, combining, as it does, the attributes of the square, which represents the Earth or created universe; the circle, which is associated with Heaven; and the cube, which symbolizes stability. Traditionally, the triumphal arch also represents the city, the realm or the empire. In 'L'Arc de Triomphe du Carrousel', the Tuileries palace is now not just undermined but reduced to an aesthetic ruin in the background serving merely to heighten the already strong impact of the Arc. In reality, the palace façade itself, despite the obvious loss of its cupola, remained very much as it had been before the fire, as examples in Soulier's *Paris incendié* collection clearly show, but by physically cutting out the upper part of the Pavillon de l'Horloge, Baldus effectively turns the central arch of the Arc du Carrousel into the focus of the picture. The hitherto secular Arc du Carrousel thus takes on the symbolic appearance of the gates of heaven, opening the way to revelation and reflecting the harmony of the universe. Baldus's Arc du Carrousel, like Soulier's view of the interior of the palace looking up and out towards the Arc, thus offers the city and the nation the possibility of regeneration and redemption, of making the transition from death to life. Baldus's message here would also appear to echo that of Du Camp in *Paris: ses organes*, and in Zola's work generally: empires may crumble and fall, but the city and the nation live on. What this image appears to be saying – in 1875 – is that while the French nation should be proud of, and *remember*, its past military glories, the true way forward is peace (represented by the allegorical charioteer on the top of the Arc), and that God (in Baldus's view at least) will lead the French people out of the ruins of the past towards salvation. Such an interpretation would be wholly in keeping with the religious revival of the period. However seductive this initial interpretation may be, a closer 'reading' of the history and architectural details of the Arc du Carrousel itself opens up the possibility of another interpretation.

The Arc du Carrousel is not generally considered to be one of Paris's principal monuments. It is dwarfed, in every sense, by contrast to the Arc de Triomphe de l'Etoile or the Tour Eiffel, for example, and consequently its history is often overlooked. And yet, an appreciation of the Arc's history and architectural detail may provide the key to understanding why Baldus (consciously or unconsciously) may have chosen this particular monument rather than, say, the Arc de Triomphe de L'Etoile (included among the earlier images in the collection), or the Vendôme Column (significantly omitted from the collection), or indeed Notre-Dame de Paris, with which to conclude his collection of the nation's architectural treasures.

The Arc du Carrousel was completed in 1808 as part of Napoleon I's project to redevelop the area between the Tuileries and the Louvre. His original intention had been to construct two triumphal archways, one dedicated to peace, the other dedicated to the glory of war but, in the event, only one arch was built, and it remained unclear as to whether it was to celebrate peace or war or both. The Arc du Carrousel was modelled on those of Septimius Severus and Constantine in Rome. It is flanked by eight Corinthian columns and bears the statues of eight soldiers of the French Imperial guard. Napoleon (with uncharacteristic self-effacement) rejected the idea of also placing a statue of himself on top of the arch, but agreed instead that he should be represented on the six bas-reliefs commemorating the battle of Austerlitz, the capitulation of Ulm, his entry into Munich, his meeting with Francis II, the signing of the peace treaty in Presburg, and his entry into Vienna. At its summit, the arch originally supported the statue, acquired by Napoleon in 1797 from Venice, of the Four Horses of the Temple of the Sun at Corinth (also known as *Les Chevaux de Saint-Marc*), with an inscription beneath it, in French (rather than Greek or Latin), celebrating the exploits of the army and Napoleon's triumph at Austerlitz.

In 1815, however, after Napoleon's defeat, and as further evidence of the political investment in such structures, the Duke of Wellington personally attended the removal of the Corinthian Horses and arranged for their return to Venice. The Allies also ordered the removal from the arch of all the imperial bas-reliefs. Between 1828 and 1830, during the restoration of the Bourbon Charles X, six new bas-reliefs, celebrating the heroic exploits of the Duc d'Angoulême, were produced as replacements but these were never to be mounted on the arch and, in fact, they can be seen on display in the exhibition area in the basement of the Louvre complex. In 1828, however, a copy of the Corinthian Horses was erected in place of the original statue with the addition of a central chariot, driven by an allegorical figure, and flanked by two more winged figures.[67] The actual significance of these figures (like the arch itself) remained open to interpretation. Some saw them as celebrating the restoration of the monarchy, others as celebrating peace, and others still as representing military victory. In 1875, therefore, Baldus could not have chosen a more fitting monument with which to complete his collection of images celebrating French architecture. The Arc du Carrousel, like the early Third Republic, is full of ambiguities and contradictions. The arch is modelled on the architecture of classical Greece and Rome but epitomizes the French Imperial style. It sports a series of bas-reliefs and a French inscription celebrating Napoleon's military exploits but is crowned with a meaningless fake Greek statue. All things considered, the Arc du Carrousel is an architectural pastiche attempting to be all things to all men – Bonapartist, royalist, republican – and succeeding, like MacMahon's *Ordre moral*, in satisfying none.

Pictures at an exhibition: Marville's hygienic view

Charles Marville is best known as having been one of Haussmann's official photographers and for his meticulous documentation of the ancient streets of Paris prior to their demolition to make way for the new city of wide boulevards. His *Album du vieux Paris*, containing some 425 of the images commissioned by Haussmann during the 1850s, was displayed in the Pavilion de la Ville de Paris alongside two series of photographs, numbering about a hundred in total, dating from 1876 to 1877, which he had produced as part of a special commission from the Municipal Council of Paris to document the new city in time for the *Exposition* in 1878. Entitled *Travaux*, this exhibit comprised views of a number of new thoroughfares and construction projects. They included, amongst others, the Boulevard Saint-Germain and rue de Rennes extensions, the rue Soufflot, the boulevard Haussmann, the avenue de l'Opéra, and the boulevard Henri IV.[68]

While Marville may not have resorted to enhancing or correcting his images by hand, a common and accepted practice among his contemporaries (Baldus is an obvious example), his close attention to framing, perspective, lighting and props, enabled him to create the perfect 'mise-en-scène' in accordance with the requirements of those who commissioned him. By photographing the new thoroughfares in landscape, for example, he was able to emphasize their width and length under a vast expanse of clear, bright sky. These typical Haussmann perspectives are depicted with scientific precision. The Paris on show is obviously a modern city where the trams run on time and the well-lit boulevards are regularly swept clean. The emphasis placed on the hygienic aspect of the new Paris is further exemplified by the fact that Marville was asked to display some of the many photographs he had taken of the city's new street lighting and 'vespasiennes' (public urinals). The squalid back streets such as the rue Beurrière, for example, which was demolished to make way for the new rue de Rennes, on the other hand, are executed in portrait style, thereby emphasizing their narrowness and darkness. Marville is even known to have sprayed the cobblestones in these old streets and alleyways with water in an attempt to render them unsanitary in appearance. The message is clear: no one but the most destitute would want to live in these streets, let alone bring up their children in them. In this way Marville provided the visual evidence that Haussmann and his Third Republic successors required to justify the demolitions.

While many of the schemes depicted in *Travaux* had been conceived and in some cases even partly executed, under Napoleon III, Marville's contemporary audience at the *Exposition universelle* in 1878 would have been in no doubt that the demolitions, building sites and new boulevards on display formed part of the restructuring of the post-Second-Empire, post-Commune, modern city. And, while Paris still contained at its heart, and for all to see, many ruins and scars from the time of the Commune, these material traces had either already become part of the 'normal' landscape or else had been appropriated for other purposes. The Tuileries palace, for example, was partly concealed behind a vast orchestra stand and auditorium,[69] while the place du Carrousel housed a giant stationary balloon which was to remain in place for many months following the close of the *Exposition*.

In the model of the new metropolis exhibited in the Pavillon de la Ville de Paris, no less than in Marville's selective view of 'le vieux Paris', the Paris of the Commune might have never existed. One reactionary visitor, Ernest Delloye, for example, who had come to Paris hoping to see photographs of the buildings destroyed by the fires of the Commune was deeply disappointed to find that such images were not on show and concluded that the organizers must have stipulated that they be purposely forgotten.[70] Furthermore, anyone, like Du Camp, who might have come searching for a celebration, or at least an acknowledgement, of the achievements of Second-Empire urban planning would have been equally disappointed.

If, as we have seen, the ironic sub-text to Walker's 'promenades' in *Le Monde illustré* sometimes served to remind that journal's intended readers of the trauma of their shared past, the discrete version of history presented in the combined *Vieux Paris* and *Travaux* exhibit, by contrast, can be said to constitute a denial of the existence of both the Second Empire and the Commune, and is symbolic of the appropriation of the city (and of its photographer), by Gambetta and the republican Municipal Council of Paris, the driving force behind the *Exposition universelle*. In this sense the exhibits are also, effectively, a response to what Nietzsche considered to be an unhealthy obsession with the past, which was preventing his generation from moving forward and attaining happiness.[71] Taking the view that history is useful only so long as it serves life and that once it no longer serves this purpose it should be abandoned, Nietzsche argues in favour of a 'hygiene of life' as the means by which to counter this 'malady of history' (p. 63). For Nietzsche, the ability to forget is not only 'essential to action of any kind' but it is also important to be able to 'forget at the right time' as well as 'to remember at the right time'; to be able to sense when 'it is necessary to feel historically and when unhistorically' (where 'unhistorical' is defined as 'the art and power of *forgetting* and of enclosing oneself within a bounded horizon') (pp. 63, 120). In praising the power of oblivion, Nietzsche goes on to single out the ancient Greeks as an example of how a people gradually learned to organize chaos by following Delphic teaching and thinking back to themselves, to their real needs and how it was 'through the higher force of their *moral* nature that the Greeks achieved victory over all other cultures' (p. 223). Nietzsche was writing with Germany in mind, but there are clear parallels to be drawn with France after 1871. The new hygienic Paris depicted in *Travaux* exemplifies Nietzsche's 'unhistorical', 'bounded horizon'; it is Paris as moral Athens as opposed to decadent Rome, Gambetta's 'Athenian Republic' as opposed to Napoleon III's 'Roman Empire'.[72] The city depicted in *Travaux* represents peace and order as opposed to war and chaos, beauty and creativity as opposed to ugliness and destruction, and healthy forgetting as opposed to unhealthy remembering. In 1878, therefore, Marville conveys through the use of his 'objective' lens the essence of that centrist bourgeois republicanism which would finally defeat *l'Ordre moral*, return Paris to its status of capital, grant amnesty to ex-Communards, and place that 'tombstone of oblivion' over the Commune itself.

Notes

1 Walter Benjamin, 'Charles Baudelaire' and 'A Small History of Photography', in *One-Way Street and Other Writings*, trans. by Edmund Jephcott and Kingsley Shorter (London: Verso, 1979), pp. 146, 250. *The Arcades Project*, 'Exposé of 1935', p. 6.

2 Benjamin, *The Arcades Project*, 'Exposé of 1935', p. 13, 'Exposé of 1939', pp. 25–6.

3 Roger Scruton, 'Photography and Representation', *Critical Inquiry*, 7 (1980–81), pp. 577–603 (589–90).

4 Susan Sontag, *On Photography*, 2nd edn (London: Penguin, 1986), pp. 4, 154.

5 Roland Barthes, *La Chambre claire: note sur la photographie* (Paris: Seuil, 1980), p. 18.

6 Scruton, pp. 593–4.

7 Sontag, p. 154.

8 Barthes, *La Chambre claire*, p. 65, and *Mythologies*, 2nd edn (Paris: Seuil, 1970), pp. 98, 152, 183.

9 Sontag, pp. 4, 17.

10 Ross, 'What Photographs Can't Do', *The Journal of Aesthetics and Art Criticism*, 41: 1 (autumn 1982), pp. 5–17 (pp. 7–8).

11 John Snyder and Neil Walsh Allen 'Photography, Vision, and Representation', *Critical Inquiry*, 2 (1975), p. 144.

12 Sontag, p. 86.

13 Pierre Bourdieu, *Un art moyen: essai sur les usages sociaux de la photographie* (Paris: Editions de Minuit, 1965), p. 25.

14 See *Annuaire général de la photographie: France, Belgique, Suisse* (Paris: Librairie Plon, 1892), pp. 370–1, and Armand Bigeon, *La Photographie devant la loi et devant la jurisprudence* (Paris: Société d'éditions scientifiques, 1892), pp. 95–8.

15 *Annuaire général de la photographie*, p. 370. See also English, p. 14.

16 Bigeon, pp. 98–9.

17 English, p. 3.

18 *Dépôt légal* records, Cabinet de la photographie et de l'estampe, Bibliothèque nationale de France.

19 The entry for the Tuileries by a German company, Brauneck Maier, does not state whether the photograph was taken before or after May 1871. *Bulletin de la Société française de photographie* (1876), pp. 19, 11, 30, 38, 298.

20 See Ernest Lacan, *Le Moniteur de la photographie*, 16 May 1878.

21 See Alphonse Davanne, *Exposition universelle interationale de Paris à Paris. Rapport sur les Epreuves et les appareils de photographie* (Paris: Imprimerie nationale, 1880), pp. 9, 44.

22 An earlier version of this analysis of Soulier's photographs, 'The Politics and Aesthetics of a Phantom Palace: Le Palais des Tuileries in Charles Soulier's *Paris incendié, mai 1871*' appeared in *Romance Studies*, 22: 3 (November 2004), pp. 197–207.

23 Luxenberg, pp. 122–4, 132–3.

24 English, pp. 46–51.

25 See Edouard Dangin, 'Notices sur les monuments et rues incendiés', in Henri de Bleignerie and Edouard Dangin, *Paris incendié 1871: album historique* (Paris: A. Jarry, 1871).

26 See Sontag, p. 5, Barthes, *La Chambre Claire*, p. 25, and also Du Camp, *LC*, II, pp. 234–5. It was not until much later in the century that Commune sympathizers were to re-use many of the same images to promote their own version of events in, for example, the anonymous album entitled, *Paris sous la Commune par un temoin fidèle: la photographie*. See English, p. 24. See also

Andy Stafford, '"La légende de l'histoire": Bernard Noël's Captions for Photography of the Paris Commune', *Contemporary French and Francophone Studies*, 10: 3 (August 2006), pp. 291–300.

27 See Michèle and Michel Auer, *Encyclopédie internationale des photographes de 1839 à nos jours*, 2 vols (Hermance, Switzerland: Camera Obscura, 1985), II; and Elizabeth Anne McCauley, *Industrial Madness: Commercial Photography in Paris 1848–1871* (New Haven, CT, and London: Yale University Press, 1994), p. 310.

28 Shelley Rice, *Parisian Views* (Cambridge, MA, and London: MIT Press, 1997), pp. 133–6.

29 Lacan, *Le Moniteur de la photographie*, 15 June 1869.

30 Lacan, *Le Moniteur de la photographie*, 1 August 1871; Gautier, p. 338.

31 Luxenberg, p. 116.

32 Auer, II.

33 The labelling and references on each mount were added later, in 1899, by cataloguers from the Victoria and Albert Museum when the prints were transferred from the National Art Library to the Print, Drawings and Paintings Collection.

34 The series comprises views of the Hôtel de Ville, Vendôme Column, Ministry of Finance, cour des Comptes, place Château d'Eau and surrounding buildings, boulevard Voltaire, Palais Royale, rue Royale, rue de Rivoli, Bibliothèque du Louvre, rue de Lille, Préfecture de Police, Colonne de juillet, boulevard and Théâtre Saint-Martin, Caisse des Dépôts et Consignateurs, Légion d'Honneur, Grenier d'Abondance, avenue de Neuilly, Porte Maillot, Point-du-Jour, destroyed houses in Auteuil, and Palais de Saint-Cloud and the surrounding area.

35 Lapostolle, 'Plus vrai que le vrai', pp. 69–70. See also Tillier, ch. XIX.

36 See Millot in Bellet and Régnier, pp. 194–8.

37 See Gen Doy, 'The Camera against the Paris Commune', in *Photography/Politics One*, ed. by Victor Burgin et al. (London: Photography Workshop, 1979), pp. 13–16; and Tillier, pp. 357–9.

38 Sontag, p. 79.

39 Luxemberg, p. 116.

40 See Roland Mortier, *La Poétique des ruines en France: ses origines, ses variations de la Renaissance à Victor Hugo* (Geneva: Droz, 1974), pp. 8, 127–9; and Luxenberg, pp. 122, 135, n. 68.

41 Gaston Bachelard, *La Psychanalyse du feu* (Paris: Gallimard, 1949), chs 1, 2.

42 Gautier, pp. 320–1, 338.

43 Graham Robb, *Victor Hugo* (London: Picador, 1997), p. 472.

44 Sontag, p. 10.

45 Serge Tisseron, *Le Mystère de la chambre claire: photographie et inconscient* (Paris: Flammarion, 1996), p. 138.

46 Casey, p. 23.

47 Tisseron, p. 140.

48 Noël, *Dictionnaire de la Commune*, p. 262.

49 Varnedoe, p. 63.

50 See Catherine Marcille, 'Le Château des Tuileries', in *Grand Louvre: sous les jardins du Carrousel, Les Dossiers d'Archéologie*, 190 (February 1994), pp. 64–71.

51 See www.tuileries.org, Section 4 'Pourquoi reconstruire?', sub-sections 4.5 'Le Patrimoine national', and 4.7 'Un Projet révolutionnaire'. The *Comité national pour la reconstruction des Tuileries* was inaugurated on 11 February 2004 under the honorary presidency of the Princess Napoléon and Alain Boumier, president of the *Académie du Second Empire*. The estimated cost of the project is 300 million euros to be paid for by sponsorship, and national and international public donations. It is intended that the building be given as a gift to the nation on its completion.

52 See Daniel, in Lambert, p. 20; and Bernard Marbot, ed., *Une invention du XIXe siècle. Expression et technique, la photographie. Collections de la Société française de photographie* (Paris: Bibliothèque nationale, 1976), p. 81.

53 See Anne de Mondenard, *Mission héliographique de 1851* (Paris: Editions du patrimoine, 2002).

54 Daniel, in Lambert, p. 65.

55 A heliogravure, or photogravure, is the result of a photomechanical process of reproduction derived from engraving methods and developed from the work of early photographers Niépce, Talbot, Baldus and Nègre. The process offers excellent definition.

56 *Bulletin de la Société française de photographie*, 19: 6 (June 1874), pp. 155, 178, 245.

57 Daniel, in Lambert, p. 96.

58 Maia-Mari Sutnik, *Edouard Baldus Heliogravures: Selections from 'Les Principaux monuments de la France'* (Toronto: Art Gallery of Toronto, 1994), p. 5, and Lambert, p. 272, n. 263. Research to date has not confirmed whether all sixty prints were ever published. Of the collections identified by Daniel, those held by the Centre Canadien d'Architecture in Montreal, the Avery Architectural and Fine Arts Library at Columbia University in New York, and the National Art Library at the Victoria and Albert Museum in London, each contain forty-five prints. The copy held by the Musée Carnavalet (ref. PH28491) certainly includes a copy of 'L'Arc de Triomphe du Carrousel' (reproduced in Frizot, p. 757), but I have not yet had the opportunity to verify the album for myself.

59 Joanne, *Paris illustré en 1870 et 1877. Guide de l'étranger et du Parisien* (Paris: Hachette, 1877), p. lxxvi.

60 See McCauley, pp. 27, 97, 100, 305.

61 Davanne, p. 31.

62 Daniel, in Lambert, p. 96.
63 See Rice, pp. 194–207; Heilbrun, in Lambert, p. 13; and Elvire Perego, in Frizot, pp. 213–14.
64 See Tersen, 'L'Opinion publique et la Commune de Paris (1871–79)', pp. 32–7; and Varnedoe.
65 Daniel, in Lambent, p. 96.
66 A similar photograph from about 1860 is reproduced in Rice, p. 23.
67 See Patrice Boussel in *Dictionnaire de Paris* (Paris: Larousse, 1964), p. 99.
68 Copies are reproduced in Thézy, pp. 322, 442–7, 477, 562, 564–7, 513.
69 Réné Delorme, 'Causerie: La fête du 30 juin', in *Les Chefs d'œuvres d'art à l'exposition universelle, 1878*, ed. by Auguste Emile Bergerat (Paris: n.pub., 1878), p. 38.
70 Ernest Delloye, *1878 Exposition: notes et souvenirs* (Paris: Baltenweck, 1878), pp. 87–8.
71 Nietzsche, 'On the Uses and Disadvantages of History', p. 120.
72 Bury, *Gambetta's Final Years*, p. 18, n. 48.

6

Conclusion

There are aspects of Paris's history which are painful, but which have to be talked about.

(Bertrand Delanoë, 17 October 2001)[1]

After years of lobbying by the Association Les Amis de la Commune, the inauguration of the place de la Commune in a small quiet square in the Butte aux Cailles, not far from the Association's headquarters in the rue des Cinq-Diamants, marked somewhat of a turning point in the repression of the memory of the Commune. As might be expected, the path to such recognition was far from smooth, however. Even after the official go-ahead for the naming of the square was given, there were still obstacles to overcome. For electoral reasons no doubt, it was the right-wing politician and the then Mayor of Paris Jean Tibéri who gave the final approval for the creation of the place de la Commune, but he drew the line at allowing the unveiling of the blue and white plaque marking the site of one of the last Communard barricades to take place on 18 March 2000 in celebration of the birth of the Commune, and 19 April was instead chosen as the inauguration date. An unofficial celebration went ahead regardless on 18 March in defiance of the mayor's orders. The erection of the plague itself was also not without incident. The first plaque to be cast and mounted was inscribed simply 'placc de la Commune de Paris' with the all too crucial date, 1871, mysteriously omitted. Protests were duly raised and a replacement was installed. Periodically the plaque disappears altogether, the thief or thieves remaining anonymous and their motives left unclear. Each time the valuable trophy is replaced.

Though not much visited by tourists, who tend to stay in the city centre, the Butte aux Cailles is in fact quite an ancient and historic site in its own right and not just because of its association with the Commune. The blue plaque in the place de la Commune therefore finds itself situated alongside one of those traditional brown shields of the sort seen at every historic location in Paris. The shield recounts the Butte's long history going back to the sixteenth century but surprisingly (or not) makes no mention at all of the Commune. As with the Mur des fédérés, one has to know the history of the Commune already in order to understand what is being commemorated by the simple description on the blue plaque: 'place de la Commune de Paris 1871'. The brown shield and the blue plaque stand together and apart, each in its own way denying the existence of the other; one celebrates a comfortable, nostalgic French *patrimoine* or heritage, while the other acts as a reminder of the city's bloody past and the persistent desire of its citizens to be seen and heard. During the official ceremony on 19 April 2000, Tibéri surprised all those present by paradoxically claiming to be an inheritor of the Commune's mantle while at the same time invoking the memory of Adolphe Thiers. He was suitably booed for his pains.

In that same year, the Commune was also commemorated at the Musée d'art et d'histoire at Saint-Denis to the north of the city where, in addition to its permanent display covering the events of 1870 and 1871, the museum also mounted an exhibition of Bruno Braquehais's photographs of the Commune. At the high-profile Musée d'Orsay, two further linked exhibitions, 'Courbet et la Commune' and 'La Commune photographiée', were also held, accompanied by a screening of Peter Watkins's controversial film, *La Commune: Paris 1871*. The following year, 2001, the Musée de l'Histoire vivante in the suburb of Montreuil to the east of Paris celebrated the life of Louise Michel. Also in 2001, and coincidentally on 18 March, Paris elected itself a new mayor, Bertrand Delanoë, the first Socialist to occupy the post since the Commune.

Later that year, on 17 October 2001, and against much opposition from the extreme Right and sections of the police department, another plaque was unveiled in the city, this time by Delanoë in recognition of those killed in another suppressed state-sanctioned atrocity. The plaque in question, placed near the Pont Saint Michel (and easily missed) marks the spot where, on 17 October 1961, a number of Algerian protestors were cast into the Seine after being brutally beaten or killed on the orders of the then Chief of Police and veteran Vichy official Maurice Papon. As with the *Semaine sanglante*, the total number of those killed on 17 October 1961 is unknown and again as in 1871 the waters of the Seine ran red with the blood of the victims whose bodies were washed up on the river's banks for weeks afterwards. The plaque reads: 'A la mémoire des nombreux Algeriens tués lors de la sanglante repression de la manifestation pacifique du 17 octobre 1961' (In memory of the numerous Algerians killed during the bloody suppression of the peaceful demonstration on 17 October 1961).[2] The decision to acknowledge the massacre in this way was taken without the approval of the centre and right-wing political parties, who also boycotted the unveiling of the plaque. Many saw the move as provocative and declared that the whole event was totally inappropriate especially in the light of the perceived terrorist threat to the city following the 11 September attacks on the Twin Towers in New York. Jean-Paul Proust, Chief of Police in 2001, declared that all the victims of the Franco-Algerian war should have been commemorated, including the policemen and gendarmes killed in the line of duty.[3] For those who supported the move, however, the plaque could only be a small step towards a total lifting of the taboo in France relating to the Algerian war of independence. Some called for open access to the archives of the period and for the full history of the conflict to be included on the school curriculum.[4] For his part, Delanoë admitted that 'there are parts of Paris's history which are painful, but which have to be talked about'[5] and that the official acknowledgement of what took place in the city on 17 October 1961 was a way of turning the page on the past, moving on and looking ahead to the future.[6]

If it was obviously too soon for Paris to stage an accompanying exhibition on the Algerian war in 2001, the Commune at least continued that year to be the subject of official commemoration, this time at the Sénat (National Assembly), the seat of government itself, from 22 November to 8 December. This brief landmark exhibition entitled 'La Commune de Paris a 130 ans – 20 peintres aujourd'hui' (The Paris Commune is 130 years old – 20 modern-day painters) was organized by Les Amis de la Commune and officially opened by Raymond Forni, the then Socialist President of the National Assembly. More exhibitions followed: 'Paris incendié, 21–28 mai 1871', again at the Musée d'art et d'histoire at Saint Denis in 2002–3, and 'La Commune de Paris, 1871' at the Hôtel de Ville in 2004, again organized by Les Amis de la Commune as part of their annual celebrations in various parts of the capital with Communard links.

Those who know the history of the Commune and who go looking for traces of it in modern-day Paris will find that its memory is certainly being kept alive by Les Amis de la Commune, the French Communist Party, and others on the Left through various events and exhibitions, ceremonies at the Mur des fédérés at Père-Lachaise on the 18 March and other memorable dates, guided tours of the city, and community theatre projects, but also through street names and unofficial markings on pavements and buildings, as well as through private displays of photographs and other memorabilia in some of the bars and cafés in the working-class districts of the city such as Belleville and La Villette. It was not until 2001, however, that the repression of the Commune was officially recognized by the state when Forni paid tribute to the thousands of anonymous and unarmed Parisians murdered in an act of unprecedented ferocity by the Versaillais.[7] Forni's reference to the Versaillais, however, was a telling reminder that all moderate republicans from Gambetta onwards have always tried to disassociate themselves and the Republic from the state's slaughter of its own citizens by placing the blame for *la Semaine sanglante* and the repression that followed squarely on the shoulders of Adolphe Thiers and his monarchist supporters, and thereby conveniently ignoring the fact that many who called themselves republicans in 1871 also supported the national government's action. If we are to believe Forni, the Commune has never disappeared from the (French) collective memory. And yet, despite Forni's endorsement, despite all the public demonstrations of remembrance in the capital from 2000 to 2004, and despite all the political activism and scholarship devoted to keeping its memory alive, particularly since May 1968, the Commune, no less than the Algerian war of independence, continues to be marginalized in the French education system and there remains much ignorance both in France and elsewhere about this 'other French revolution' and the terrible retribution meted out by the state to its own people.[8]

Some might argue along with Nietzsche that it is unhealthy and counter-productive for nations to remember too much, that there comes a time to cast off those chains that bind us to the past. Henri Rousso's solution to overcoming the problem of remembering past crimes, written with the Holocaust and France's collaboration during the Second World War specifically in mind, strikes one as more compelling, however. According to Rousso, we should not forget such crimes, nor should we try to live as if they had never happened, but instead we should learn to live with the memories in the knowledge that it is impossible ever to make up for them or to change the past.[9]

If the events of the *Semaine sanglante* and its aftermath may appear to belong to some long distant past, we need only to think of the civil war in Spain in 1936, France and Algeria in the 1950s and 1960s, the Troubles in Northern Ireland, the repression of student protestors in Tiananmen Square in 1989, the internecine conflicts in Yugoslavia, Rwanda and Chechnya in the 1990s, the containing conflicts in the Middle East, and the torching of Paris's working-class suburbs in 2005 and 2006 by alienated young people living on the margins of society, to realize that the issues raised by the Commune remain as pertinent today as they were during the early Third Republic. An understanding of the ways in which memories of the Commune were constructed and promulgated, repressed and suppressed, helps to shed light on these other conflicts, therefore, and also raises some broader questions relating to political and social exclusion, censorship, government propaganda and the role of the media, historical revisionism, conflicts between different versions of 'memory' and 'history', the ways in which individuals and societies choose to deal with inconvenient memories and to explain their own past to themselves, and how, as Halbwachs suggests, the constructed histories or school textbook accounts of a nation's past are typically the creation of the dominant social class.

Notes

1 Cited on http://news.bbc.co.uk/2/hi/world/monitoring/media_reports/1604970.stm (accessed 20 April 2006).
2 Ibid. As noted and translated by the BBC.
3 *Le Monde*, 17 October 2001 noted on www.algeria-watch.org/farticle/1954–62/17oct_polemique.htm (accessed 20 April 2006).
4 Ibid.
5 Cited on http://news.bbc.co.uk/2/hi/world/monitoring/media_reports/1604970.stm (accessed 20 April 2006).
6 Noted on www.humanite.fr/journal/2001-10-16/2001-10-16-251944 (accessed 20 April 2006).
7 See Forni's speech reproduced in the catalogue to the exhibition, 'La Commune de Paris a 130 ans – 20 peintres aujourd'hui'. My thanks to Madame Laurence Goux of the Musée d'art et d'histoire at Saint-Denis for kindly giving me a copy of the speech and to Les Amis de la Commune for giving me a copy of the catalogue itself together with much more useful documentation.
8 See Bernard Frederick in *L'Humanité*, 20 April 2000. The article can be accessed at www.humanite.presse.fr/journal/2000-04-20/2000-04-20-223878. See also Shafer, p. 184.
9 Rousso, 'Mémoire et oubli', in *Pourquoi se souvenir?*, ed. by Françoise Barret-Ducrocq (Paris: Bernard Graset, 1999), p. 112.

Bibliography

Manuscripts and photographs

Du Camp, Maxime
Paris, Bibliothèque de l'Institut, fonds Maxime Du Camp, portefeuille des *Convulsions de Paris*, 3723, 3745
Paris, Bibliothèque de l'Institut, fonds Maxime Du Camp, correspondence with Prosper de Barante, 2715

Baldus, Edouard-Denis
London, National Art Library, Victoria and Albert Museum, *Les Principaux Monuments de France* (1875), 106 c.23

Soulier, Charles
London, Print, Drawings, and Paintings Collection, Victoria and Albert Museum, *Paris Incendié, mai 1871*, MX14 X83B

Primary texts

Alexis, Paul, '*Naturalisme pas mort': Lettres inédites de Paul Alexis à Emile Zola 1871–1900*, ed. by B.H. Bakker (Toronto: University of Toronto Press, 1971)

Annuaire de la presse, 1881 (Paris: L'Agence télégraphique universelle, 1881)

Annuaire général de la photographie: France, Belgique, Suisse (Paris: Librairie Plon, 1892)

Barante, Amable Guillaume Prosper Brugière de, *Histoire des ducs de Bourgogne de la maison de Valois 1364–1477*, 13 vols, 3rd edn (Paris: Ladvocat, 1825–26)

Bergerat, Auguste Emile, *Les Chefs d'œuvres d'art à l'exposition universelle, 1878* (Paris: n.pub., 1878)

Bibliography

Bleignerie, Henri de and Edouard Dangin, *Paris incendié 1871: album historique* (Paris: A. Jarry, 1871)

Bulletin de la Société française de photographie, 18–20 (1869–78)

Coppée, François, *Œuvres: Théâtre: 1869–72* (Paris: Alphonse Lemerre, n.d.)

Coppée, François, *Œuvres: Poèsies II, 1869–1875* (Paris: Alphonse Lemerre, n.d.)

Coppée, François, *François Coppée: Lettres à sa mère et à sa sœur: 1862–1908*, ed. by Jean Monval (Paris: Alphonse Lemerre, 1914)

Davanne, Alphonse, *Exposition universelle internationale de Paris à Paris. Rapport sur les épreuves et les appareils de photographie* (Paris: Imprimerie nationale, 1880)

Dayot, Armand, *L'Invasion, le Siège, la Commune, 1870–1871* (Paris: Flammarion, 1895(?))

Delloye, Ernest (Baron de Marcq), *1878 Exposition: notes et souvenirs* (Paris: Baltenweck, 1878)

Discours prononcés dans la séance publique tenue par l'Académie française pour la réception de Maxime Du Camp, le 23 décembre 1880 (Paris: Firmin-Didot, 1880)

Discours prononcés dans la séance publique tenue par l'Académie française pour la réception de M. Paul Bourget, le 13 juin 1895 (Paris: Firmin-Didot, 1895)

Du Camp, Maxime, *Les Ancêtres de la Commune: L'Attentat Fieschi* (Paris: Charpentier, 1877)

Du Camp, Maxime, *Les Chants modernes* (Paris: Librairie nouvelle, 1860)

Du Camp, Maxime, *Les Convulsions de Paris*, 4 vols, 1st edn (Paris: Hachette, 1878–80)

Du Camp, Maxime, *Les Convulsions de Paris*, 4 vols, 5th edn (Paris: Hachette, 1881)

Du Camp, Maxime, *Paris After the Prussians*, trans. by Philip A. Wilkins (London and Melbourne: Hutchinson, 1940)

Du Camp, Maxime, *Paris: ses organes, ses fonctions et sa vie dans la seconde moitié du XIXe siècle*, 6 vols, 1st edn (Paris: Hachette, 1869–76)

Du Camp, Maxime, *Paris: ses organes, ses fonctions et sa vie dans la seconde moitié du XIXe siècle*, 6 vols (Paris: Hachette, 1884–95): I (1893), II (1883), III (1895), IV (1894), V (1884), VI (1884)

Du Camp, Maxime, *Souvenirs littéraires*, 2 vols (Paris: Hachette, 1882–83)

Du Camp, Maxime, *Un Voyageur en Egypte vers 1850: 'Le Nil' de Maxime Du Camp*, ed. by Michel Dewachter et al. (n.p.: Sand/Coni, 1987)

L'Exposition de Paris (1878) (Paris: Librairie illustrée and Librairie M. Dreyfous, 1878)

Flaubert, Gustave, *Correspondance supplément: juillet 1877–mai 1880*, ed. by René Dumesnil et al. (Paris: Editions Conrad, 1951)

Flaubert, Gustave, *Correspondances, Flaubert-Alfred Le Poittevin, Flaubert-Maxime Du Camp*, ed. by Yvan Leclerc (Paris: Flammarion, 2000)

Flaubert, Gustave, *Œuvres complètes de Gustave Flaubert: Correspondance (1877–1880)* (Paris: Louis Conrad, 1930)

Bibliography

Flourens, Gustave, *Paris livré*, 6th edn (Paris: A. Le Chevalier, 1873)

Gautier, Théophile, *Tableaux de Siège: Paris, 1870–1871*, 2nd edn (Paris: Charpentier, 1895)

Joanne, Adolphe, *Paris illustré en 1870. Guide de l'étranger et du Parisien* (Paris: Hachette, 1871)

Joanne, Adolphe, *Paris illustré en 1870 et 1877. Guide de l'étranger et du Parisien* (Paris: Hachette, 1877)

Lissagaray, Prosper-Olivier, *Histoire de la Commune de 1871* (Paris: Maspero, 1970)

Lissagaray, Prosper-Olivier, *Les Huit Journées de mai derrière les barricades (1871)* (Paris: Editions d'histoire sociale, 1968)

Lorédan, Larchey, *Mémorial des deux sièges de Paris, 1870–71* (Paris: 1872)

Maisonneufve, V.-F., *La Nouvelle-Calédonie et les îles de déportation* (Paris: Au bureau de *l'Eclipse*, 1872)

Maisonneufve, V.-F., *La Presse populaire: Tony Révillon* (Paris: Lachaud, 1869)

Marx, Karl, *The Civil War in France (1871)*, ed. by Frederick Engels, 2nd edn (Moscow: Progress Publishers, 1977)

Mendès, Catulle, *Les 73 journées de la Commune (du 18 mars au 20 mai 1871)* (Paris: Lachaud, 1871)

Michel, Louise, *La Commune: histoire et souvenirs*, 2 vols (1898) (Paris: Maspero, 1970)

Morisot, Berthe, *Correspondance de Berthe Morisot avec sa famille et ses amis*, ed. by Denis Rouart (Paris: Quatre Chemins Editart, 1950)

Nass, Lucien, *Le Siège de Paris et la Commune* (Paris: Plon, 1914)

Le Monde Illustré, 1871–79

Le Moniteur de la photographie: revue intérnationale des progrès du nouvel art, 1869–78

Prolès, Charles, *Gustave Flourens. Insurrection crétoise 1867–68. Siège de Paris 1870–71* (Paris: Chamel, 1898)

Renan, Ernest, *Qu'est-ce qu'une nation?*, ed. by Joël Roman (Paris: Presses Pocket, 1992)

Robida, Albert, *Album du Siège et de la Commune*, ed. by Lucien Scheler, 2 vols (Paris: Librairie Historique and Librairie Thomas-Scheler, 1971)

Le Siècle, 1871 and 1879

Taine, Hippolyte, *Essais de critique et d'histoire* (1855), 3rd edn (Paris: Hachette, 1874)

Taine, Hippolyte, *Histoire de la littérature anglaise*, 5 vols, 2nd edn (Paris: Hachette, 1899)

Taine, Hippolyte, *Les Origines de la France contemporaine* (Paris: Hachette, 1876)

Thierry, Jacques Nicolas Augustin, *Œuvres* (Brussels: Human, 1839)

Vallès, Jules, *L'Insurgé*, ed. by Marie-Claire Bancquart (Paris: Gallimard, 1975)

Vallès, Jules, *Le Tableau de Paris* (Paris: Editions de Delphes, 1964)

Zola, Emile, *La Débâcle*, ed. by Robert Lethbridge, trans. by Elinor Dorday (Oxford: Oxford University Press, 2000)

Zola, Emile, *Ecrits sur l'art*, ed. by Jean-Pierre Leduc-Adine (Paris: Gallimard, 1991)

Zola, Emile, *Emile Zola: Correspondance*, ed. by B.H. Bakker, 10 vols (Montreal: University of Montreal, 1978–95)

Zola, Emile, *Œuvres complètes*, ed. by Henri Mitterand, 15 vols (Paris: Cercle du livre précieux, 1966–69)

Zola, Emile, *Les Rougon-Macquart*, ed. by Henri Mitterand, 5 vols (Paris: Gallimard, 1960–67)

Zola, Emile, *Le Ventre de Paris*, ed. by Marc Baroli (Paris: Lettres Modernes Minard, 1969)

Zola, Emile, *Le Ventre de Paris*, ed. by R.A. Jouanny (Paris: Garnier Flammarion, 1971)

Secondary texts: history, representation and interpretation of the Commune

The following is not intended to be an exhaustive list.

Baas, Jacquelynn, 'Edouard Manet and *Civil War*', *Art Journal*, 45: 1 (spring 1985), pp. 36–42

Bajac, Quentin, ed., *La Commune photographiée* (Paris: Editions de la Réunion des musées nationaux, 2000)

Bellet, Roger and Philippe Régnier, eds, *Ecrire la Commune: Temoignages, récits et romans (1871–1881–1931)* (Tusson, Charante: Editions De Lérot, 1994)

Boime, Albert, *Art and the French Commune: Imagining Paris after War and Revolution* (Princeton: Princeton University Press, 1995)

Braire, Jean, *Sur les traces des Communards: enquête dans les rues de Paris d'aujourd'hui* (Paris: Editions Amis de la Commune, 1988)

Doy, Gen, 'The Camera against the Paris Commune', in *Photography/Politics One*, ed. by Victor Burgin et al. (London: Photography Workshop, 1979), pp. 13–26

Dupuy, Aimé, *1870–1871: La Guerre, la Commune et la presse* (Paris: Armand Colin, 1959)

Eichner, Carolyn J., *Surmounting the Barricades: Women in the Paris Commune* (Bloomington: Indiana University Press, 2004)

English, Donald E., *Political Uses of Photography in the Third French Republic, 1871–1914* (Ann Arbor, MI: University of Michigan Research Press, 1981)

Europe, 499–500 (November–December 1970)

Gaudin, Pierre, and Claire Revercheron, 'Une image renversée: les photographies des barricades de la Commune', in *La Barricade*, ed. by Alain Corbin and Jean-Marie Mayeur (Paris: La Presse de la Sorbonne, 1997), pp. 337–40

Bibliography

Gautrand, Jean-Claude, '1870–1871: Les Photographes et la Commune', *Photo-Ciné-Revue* (February 1972), pp. 53–63

Glazer, Catherine, 'De la Commune comme maladie mentale', *Romantisme*, 48 (1985), pp. 63–70

Gonzalez, Sylvie and Bertrand Tillier, *Le Siège et la Commune de Paris 1870–1781* (Paris: Musée d'art et d'histoire, Saint-Denis, 2001)

Gould, Roger V., *Insurgent Identities: Class, Community, and Protest in Paris from 1848 to the Commune* (Chicago: University of Chicago Press, 1995)

Gullickson, Gay L., *Unruly Women of Paris: Images of the Commune* (Ithaca, NY, and London: Cornell University Press, 1996)

Harvey, David, *Consciousness and the Urban Experience* (Oxford: Blackwell, 1985)

Horne, Alistair, *The Fall of Paris: The Siege and the Commune, 1870–71* (London: Macmillan, 1965)

Hugues, Nouhaud, 'Témoignage ou esthétique de la ruine photographiée: A. Liébert et la guerre de 1870–71' (unpublished maîtrise d'histoire de l'art, Paris X Nanterre, Bibliothèque Nationale, June 1993)

Jellinek, Frank, *The Paris Commune* (London: Victor Gollancz, 1937)

Joughin, Jean T., 'The Paris Commune in French Politics 1871–1880', *The Johns Hopkins University Studies in Historical and Political Science*, 73: 1 (1955)

Lapostolle, Christine, 'De la barricade à la ruine', *La Recherche photographique*, 6 (June 1989), pp. 20–8

Lapostolle, Christine, 'Plus vrai que le vrai: stratégie photographique et Commune de Paris', *Actes de la recherche en sciences sociales*, 73 (June 1988), pp. 67–76

Larguier, Gilbert and Jérôme Quaretti, eds, *La Commune de 1871: Utopie ou modernité?* (Perpignan: Presses universitaires de Perpignan, 2000)

Lee, Daryl, 'Braquehais: photographie, ruines, Paris', in *Bruno Braquehais, un photographe de la Commune. Exposition du 9 mars au 19 juin 2000, Musée d'art et d'histoire, Saint-Denis*, ed. by Sylvie Gonzales (Saint-Denis: n. pub., 2000), pp. 3–5

Lefebvre, Henri, *La Proclamation de la Commune* (Paris: Gallimard, 1965)

Leith, James A., ed., *Images of the Commune* (Montreal and London: McGill-Queen's University Press, 1978)

Lidsky, Paul, *Les Ecrivains contre la Commune*, 2nd edn (Paris: La Découverte, 1999)

Luxenberg, Alisa, 'Creating *Désastres*: Andrieu's Photographs of Urban Ruins in the Paris of 1871', *Art Bulletin*, 80: 1 (March 1998), pp. 113–36

Matsuda, Matt, *The Memory of the Modern* (Oxford: Oxford University Press, 1996)

Milner, John, *Art, War and Revolution in France 1870–1871: Myth, Reportage and Reality* (New Haven, CT, and London: Yale University Press, 2000)

Bibliography

Noël, Bernard, *Dictionnaire de la Commune*, 2 vols (Paris: Flammarion, 1978)

Noël, Bernard and Jean-Claude Gautrand, *La Commune, Paris 1871* (Paris: Natan Collection Photo Poche, 2000)

Péridier, Jean, *La Commune et les artistes: Pottier-Courbet-Vallès-J.-B. Clément* (Paris: Nouvelles éditions latines, 1980)

Petitjean, Joël, 'Albums, recueils, et livres illustrés', *La Recherche photographique*, 6 (June 1989), pp. 29–31

Petitjean, Joël, 'Recherches sur la photographie et la Commune' (unpublished doctoral dissertation, Université de Paris IV-Sorbonne, U.F.R. Histoire de l'Art-Archéologie, 1995)

Rebérioux, Madelaine, 'Roman, théâtre et chanson: quelle Commune?', *Le Mouvement social*, 79 (April/June, 1972), pp. 273–92

Rifkin, Adrian, 'Cultural Movement and the Paris Commune', *Art History*, 2 (1979), pp. 51–61

Rifkin, Adrian, 'No Particular Thing to Mean', *Block*, 8 (1983), pp. 36–45

Rifkin, Adrian, 'Well Formed Phrases: Some Limits of Meaning in Political Print at the End of the Second Empire, *The Oxford Art Journal* 8: 1 (1985), pp. 20–8

Riot-Sarcey, Michèle, 'De la "tricoteuse" à la "pétroleuse" ou les figures répulsives de la "femme publique"', *La Revue du Musée d'Orsay*, 10 (spring 2000), pp. 54–61.

Roberts, J.M., 'La Commune par la droite: dimensions d'une mythologie', *Revue d'histoire moderne et contemporaine*, 19 (1972), pp. 187–205

Roche, Anne and Gérard Delfau, 'La Commune et le roman français', *Le Mouvement social*, 79 (April/June 1972), pp. 293–316

Roos, Jane Mayo, *Early Impressionism and the French State (1866–1874)* (Cambridge and New York: Cambridge University Press, 1996)

Roos, Jane Mayo, 'Within the "Zone of Silence": Monet and Manet in 1878', *Art History*, 11: 3 (September 1988), pp. 374–407

Ross, Kristin, *The Emergence of Social Space: Rimbaud and the Paris Commune* (Minneapolis: University of Minnesota Press, 1988)

Rougerie, Jacques, *La Commune de 1871* (Paris: Presses universitaires de France, 1988)

Rougerie, Jacques, 'Ce que l'on peut savoir aujourd'hui de la Commune', *La Revue du Musée d'Orsay*, 10 (spring 2000), pp. 46–53

Schivelbusche, Wolfgang, *The Culture of Defeat: On National Trauma, Mourning, and Recovery*, trans. by Jefferson Chase (London: Granta Books, 2003)

Schulkind, Eugene, ed., *The Paris Commune of 1871: The View from the Left* (London: Jonathan Cape, 1972)

Serman, William, *La Commune de Paris (1871)* (Paris: Fayard, 1986)

Shafer, David A., *The Paris Commune: French Politics, Culture, and Society at the Crossroads of the Revolutionary Tradition and Revolutionary Socialism* (New York and Basingstoke: Palgrave MacMillan, 2005)

Bibliography

Stafford, Andy, '"La légende de l'histoire": Bernard Noël's Captions for Photography of the Paris Commune', *Contemporary French and Francophone Studies*, 10: 3 (August 2006), pp. 291–300

Starr, Peter, *Commemorating Trauma: The Paris Commune and its Cultural Aftermath* (New York: Fordham University Press, 2006)

Taithe, Bertrand, *Citizenship & Wars: France in Turmoil 1870–1871* (London and New York: Routledge, 2001)

Taithe, Bertrand, *Defeated Flesh: Welfare, Warfare and the Making of Modern France* (Manchester: Manchester University Press, 1999)

Tersen, Georges, 'L'Opinion publique et la Commune de Paris (1871–79)', *Bulletin de la société d'études historiques, géographiques et scientifiques de la région parisienne*, 106 (January–March 1960), pp. 15–27; 107–8 (April–September 1960), pp. 26–36; 109 (October–December 1960), pp. 25–31; and 114–15 (January–June 1962), pp. 24–33

Thomas, Edith, *Les Pétroleuses* (Paris: Gallimard, 1963)

Tillier, Bertrand, *La Commune de Paris: Révolution sans images?* (Seyssel: Champ Vallon, 2004)

Tombs, Robert, *The Paris Commune, 1871* (London: Longman, 2000)

Tombs, Robert, *The War Against Paris* (Cambridge and London: Cambridge University Press, 1981)

Wiener, John, 'Paris Commune Photos at a New York Gallery: An Interview with Linda Nochlin', *Radical History Review*, 32 (1985), pp. 59–70

Wilson, Colette, 'City Space and the Politics of Carnival in Zola's *L'Assommoir*', *French Studies*, 58: 3 (2004), pp. 343–56

Wilson, Colette, '"La Dernière étape des fédérés au Père-Lachaise": The Contribution of *Le Monde illustré* to the Right-Wing Myth of Paris and the Commune', in *Reading and Writing the Forbidden: Essays in French Studies*, edited by Bénédicte Facques et al. (Reading: The 2001 Group, 2003), pp. 103–16

Wilson, Colette, 'Florent/Flourens: du nouveau sur la dimension politique du *Ventre de Paris*', *Les Cahiers naturalistes*, 79 (2005), pp. 77–87

Wilson, Colette, 'Memory and the Politics of Forgetting: Paris, the Commune, and the 1878 *Exposition Universelle*', *Journal of European Studies*, 35: 1/2 (2005), pp. 173–89

Wilson, Colette, '*Une page d'amour*: un panorama politique', *Les Cahiers naturalistes*, 76 (2002), pp. 177–91

Wilson, Colette, 'The Politics and Aesthetics of a Phantom Palace: Le Palais des Tuileries in Charles Soulier's *Paris incendié, mai 1871*', *Romance Studies*, 22: 3 (November 2004), pp. 197–207

Winks, Christopher, 'Ruins and Foundation Stones: The Paris Commune and the Destruction of the Vendôme Column', in *Revolutionary Romanticisms*, ed. by Max Blechman (San Francisco: Cityheights Books, 1999)

Bibliography

Other secondary texts

Agulhon, Maurice, *Marianne au combat: L'Imagerie et la symbolique républicaines de 1789 à 1880* (Paris: Flammarion, 1979)

Albalat, Antoine, *Gustave Flaubert et ses amis* (Paris: Plon, 1927)

Albert, Pierre, *La Presse française* (Paris: La Documentation française, 1990)

Alméras, Henri D', *La Vie parisienne pendant le Siège et sous la Commune* (Paris: Albin Michel, 1927)

Anderson, Benedict, *Imagined Communities: Reflections on the Origin and Spread of Nationalism* (London and New York: Verso, 1999)

Aubenas, Sylvie and Jacques Lacarrière, *Voyage en Orient* (Paris: Hazan, 1999)

Auer, Michèle and Michel Auer, *Encyclopédie internationale des photographes de 1839 à nos jours*, 2 vols (Hermance, Switzerland: Camera Obscura, 1985)

Bachelard, Gaston, *La Psychanalyse du feu* (Paris: Gallimard, 1949)

Baguley, David, 'Image et symbole: la tache rouge dans l'œuvre de Zola', *Les Cahiers naturalistes*, 39 (1970), pp. 36–41

Baguley, David, *Napoleon III and his Regime: An Extravaganza* (Baton Rouge: Lousiana State University Press, 2000)

Baguley, David, 'Rite et tragédie dans *L'Assommoir*', *Les Cahiers naturalistes*, 52 (1978), pp. 80–96

Baguley, David, 'Le Supplice de Florent: à propos du *Ventre de Paris*', *Europe*, 468–9 (April–May 1968), pp. 91–7

Baguley, David, *Zola: 'L'Assommoir'* (Cambridge: Cambridge University Press, 1992)

Bakhtin, Mikhail, *Problems of Dostoevesky's Poetics*, trans. by R.W. Rotsel (n.p.: Ardis, 1973)

Bakhtin, Mikhail, *Rabelais and his World*, ed. by Krystyna Pomorska and Michael Holquist, trans. by Helene Iswolsky (Bloomington: Indiana University Press, 1984)

Bancquart, Marie-Claire, *Paris 'fin-de-siècle': de Jules Vallès à Remy de Gourmont*, 2nd edn (Paris: Editions de la Différence, 2002)

Barret-Ducrocq, Françoise, ed., *Pourquoi se souvenir?* (Paris: Bernard Graset, 1999)

Barrows, Susanna, 'After the Commune: Alcoholism, Temperance, and Literature in the Early Third Republic', in *Consciousness and Class Experience in Nineteenth-Century Europe*, ed. by John M. Merriman (New York and London: Holmes and Meier, 1979), pp. 205–18

Bart, B., 'Is Maxime Du Camp a Reliable Witness?', *Modern Languages Review*, 47 (1953), pp. 17–25

Barthes, Roland, *La Chambre claire: note sur la photographie* (Paris: Seuil, 1980)

Barthes, Roland, *Essais critiques IV. Le Brunissement de la langue* (Paris: Seuil, 1984)

Barthes, Roland, *Mythologies*, 2nd edn (Paris: Seuil, 1970)

Barthes, Roland, *S/Z* (Paris: Seuil, 1970)

Becker, Colette, 'L'Audience d'Emile Zola', *Les Cahiers naturalistes*, 47 (1974), pp. 40–69

Bell, David F., *Models of Power: Politics and Economics in Zola's 'Rougon-Macquart'* (Lincoln, NE, and London: University of Nebraska Press, 1988)

Bellanger, Claude et al., eds, *Histoire générale de la presse française*, 4 vols (Paris: Presses universitaires de France, 1972)

Benjamin, Walter, *The Arcades Project*, trans. by Howard Eiland and Kevin McLaughlin (Cambridge, MA, and London: Belknap Press of Harvard University Press, 1999)

Benjamin, Walter, *Charles Baudelaire: A Lyric Poet in the Era of High Capitalism*, trans. by Harry Zohn (London and New York: Verso, 1989)

Benjamin, Walter, *One-Way Street and Other Writings*, trans. by Edmund Jephcott and Kingsley Shorter (London: Verso, 1979)

Benjamin, Walter, 'A Small History of Photography', trans. by Phil Patton, *Artform*, 15 (February 1977), pp. 46–51

Benrekassa, Georges, et al., 'Le Premier Centenaire de la mort de Rousseau et de Voltaire: Significations d'une commémoration', *Revue d'histoire littéraire de la France*, 79: 2–3 (March/June 1979), pp. 265–95

Berg, William J., *The Visual Novel: Emile Zola and the Art of His Times* (University Park: Pennsylvania State University Press, 1992)

Bergson, Henri, *Matière et mémoire: essaie sur la relation du corps à l'esprit* (Paris: Quadrige/Presses universitaires de France, 1997)

Bernard, Claudie, *Le Passé recomposé: Le Roman historique français du dix-neuvième siècle* (Paris: Hachette Supérieur, 1996)

Bigeon, Armand, *La Photographie devant la loi et devant la jurisprudence* (Paris: Société d'éditions scientifiques, 1892)

Bourdieu, Pierre, *Un art moyen: essai sur les usages sociaux de la photographie* (Paris: Editions de Minuit, 1965)

Brombert, Beth Archer, *Edouard Manet: Rebel in a Frock Coat* (Chicago: University of Chicago Press, 1996)

Brown, Frederick, *Zola: A Life* (London: Macmillan, 1995)

Brown, Marilyn R., 'Manet, Nodier and *Polichinelle*', *Art Journal*, 45: 1 (spring 1985), pp. 43–8

Brun, Philippe, *Albert Robida (1848–1926): Sa vie, son œuvre suivi d'une bibliographie complète de ses écrits et dessins* (n.p.: Promodis, 1984)

Burke, Peter, *Popular Culture in Early Modern Europe* (Aldershot: Ashgate, 1999)

Bury, J.P.T., *Gambetta and the Making of the Third Republic* (London: Longman, 1973)

Bury, J.P.T., *Gambetta's Final Years: 'The Era of Difficulties' 1877–1882* (London and New York: Longman, 1982)

Bury, J.P.T., *Napoleon III and the Second Empire* (London: English Universities Press, 1964)

Candau, J., *Anthropologie de la mémoire* (Paris: Presses universitaires de France, 1996)

Carter, A.E., *The Idea of Decadence in French Literature: 1830–1900* (Toronto: University of Toronto Press, 1958)

Casey, Edward S., *Remembering: A Phenomenological Study*, 2nd edn (Bloomington and Indianapolis: Indiana University Press, 2000)

Castells, Manuel, *The City and the Grassroots: A Cross-cultural Theory of Urban Social Movements* (London: Edward Arnold, 1983)

Certeau, Michel de, et al., *L'Invention du quotidien*, 2 vols (Paris: Gallimard, 1994)

Chaitin, Gilbert D., 'Listening Power: Flaubert, Zola, and the Politics of *style indirect libre*', *The French Review*, 72: 6 (May 1999), pp. 1023–37

Citron, Pierre, *La Poésie de Paris dans la littérature française de Rousseau à Baudelaire* (Paris: Editions de Minuit, 1961)

Clark, Roger, *Zola: 'L'Assommoir'* (Glasgow: University of Glasgow, French and German Publications, 1990)

Collins, Irene, *The Government and the Newspaper Press in France, 1814–1881* (London: Oxford University Press, 1959)

Condé, Michel, 'Représentations sociales et littéraires de Paris à l'époque romantique', 'La Ville et son paysage', *Romantisme*, 83 (1994), pp. 49–58

Connerton, Paul, *How Societies Remember* (Cambridge: Cambridge University Press, 1989)

Cook, Robert, *Civil War America: Making a Nation 1848–1877* (London: Pearson Longman, 2003)

Davis, Natalie Zemon, *Society and Culture in Early Modern France* (Cambridge: Polity, 1987)

Deffoux, Léon, *La Publication de 'L'Assommoir'* (Paris: Société d'éditions littéraires et techniques, 1931)

Derrida, Jacques, *De la grammatologie* (Paris: Les éditions de minuit, 1967)

Descotes, M., *Les Grands Rôles du théâtre de Corneille* (Paris: Presses universitaires de France, 1962)

Dictionnaire de Paris (Paris: Larousse, 1964)

Di Stefano, Rosa M., 'Maxime Du Camp d'après sa correspondance avec Flaubert', *Les Amis de Flaubert*, 54 (1979), pp. 7–18

Donaldson-Evans, Mary, 'The Morbidity of Milieu: *L'Assommoir* and the Discourse of Hygiene', in *Literary Generations*, ed. by Alain Toumayoan (Lexington: French Forum, 1992), pp. 150–62

Dreyfous, Maurice, *Ce qui me reste à dire*, 2 vols, 3rd edn (Paris: Paul Ollendorff, 1912)

Dubief, Eugène, *Le Journalisme* (Paris: Hachette, 1892)

Dubois, Jacques, *'L'Assommoir' de Zola*, 2nd edn (Paris: Belin, 1993)

Duchet, Claude, 'Pathologie de la ville zolienne', in *Du Visible à l'invisible: pour Max Milner*, ed. by Stéphane Michaud (n.p.: José Corti, 1988), pp. 83–96

Bibliography

Dufreigne, Pierre, 'Images d'un Paris perdu', *L'Express*, 17 November 1994, pp. 120–2

Durkheim, Emile, 'Représentations individuelles et représentations collectives', in *Sociologie et philosophie* (Paris: Presses universitaires de France, 1967), pp. 1–38

Faguet, Emile, *Propos littéraires*, 5 vols (Paris: Société française d'imprimerie et de librairie, 1902–9)

Ferguson, Priscilla Parkhurst, *Paris as Revolution: Writing the 19th-Century City* (Berkeley, Los Angeles and London: University of California Press, 1994)

Finot, André, *Maxime Du Camp* (Paris: Les Amis de Flaubert, 1949)

Foncier mensuel (November 1994)

Forni, Raymond, Président de l'Assemblée nationale, text of speech given at the Hôtel de Lassay, 21 November 2001. Copy courtesy of the Musée d'art et d'histoire de Saint-Denis

Fraisse, Geneviève and Michelle Perrot, eds, *A History of Women in the West: IV. Emerging Feminism from Revolution to World War* (Cambridge, MA, and London: Belknap Press, 1992)

Frizot, Michel, ed., *A New History of Photography* (Cologne: Könemann Verlagsgesellschaft, 1998)

Gacon, Stéphane, 'L'Oubli institutionnel', in *Oublier nos crimes: L'Amnésie nationale: une spécificité française?*, ed. by Dimitri Nicolaïdis (Paris: Editions Autrement, 1994), pp. 98–111

Gaillard, Jeanne, 'Zola et l'Ordre moral', *Les Cahiers naturalistes*, 54 (1980), pp. 25–32

Gerhardi, Gerhard C., 'Zola's Biological Vision of Politics: Revolutionary Figures in *La Fortune des Rougon* and *Le Ventre de Paris*', *Nineteenth-Century French Studies*, 2–4 (spring–summer 1974), pp. 164–80

Goldstein, Robert Justin, *Censorship of Political Caricature in Nineteenth-century France* (Kent, OH: Kent State University Press, 1989)

Grand Louvre: sous les jardins du Carrousel, *Les Dossiers d'Archéologie*, 190 (February 1994)

Grant, Elliott M., 'Zola and the Sacré-Cœur', *French Studies*, 20 (1966), pp. 243–52

Green, Anne, *Flaubert and the Historical Novel: 'Salammbô' Reassessed* (Cambridge: Cambridge University Press, 1982)

Green, Anne, 'France Exposed: Madame Bovary and the Exposition Universelle', *The Modern Language Review*, 99: 4 (October 2004), pp. 915–23

Gretton, Tom, 'Difference and Competition: the Imitation and Reproduction of Fine Art in a Nineteenth-century Illustrated Weekly News Magazine', *Oxford Art Journal*, 23: 2 (2000), pp. 143–62

Guedj, Aimé, 'Les Révolutionnaires de Zola', *Les Cahiers naturalistes*, 36 (1968), pp. 123–37

Bibliography

Guéry, Louis, *Visages de la presse: La Présentation des journaux des origines à nos jours* (Paris: Editions du Centre de formation et de perfectionnement des journalistes, 1997)

Gural-Migdal, Anna, 'Représentation utopique et ironie dans *Le Ventre de Paris*', *Les Cahiers naturalistes*, 74 (2000), pp. 145–61

Gural-Migdal, Anna, ed., *Writing the Feminine in Zola and Naturalist Fiction* (Bern: Peter Lang, 2003)

Halbwachs, Maurice, *Les Cadres sociaux de la mémoire*, ed. by Gérard Namer (Paris: Albin Michel, 1997)

Halbwachs, Maurice, *La Mémoire collective*, ed. by Gérard Namer (Paris: Albin Michel, 1997)

Hamon, Philippe, *Expositions, littérature, et architecture au XIXe siècle* (Paris: José Corti, 1989)

Harrow, Susan, 'The Matter with Jeanne: Narrative and the Nervous Body in Zola's *Une page d'amour*', *Excavatio*, 12 (1999), pp. 60–8

Hemmings, F.W.J., *Emile Zola*, 2nd edn (Oxford: Oxford University Press, 1970)

Hertz, Neil, 'Medusa's Head: Male Hysteria under Political Pressure', in *The End of the Line: Essays on Psychoanalysis and the Sublime*, ed. by Neil Hertz (New York: Columbia University Press, 1985), pp. 169–73

Heylli, Georges d', ed., *Dictionnaire des pseudonyms* (Geneva: Slatkine reprints, 1971)

Holt, Richard, *Sport and Society in Modern France* (Hamden, CT: Archon Books, 1981)

House, John, *Impressionism, Paint and Politics* (New Haven, CT, and London: Yale University Press, 2004)

Hungerford, Constance, 'Charles Marville, Popular Illustrator: The Origins of a Photographic Sensibility', *History of Photography* (July–September 1985), pp. 227–46

Hungerford, Constance Cain, *Ernest Meissonier: Master in his Genre* (Cambridge: Cambridge University Press, 1999)

Huyssen, Andreas, *Present Pasts: Urban Palimpsests and the Politics of Memory* (Stanford, CA: Stanford University Press, 2003)

Huyssen, Andreas, *Twilight Memories: Marking Time in a Culture of Amnesia* (New York and London: Routledge, 1995)

Jameson, Fredric, *The Political Unconscious: Narrative as a Socially Symbolic Act* (Ithaca, NY: Cornell University Press, 1981)

Jeffords, Susan, *The Remasculinization of America: Gender and the Vietnam War* (Bloomington, IN: Indiana University Press, 1995)

Jonas, Raymond, *France and the Cult of the Sacred Heart: An Epic Tale for Modern Times* (Berkeley, Los Angeles and London: University of California Press, 2000)

Joutard, Philippe, et al., *La Saint-Barthélemy ou les résonances d'un massacre* (Neuchâtel: Delachaux et Niestlé, 1976)

Bibliography

Jullian, Camille, *Extraits des historiens français du XIXe siècle* (Paris: Hachette, 1897)

Kasl, Ronda, 'Edouard Manet's *Rue Mosnier*: "Le pauvre a-t-il une patrie?"', *Art Journal*, 45: 1 (spring 1985), pp. 49–58

Kidd, William, 'Marianne: from Medusa to Messalina. Psycho-sexual imagery and political propaganda in France 1789–1945', *Journal of European Studies*, 34: 4, pp. 333–48

Kranowski, Nathan, *Paris dans les romans d'Emile Zola* (Paris: Presses Universitaires de France, 1968)

Kuhn, Annette, *Family Secrets: Acts of Memory and Imagination* (London and New York: Verso, 2002)

Ladurie, Emmanuel Le Roy, *Le Carnaval de Romans: De la Chandeleur au mercredi des Cendres, 1579–1580* (Paris: Gallimard, 1979)

Lambert, Phyllis, et al., *Edouard Baldus, photographe* (New York, Montreal, Paris: Réunion des Musées nationaux, 1994)

Langford, Rachael, *Jules Vallès and the Narration of History: Contesting the French Third Republic in the 'Jacques Vingtras' Trilogy* (Bern: Lang, 1999)

Lanoux, Armand, *Bonjour Monsieur Zola* (Paris: Le Livre Contemporain-Amiot-Dumont, 1954)

Lavielle, Emile, *Le Ventre de Paris* (Rosny: Bréal, 1999)

Lefebvre, Henri, *Espace et politique*, 2nd edn (Paris: Anthropos, 2000)

Lefebvre, Henri, *La Production de l'espace* (Paris: Anthropos, 1974)

Lefebvre, Henri, *La Somme et le reste* (1959) (Paris, Méridiens, Klincksieck, 1989)

Lefebvre, Henri, *La Vie quotidienne dans le monde moderne* (Paris: Gallimard, 1968)

Le Goff, Jacques, *Histoire et mémoire* (Paris: Gallimard, 1988)

Lejeune, Paule, *Germinal, un roman antipeuple* (Paris: Nizet, 1978)

Lethbridge, Robert, 'La Préparation de *La Curée*: mise au point d'une chronologie', *Les Cahiers naturalistes*, 51 (1976), pp. 37–48

Lethbridge, Robert, 'Reading the Songs of *L'Assommoir*', *French Studies*, 45 (1991), pp. 435–47

Lethbridge, Robert, 'Reflections in the Margin: Politics in Zola's *L'Assommoir*', *Australian Journal of French Studies*, 30: 2 (1993), pp. 222–32

Lethbridge, Robert, 'A Visit to the Louvre: *L'Assommoir* Revisited', *Modern Language Review*, 87 (1992), pp. 41–55

Lightbody, Charles Wayland, *The Judgements of Joan: Joan of Arc, a Study in Cultural History* (London: Allen and Unwin, 1961)

Lipton, Eunice, *Looking into Degas: Uneasy Images of Women and Modern Life* (Berkeley, Los Angeles, London: University of California Press, 1986)

Loftus, W., 'The Veracity of Maxime Du Camp's Reminiscences of Gustave Flaubert, 1849–51', *Les Bonnes Feuilles* (1974), pp. 61–72

Lumbroso, Olivier, 'Le Passage des panoramas (poétique et fonctions des vues panoramiques dans *Les Rougon-Macquart*)', *Littérature*, 116 (December 1999), pp. 17–46

Mainardi, Patricia, *Art and Politics of the Second Empire: The Universal Expositions of 1855 and 1867* (New Haven, CT, and London: Yale University Press, 1987)

Man, Paul de, 'Literary History and Literary Modernity', *Daedalus, Journal of the American Academy of Arts and Sciences*, 99 (1970), pp. 384–404

Marbot, Bernard, ed., *Une invention du XIXe siècle. Expression et technique, la photographie. Collections de la Société française de photographie* (Paris: Bibliothèque nationale, 1976)

Marchandiau, Jean-Noël, *L'Illustration 1843–1944: vie et mort d'un journal* (Toulouse: Editions Privat, 1987)

Max, Stefan, *Les Métamorphoses de la grande ville dans 'Les Rougon-Macquart'* (Paris: Nizet, 1966)

McCauley, Elizabeth Anne, *Industrial Madness: Commercial Photography in Paris 1848–1871* (New Haven, CT, and London: Yale University Press, 1994)

Minogue, Valerie, *Zola: 'L'Assommoir'* (London: Grant and Cutler, 1991)

Minot, Leslie Ann, 'Women and the Commune: Zola's revisions', *Excavatio*, 10 (1997), pp. 57–65

Mitterand, Henri, *Zola journaliste: de l'affaire Manet à l'affaire Dreyfus* (Paris: Armand Colin, 1962)

Mitterand, Henri, *Zola: L'Histoire et la fiction* (Paris: Presses universitaires de France, 1990)

Mitterand, Henri, *Zola: 1. Sous le regard d'Olympia 1840–1871* (Paris: Fayard, 1999)

Mondenard, Anne de, *Mission héliographique de 1851* (n.p.: Editions du patrimoine, 2002)

Monselet, André, *Charles Monselet: sa vie, son œuvre* (Paris: Emile Testard, 1892)

Mortier, Roland, *La Poétique des ruines en France: ses origines, ses variations de la Renaissance à Victor Hugo* (Geneva: Droz, 1974)

Mortimer, Armine Kotin, *La Clôture narrative* (Mayenne: José Corti, 1985)

Mouillaud, Maurice, 'Le Journal: un texte sous tension', in *Textologie du journal*, ed. by Pierre Rétat (Paris: Minard, 1990)

Mucchielli, Laurent, 'Pour une psychologie collective: l'héritage durkheimien d'Halbwachs et sa rivalité avec Blondel durant l'entre-deux guerres', *Revue d'histoire des sciences humaines*, 1 (1999), pp. 103–41

Nelson, Brian, *Zola and the Bourgeoisie: A Study of Themes and Techniques in 'Les Rougon-Macquart'* (London: Macmillan, 1983)

Nietzsche, Friedrich, *On the Genealogy of Morals*, ed. and trans. by Douglas Smith (Oxford and New York: Oxford University Press, 1996)

Nietzsche, Friedrich, *Untimely Meditations*, ed. by J.P. Stern, trans. by R.J. Hollingdale (Cambridge: Cambridge University Press, 1983)

Bibliography

Noël, Louis, *François Chifflart: peintre et graveur français, 1825–1901* (Lille: Imprimerie Vandroth-Fauconnier, 1902)

Nora, Pierre, ed., *Les Lieux de mémoire*, 3 vols (Paris: Gallimard, 1984–93)

Osterwalder, Marcus, ed., *Dictionnaire des illustrateurs, 1800–1914* (Neuchâtel: Ides et Calendes, 1989)

Otis, Laura, *Organic Memory: History and the Body in the Late Nineteenth and Early Twentieth Centuries* (Lincoln, NE, and London: University of Nebraska Press, 1994)

Packard, Noel and Chirstopher Chen, 'From Medieval Mnemonics to a Social Construction of Memory', *American Behavioral Scientist*, 48: 10 (June 2005), pp. 1297–319

Paivio, Allan, *Mental Representation: A Dual Coding Approach*, 2nd edn (Oxford: Oxford University Press, 1990)

Paivio, Allan and Csapo Kalman, 'Picture Superiority in Free Recall: Imagery or Dual Coding?', *Cognitive Psychology*, 5 (1973), pp. 176–206

Pascal, Roy, *The Dual Voice: Free Indirect Speech and its Functioning in the Nineteenth-century European Novel* (Manchester: Manchester University Press, 1977)

Pellini, Pierluigi, ' "Si je triche un peu": Zola et le roman historique', *Les Cahiers naturalistes*, 75 (2001), pp. 7–28

Petrey, Sandy, 'Historical Reference and Stylistic Opacity in *Le Ventre de Paris*', *Kentucky Romance Quarterly*, 24: 3 (1977), pp. 325–40

Pilbeam, Pamela, *Republicanism in Nineteenth-Centruy France* (London: Macmillan, 1995)

Pinkney, David H., *Napoleon III and the Rebuilding of Paris* (Princeton: Princeton University Press, 1958)

Prendergast, Christopher, 'Le Panorama, la peinture et la faim: le début du *Ventre de Paris*', *Les Cahiers naturalistes*, 67 (1993), pp. 65–71

Prendergast, Christopher, *Paris and the Nineteenth Century* (Cambridge, MA, and Oxford: Blackwell, 1995)

Radstone, Susannah, ed., *Memory and Methodology* (Oxford: Berg, 2000)

Radstone Susannah and Katherine Hodgkin, eds, *Regimes of Memory* (London: Routledge, 2003)

Randell, Keith, *France: The Third Republic 1870–1914* (London: Edward Arnold, 1986)

Rearick, Charles, 'Festivals in Modern France: The Experience of the Third Republic', *Journal of Contemporary History*, 12 (1977), pp. 435–60

Redfern, Walter, *Feet First: Jules Vallès* (Glasgow: University of Glasgow French and German Publications, 1992)

Reffait, Christophe, 'La renaissance de la nation selon *La Débâcle* de Zola', *Journal of the Society of Dix-Neuviémistes*, 6 (2006), pp. 42–54

Régnier, Philippe, ed., *La Caricature entre République et censure. L'Imagerie satirique en France de 1830–1880: un discours de résistance?* (Lyon: Presses universitaires de Lyon, 1996)

Régnier, Philippe, 'La fonction de la *Revue des deux mondes* entre 1829 et 1870', in *Philologiques III. Qu'est-ce qu'une* littérature *nationale? Approches pour une théorie interculturelle du champ littéraire*, ed. by Michel Espagne and Michael Werner (Paris: Editions de la Maison des Sciences de l'Homme, 1994), pp. 289–314

Reid, James H., *Narration and Description in the French Realist Novel: The Temporality of Lying and Forgetting* (Cambridge: Cambridge University Press, 1993)

Rice, Shelley, *Parisian Views* (Cambridge, MA, and London: MIT Press, 1997)

Ricœur, Paul, *Temps et récit*, 3 vols (Paris: Seuil, 1985)

Ripoll, Roger, 'Zola et les Communards', *Europe*, 468–9 (April–May 1968), pp. 17–26

Robb, Graham, *Victor Hugo* (London: Picador, 1997)

Roberts-Jones, Philippe, *De Daumier à Lautrec: Essai sur l'histoire de la caricature française* (Paris: Les Beaux Arts, 1960)

Roberts-Jones, Philippe, *La Presse satirique illustrée entre 1860 et 1890* (Paris: Institut français de la presse, 1956)

Robida, Fred, 'Albert Robida en 1870–71', *Europe*, 19 (1971), pp. 63–75

Rod, Edouard, *A Propos de 'L'Assommoir'* (Paris: Marpon and Flammarion, 1879)

Ross, Stephanie, 'What Photographs Can't Do', *The Journal of Aesthetics and Art Criticism*, 41: 1 (autumn 1982), pp. 5–17

Ruddick, Sara, *Maternal Thinking: Toward a Politics of Peace* (Boston, MA: Beacon Press, 1989)

Sala, George Augustus, *Paris Herself Again 1878–1879* (London: Golden Gallery Press, 1948)

Sautet, Marc, *Nietzsche et la Commune* (Paris: Le Sycomore, 1981)

Scarpa, Marie, *Le Carnaval des Halles: Une éthnocritique du 'Ventre de Paris' de Zola* (Paris: CNRS, 2000)

Schroder-Gudehus, Brigitte and Anne Rasmussen, *Les Fastes du progrès: Le Guide des expositions universelles, 1851–1992* (Paris: Flammarion, 1992)

Scruton, Roger, 'Photography and Representation', *Critical Inquiry*, 7 (1980–81), pp. 577–603

Senneville, Gérard de, *Maxime Du Camp: Un spectateur engagé du XIXe siècle* (Paris: Editions Stock, 1996)

Shepard, Roger N., 'Recognition Memory for Words, Sentences, and Pictures', *Journal of Verbal Learning and Verbal Behavior*, 6 (1967), pp. 156–63

Showalter, Elaine, *Sexual Anarchy* (London: Bloomsbury, 1991)

Shryock, Richard, 'Zola's Use of Embedded Narrative in *Le Ventre de Paris*: Florent's Tale', *The Journal of Narrative Technique*, 22 (winter 1992), pp. 48–56

Smith, Marilyn Chapnik, and Lochlan E. Magee, 'Tracing the Time Course of Picture-Word Processing', *Journal of Experimental Psychology: General*, 109: 4 (December 1980), pp. 373–92

Bibliography

Snyder, John and Neil Walsh Allen, 'Photography, Vision, and Representation', *Critical Inquiry*, 2 (1975), pp. 143–69

Sontag, Susan, *On Photography*, 2nd edn (London: Penguin, 1986)

Sprinker, Michael, *History and Ideology in Proust: 'A la recherche du temps perdu' and the Third French Republic* (Cambridge: Cambridge University Press, 1994)

Starkie, Enid, *Flaubert: The Making of the Master* (London: Weidenfeld and Nicolson, 1967)

Stallybrass, Peter and Allon White, *The Politics of Transgression* (London: Methuen, 1986)

Sueur, Valérie, *François Chifflart graveur et illustrateur* (Paris: Réunion des Musées nationaux, 1994)

Sutnik, Maia-Mari, *Edouard Baldus Héliogravures: Selections from 'Les Principaux monuments de France'* (Toronto: Art Gallery of Toronto, 1994)

Swart, Koenraad W., *The Sense of Decadence in Nineteenth-Century France* (The Hague: Martinus Nijhoff, 1964)

Terdiman, Richard, *Discourse/Counter-Discourse: Theory and Practice of Symbolic Resistance in Nineteenth-Century France* (Ithaca, NY, and London: Cornell University Press, 1985)

Theweleit, Klaus, 'The Bomb's Womb and the Genders of War (War Goes on Preventing Women from Becoming the Mothers of Invention)', in *Gendering War Talk*, ed. by Miriam Cooke and Angela Woollacot (Princeton: Princeton University Press, 1993)

 Thézy, Marie de, *Marville. Paris* (Paris: Hazan, 1994)

Thibault, Jean-François, 'Zola et l'horizon parisien', *French Literature Series*, 24 (1997), pp. 33–49

Thiesse, Anne-Marie, *Le Roman du quotidien: lecteurs et lectures populaires à la Belle Epoque* (Paris: Seuil, 2000)

Tillier, Bertrand, *La Commune de Paris: Révolution sans images?* (Seyssel: Champ Vallon, 2004)

Tisseron, Serge, *Le Mystère de la chambre claire: photographie et inconscient* (Paris: Flammarion, 1996)

Varnedoe, Kirk, 'The Tuileries Museum and the Uses of Art History in the Early Third Republic', in *Saloni, gallerie, musei e loro influenza sullo sviluppo dell-arte dei secoli XIX e XX.*, ed. by Francis Haskell (Bologna: CIHA, 1979), pp. 63–8

Vice, Sue, *Introducing Bakhtin* (Manchester and New York: Manchester University Press, 1997)

Walter, Rodolphe, 'Zola et la Commune: un exil volontaire', *Les Cahiers naturalistes*, 43 (1970), pp. 25–37

Watelet, Jean, *La Presse illustrée en France, 1814–1914*, 11 vols (unpublished doctoral dissertation, Université Panthéon-Assas, Paris II, 17 January 1998)

Wetherill, Michael, 'Visions conflictuelles: Le Paris de Flaubert, Zola, Monet, Degas, Caillebotte', in *Le Champ littéraire 1860–1900: Etudes offertes à Michael*

Pakenham, ed. by Keith Cameron and James Kearns (Amsterdam: Rodopi, 1996)

White, Hayden, *The Content of the Form: Narrative Discourse and Historical Representation* (Baltimore: Johns Hopkins University Press, 1987)

White, Hayden, *Metahistory: The Historical Imagination in Nineteenth-century Europe* (Baltimore: Johns Hopkins University Press, 1973)

Woodward, Christopher, *In Ruins* (London: Chatto & Windus, 2001)

Wolf, Nelly, *Le Peuple dans le roman français de Zola à Céline* (Paris: Presses universitaires de France, 1990)

Woollen, Geoff, 'Les "transportés" dans l'œuvre de Zola', *Les Cahiers naturalistes*, 72 (1998), pp. 317–33

Woollen, Geoff, 'Zola's Halles, a *Grande Surface* before their time', *Romance Studies*, 18 (2000), pp. 21–30

Yates, Frances, *The Art of Memory* (London: Routledge and Paul Kegan, 1966)

Index

Note: 'n.' after a page reference indicates the number of a note on that page; page numbers in *italic* refer to illustrations.

Index